JOURNAL OF
AN EXPLORING TOUR
Beyond the Rocky Mountains

Idaho Yesterdays
A Series Edited by Judith Austin
Idaho State Historical Society

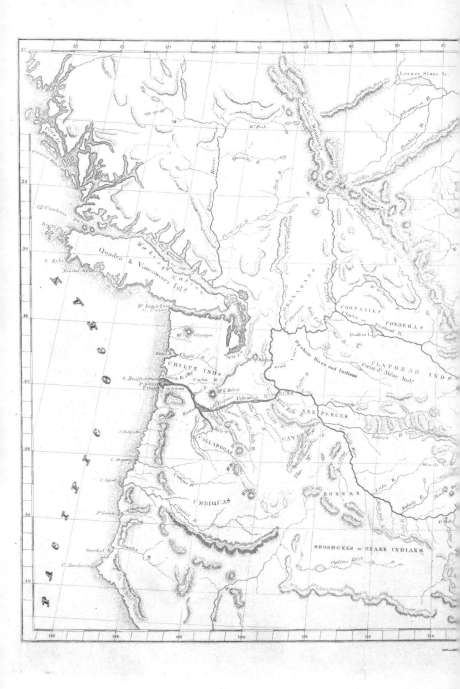

Samuel Parker's map (1838) of Oregon Territory.

JOURNAL OF
AN EXPLORING TOUR
Beyond the Rocky Mountains

Samuel Parker
Introduction by Larry R. Jones

University of Idaho Press
Moscow, Idaho

From the third edition, originally published by Mack,
Andrus, & Woodruff, Ithaca, New York, 1842.
University of Idaho Press reprint edition 1990.
Introduction by Larry R. Jones
©1990 by the University of Idaho.

Idaho Yesterdays is a reprint series developed by the Idaho
State Historical Society and published by the University of Idaho Press
with the assistance of the Idaho Centennial Foundation.
Series design by Karla Fromm
Printed in the United States of America
94 93 92 91 90   5 4 3 2 1

Library of Congress Cataloging in Publication Data

Parker, Samuel, 1779–1866.
    Journal of an exploring tour beyond the Rocky Mountains / Samuel
Parker; introduction by Larry R. Jones.
        p. cm.–(Idaho yesterdays)
    Reprint. Originally published: 3rd ed. Ithaca, N.Y.: Mack,
Andrus, & Woodruff, 1842.
    Includes bibliographical references.
    ISBN 0–89301–140–1: $19.95
    1. Northwest, Pacific–Description and travel. 2. Overland
journeys to the Pacific. 3. Indians of North America–West (U.S.)
4. Indians of North America–Languages–Glossaries, vocabularies,
etc. 5. Hawaii–Description and travel–To 1950. 6. Parker,
Samuel, 1779-1866–Journeys. I. Title. II. Series: Idaho
yesterdays (Moscow, Idaho)
F880.P23 1990
917.9504'3–dc20   90–46021
                                                           CIP

CONTENTS.

CHAPTER I.

The Tour commenced by way of Buffalo, Erie, and Pittsburgh; passage to Cincinnati in the steam-boat Ohioan; the steam-boat takes fire; Cincinnati; Falls of the Ohio; the Ohio river; Ohio and Kentucky; confluence of the Ohio and Mississippi rivers; Point Girardou; beautiful appearance of fire on the prairie; St. Genevieve, old custom; Herculaneum; gambling on board the steam-boats; St. Louis; Dr. M. Whitman; Mr. Fontenelle. 17

CHAPTER II.

Leave St. Louis for Liberty; passage up the Missouri; snags; a walk on shore; Jefferson city; river scenery; steam-boat Siam; sand bars; Lexington; steamboat disaster; Liberty; Navahoe Indians; ride to Cantonment Leavenworth; amusing provincialisms; caravan commence their journey; first encampment; Iowa Indians; Blacksnake hills; Nodaway river; Elk; cross the Neshnabotana; rich soil; rapid rise of the north branch of Neshnabotana; mode of living; mounds of the west; crossing of the Missouri; Bellevue; Missionaries. 26

CHAPTER III.

Continuance at Council Bluffs; interesting scenery; Indian curiosity; information obtained about several Indian tribes; spasmodic cholera; an Indian chief killed; leave Bellevue for the Black Hills; storm of rain; heavy thunder

CHAPTER IV.

CHAPTER V.

CHAPTER VI.

CHAPTER VII.

CHAPTER VIII.

CHAPTER IX.

CHAPTER X.

CHAPTER XI.

CHAPTER XXIII.

CHAPTER XXIV.

CHAPTER XXV.

CHAPTER XXVI.

Idaho Yesterdays
Introduction

LARRY R. JONES

ON March 14, 1835, fifty-five-year-old Samuel Parker set out from Ithaca, New York, on a twenty-eight-thousand-mile adventure that would take over two years and carry him across the North American continent and then around South America on his return home by ship. His initial purpose was to determine where Protestant Christian missions to the Indians might best be established. But Parker was an acute observer of both landscape and people, and his journal—which begins with his departure from Ithaca and ends with his landing at New London, Connecticut, on May 23, 1837—records the lives of Indians and fur traders; describes major emigrant landmarks such as Chimney Rock, Courthouse Rock, and Scotts Bluff; discusses experiences both spiritual and eminently practical; and offers guidance to future emigrants and expansionists alike. Neither illness nor the difficult conditions of the journey hindered his daily observations and recordings, and his sense of duty and strong religious convictions bolstered him in hard times.

Parker came honestly by his determination and willingness to journey into the wilderness. Born at Ashfield, Massachusetts, on April 23, 1779, he was descended from a Puritan grandfather who landed at Charlestown not long after the settlement of Plymouth and a father who fought in the Revolution. His formal education and preparation for the ministry were stop-and-start: tutorial preparation for college was halted by illness for three years, so he finally entered Williams College as a sophomore in 1803. After graduation he taught for a year at an academy in Brattleboro, Vermont, and then moved to Shelboro, Massachusetts, to begin private theological study.

After a year, Parker found himself without sufficient funds to continue his course of study but, because of a shortage of ordained clergy, received a licence to preach from the Northern Congregational Association of Hampshire County, Massachusetts. He was assigned as a home missionary in western New York and northern Pennsylvania in 1808 and preached at various churches in the area until the spring of 1809. Then he entered Andover (Massachusetts) Theological Seminary as a member of the institution's first senior class.

Following his stint at Andover, Parker was sent by the Massachusetts Missionary Society to middle and southern New York State, and in 1812 he was ordained and installed at the Congregational church in Danby, New York. Despite this Congregationalist affiliation, he joined a presbytery in 1814 and was carried on the rolls of the Presbyterian Church until his death.

Parker's marital life had no more even a beginning. Early in his pastorate at Danby, he married a young woman from his home town who was already ill at the time of their marriage and who died en route to Danby. In December of 1815 he was married again—to Jerusha Lord, a niece of Noah Webster. The Parkers had three children. A daughter, named after her mother, eventually settled with her husband in Ithaca, New York. Son Samuel became a physician and later wrote about his father's travels and achievements; son Henry became a clergyman, scientist, and author.

The family remained at Danby for fifteen years. The next change in their lives came when Parker became the financial agent for Auburn Theological Seminary in Auburn, New York. At the same time they moved to Ithaca, some forty miles south of Auburn, where Samuel maintained a residence the rest of his life. While serving as agent for the seminary, he also pastored churches for three and a half years. Then, because of his wife's poor health, he returned to Ithaca to teach in a girls' school.[1]

Shortly before going back to Ithaca, Parker read the now famous article in the March 1, 1833, issue of the *Christian Advocate and Journal* that told of a Nez Perce-Flathead Indian delegation arriving in St. Louis in 1831 seeking someone to teach their people the religion of the whites. The story initiated missionary efforts in the Oregon country; it also occupied Parker's thoughts and actions until his death. He wrote the American Board of Commissioners for Foreign Missions (known as the ABCFM) on April 10, 1833, volunteering to explore the western regions and, if a mission were deemed appropriate, to return later with his family to establish one.

The ABCFM decided that because of his age and family commitments it could not approve Parker's application. Undaunted, on January 6, 1834, he addressed the congregation of the Ithaca Presbyterian Church on the need to establish a mission in the Oregon country and to Christianize the natives. His message aroused the missionary spirit of the gathering, which voted to sponsor such an endeavor. Parker resumed negotiations with the ABCFM; this time, with the pledged monetary support of the Ithaca church, the board agreed to his proposal for an exploratory tour.

Meanwhile, also in response to the *Christian Advocate's* call, the Methodist Church commissioned Jason Lee on May 25,

1833, to travel overland and establish a mission among North-west Indians. Lee and four companions left St. Louis on April 28, 1834, and became the first Protestant missionaries to cross the Rocky Mountains. A week later, Parker and two associates — the Reverend John Dunbar and Samuel Allis, a saddler — left Ithaca amidst great fanfare from the populace. When they reach-ed St. Louis, the trio discovered that they had just missed the westbound fur caravan that included Lee and his group, trader Nathaniel Wyeth, and members of the American Fur Company.

Since it was inadvisable to travel any great distance without the protection of such a caravan, the group from Ithaca broke up. Dunbar and Allis went some 450 miles northwest to Council Bluffs to take up a mission among the Indians of that area. Par-ker returned to Ithaca, still intent on establishing a mission be-yond the Rocky Mountains. The ABCFM continued to favor the project and sent him on a tour of western New York to solicit funds and recruit additional missionaries (including Marcus Whit-man and Narcissa Prentiss) for a trip west the following year. Then he left Ithaca once again for the West — this time without any ceremony.

The relationship between Parker and Whitman proved a dif-ficult one at times and a considerable burden to the latter in his dealings with the ABCFM, but it began well enough. Both men arrived in St. Louis early enough to join the annual fur caravan of the American Fur Company, which under the guidance of Lucien Fontenelle departed by steamboat for Liberty, Missouri, on April 7. From Liberty the group traveled overland to Bellevue, Nebraska, where they encountered the cholera that was prevalent all along the Missouri that year. Whitman made good use of his medical training to treat successfully a number of the caravan, including Fontenelle. That success at Bellevue, and the medical

treatment rendered later at the fur-trade rendezvous, greatly aided
Parker's work and that of the missionaries who followed in 1836:
Whitman's medical knowledge gained them respect and helped
to make new friends who thereafter freely offered their services
to the missionaries.

Parker was slow to acknowledge the impact of Whitman's skills.
In the first published edition of his journal, he remarked somewhat casually on how Whitman's efforts enabled them to continue on their journey: without the medical intervention, the fur
company would likely have cancelled the trip. In the following
editions of his book—perhaps realizing, after some reflection on
his travels, just how fortunate they were in being able to assist
Fontenelle and his men—Parker offered more detail on the sig-
nificance of the events at Bellevue:

> This afflicative scourge [cholera], so far as it respected
> Dr. W. and myself, was providential. The assistance we ren-
> dered the sick, and the medical skill of the Doctor, con-
> verted those into permanent friends, who had so disliked
> the restraints which our presence imposed upon them, that,
> as they afterwards confessed, they had plotted our death,
> and intended on the first convenient occasion to put their
> purpose in execution (p. 46).

The large, slow-moving caravan departed from Bellevue on June
22; Parker and Whitman left the following day and soon caught
up. The group followed a route utilized by some Oregon-bound
emigrants and popularized by Mormons and California-bound
gold-seekers: they traveled on the north side of the Platte River
and the North Fork of the Platte until they crossed the latter
to visit Fort William (later Fort Laramie).[2] (California-bound
traffic generally crossed the North Fork to obtain supplies at Fort

Laramie, while the Mormon emigrants tended to remain on the north bank of the North Fork.)

At Fort William Lucien Fontenelle turned the leadership of the caravan over to Thomas Fitzpatrick, who developed a friendship with the missionaries that would prove invaluable to Whitman. Under Fitzpatrick the caravan followed the route that became known as the Oregon Trail, staying on the south bank of the North Fork of the Platte to a crossing just south of modern Casper, Wyoming. From there it headed southwest to Independence Rock and the Sweetwater River, which it followed to South Pass. Parker was impressed with the easy ascent and crossing of the Continental Divide at South Pass and, after viewing the lack of obstructions, professed that a railroad could someday be constructed from the Atlantic to the Pacific.

After South Pass, the group diverted from the Oregon Trail and headed northwest to the rendezvous site on the Green River near present-day Daniel, Wyoming.[3] While at the rendezvous — a great annual gathering of trappers, traders, and Indians — Parker spent his time collecting information on the various Indian tribes present, and Whitman was kept busy administering to the medical needs of the trappers. One of Whitman's most notable medical achievements was the extraction of an iron arrowhead from the back of Jim Bridger. Once again Whitman's skills favorably impressed the fur trappers and the Indians and helped to insure the success of the mission.

A large contingent of Nez Perce and Flathead at the rendezvous prevailed upon the missionaries to settle among their people, whom Jason Lee had bypassed in favor of settling in the Willamette Valley. Whitman, Parker decided, would return east for reinforcements; he himself would travel on alone with the Nez Perce and Flathead, explore the territory, and select suitable sites for the establishment of missions. Whitman expressed understandable concern: here was a fifty-six-year-old man, unaccustomed to the rigors and nuances of wilderness travel, who had previously relied upon the good graces of the fur trappers and Whitman for safety, the preparation of his meals, and the care of his camp equipment; now he planned to continue on west under the care of "uncivilized" Indians. But Parker persisted, proclaiming that his Christian faith would sustain him in his travels. He was not to be denied an opportunity to explore further west and ultimately bring Christianity to the Indians. When they parted, perhaps partly as reassurance, Parker agreed to meet Whitman and the additional missionaries at the next season's rendezvous.

The Nez Perce and Flathead contingent themselves soon put any fears to rest. The former appointed a member of their band to assist Parker throughout the journey, and all took great pains to assure that all his needs were met. The Indians prepared his meals, provided him with fresh mounts, packed his gear, and set up his camp, and many of the women provided him with fresh flowers and berries when available. They even adhered to his insistence on no travel on the sabbath, although they did not fully understand the reason for such a gesture.

Parker and the Indians traveled as far as Jackson Hole with a group of fur trappers under the direction of Jim Bridger. They then crossed into later Idaho as they proceeded west through Teton Pass and entered the Teton Basin (known as Pierres Hole to the fur trappers), site of the battle in which participants in the 1833 rendezvous engaged a party of Blackfoot warriors. After viewing the site, Parker discounted the popularized version of the encounter, which had the Blackfoot warriors entrenched in a densely wooded swamp, and provided a more accurate description of the battleground. From there the procession followed the Teton River northwest, crossing Henry's Fork and continuing on to Birch Creek (at the time identified as Cote's Defile). Here they rested and waited for another band of Nez Perce to join them.

A visitor to their camp on Sunday, September 6, would have witnessed what must have been an interesting worship service. The Indians constructed a shelter one hundred feet long and twenty feet wide, to hold a gathering of over four hundred, and covered the ground with furs. The congregation remained kneeling and demonstrated great patience throughout a long oration by Parker. An intepreter had recently arrived from Fort Hall, and the addition of his rendition of Parker's remarks must have made for a long service. Parker was deeply moved by the whole experience and felt that the gathering had made his trip across the Rocky Mountains truly worthwile.

The next day the company continued up Birch Creek until they crossed the divide into the Lemhi Valley. While following the Lemhi River to the Salmon River, they encountered a herd of buffalo near modern Leadore; Parker observed the methods used by the Indians to pursue the game and prepare the meat. After the hunt, the Flathead contingent and a good portion of the Nez Perce departed to pursue more buffalo. Parker and the remaining Nez Perce traveled down the Salmon River, and he made note of Captain B. L. E. Bonneville's abandoned 1832 winter post and a deposit of salt on the south side of the river.

Shortly after leaving the Salmon at North Fork, Parker and ten Indians left the main band in order to make better time. The smaller group followed up the North Fork to Hughes Creek and then headed northwest again up the creek and across the divide into Montana. They reentered Idaho through Nez Perce Pass and continued on westward over the Nez Perce Trail. (There is still much speculation as to why the Lewis and Clark expedition in 1805 and 1806 did not follow this route, as it is more direct than the Lolo Trail.) The party eased their way around and over the mountains, passing Red River Hot Springs and the site of Elk City before reaching the South Fork of the Clearwater River.[4] They crossed the river just north of modern Stites and then traveled across Camas Prairie to Webb Creek, which they followed down to the site of Lewiston and the junction of the Clearwater with the Snake. The party crossed the Snake and followed it down to Hudson's Bay Company Fort Walla Walla, where Parker bade goodbye to his Nez Perce escort and promised them that missionaries would soon be among them.

Three Walla Walla Indians accompanied Parker on the last leg of his westward journey, down the Columbia River to Fort Vancouver. Dr. John McLoughlin, the Hudson's Bay Company's chief factor there, welcomed him and offered him the hospitality of the fort—as he would succeeding American travelers. During the winter of 1835-36, Parker went on various exploring tours, supplied by the Hudson's Bay Company; preached; interviewed many of the company's employees about the various Indian tribes and the geography and geology of the country; and began a daily meteorological table. He visited Fort George (Astoria) and Jason Lee's mission on the Willamette. These visits and interviews led him to predict accurately the demise of the fur trade and the rise of commercial enterprises along the Columbia River.

When spring came, Parker left the fort for a tour of the country upriver. He stayed at Fort Walla Walla for a short time, preaching to the Indians, and then a delegation of Nez Perce escorted him back to the junction of the Clearwater and the Snake. They were willing to take him on to that year's rendezvous over the route traversed the previous year but not to lead

him eastward through the Snake River country that he wished
to cross, so Parker decided to forego an overland trip to the rendezvous and returned to Fort Walla Walla, where he secured
guides to take him overland northward to Fort Colville. It is un-
fortunate that he was unable to procure Nez Perce support for
a trip east across the Snake River Plain, as his excellent descriptions would have been a welcome addition to the literature of
the area.

Parker returned from Fort Colville via the Columbia: he obtained a boat at Fork Okanagan and floated down the river to
Fort Vancover. On June 18, 1836, he began the long voyage
home. The steamship *Beaver* carried him to Fort George, where
he transferred to the sailing ship *Columbia* for the journey to
Hawaii. Problems with connections kept him in the islands for
five months, but his prolonged visit provided an opportunity to
record his views on island activities and to work on his journal.
He finally sailed for home on December 17 aboard the *Phoe-
nix Allyn*, traveling via Tahiti and Cape Horn.

The decision to return by ship rather than overland came as
a surprise to Whitman, who expected to meet Parker at the 1836
rendezvous. Although Parker sent a letter explaining the situation, Whitman was not pleased. His dissatisfaction with Parker's
actions would deepen: the very positive tone of Parker's journal—
which was also his official report to the ABCFM—would create
problems for the missionaries who actually settled in the Oregon country and for Whitman in particular. Glowing report of
the resources available in the Oregon country—and Parker's state-
ment that he had to spend only two dollars for services and goods
after leaving Council Bluffs—made matters very difficult for
Whitman when the latter requested funds from the ABCFM for
the operation and survival of his missionary efforts.

Parker's missionary zeal and exploring tour paved the way for subsequent missionary stations, and his specific recommendations were carried out promptly. He recommended the area at the junction of the Clearwater and the Snake as the site for a Nez Perce mission station; Henry and Eliza Spalding would establish such a mission the next year on nearby Lapwai Creek. After his first visit to Fort Walla Walla, he recommended that area; the following year Marcus and Narcissa Whitman established a mission at Waiilatpu, not too far from the fort. On his travels from Fort Vancouver, he was much impressed with the country around Spokane and recommended it; in 1839, Elkanah and Mary Walker started a mission at Tshimakain, just north of modern Spokane.

But Samuel Parker never returned west himself as a missionary: he spent the remainder of his life in Ithaca preaching, publishing his journal, and giving speeches throughout the East promoting Oregon. Marcus Whitman's efforts and his role in the settlement of Oregon have been well documented, but Parker's influence has been largely overlooked. His book, with its optimistic reports of the country and its native inhabitants, coupled with his numerous public presentations, helped to encourage the settlement of Oregon. The published journal included, to the great benefit of potential emigrants, the most informative map of the Oregon Territory then in existence.

The popularity of *Journal of an Exploring Expedition* enabled it to go through five American and three European editions. After the first edition, Parker enlarged some parts and edited others, but, as he stated in the preface, he continued to adhere to the facts and "this scrupulous regard to truth is the principal merit claimed for the volume" (p. 2). The first American edition was published in 1838 and contained 371 pages; subsequent editions followed at two-year intervals. The final edition (1846) contained 422 pages. All three European editions were heavily edited: Dublin, 1840, 209 pages; Dresden, 1840, 241 pages; and Edinburgh, 1841, 78 pages. In 1967 a limited edition of the 1838 version was published by Ross & Haines of Minneapolis with an index but no introduction. The reprinting of the third edition will now make available this important descriptive account of western travels to a wider audience.

NOTES

[1]*Presbyterian Historical Almanac 1867*, 315-17, copy in Clifford M. Drury Collection, Idaho State Historical Society, Boise. See also the Suggested Readings below for further information on Parker's life.

[2]Merrill Mattes, eminent historian of the overland migration, calls it the Northern Route or Council Bluffs road and estimates that one-third of the overland traffic used it, with the heaviest usage in the first half of the 1850s. Phone conversation with the author, April, 1990.

[3]In 1857, Frederick Lander utilized a portion of this route while surveying a new road to California that was officially designated the Fort Kearney, South Pass, and Honey Lake Road but became popularly known as the Lander Road.

[4]Today, a Forest Service road closely follows the route and is one of Idaho's most scenic roads.

SUGGESTED READINGS

Davidson, Stanley. "Worker in God's Wilderness." *Montana the Magazine of Western History* (January, 1957), 7:8-17.

Drury, Clifford M. *Marcus Whitman, M.D.* Caldwell, Idaho: The Caxton Printers, Ltd., 1937.

_____. *Marcus and Narcissa Whitman and the Opening of Old Oregon.* 2 vols. Glendale, California: The Arthur H. Clark Company, 1958.
_____. "Samuel Parker." *The Presbyterian Banner,* June 27, 1935, pp. 6-7.

Eells, Myron. *Marcus Whitman, Pathfinder and Patriot.* Seattle: The Alice Harriman Company, 1909.

_____. "Rev. Samuel Parker." *Whitman College Quarterly* (1898), 2:3-34.

Manuscript collections that contain material related to Parker can be found at the Houghton Library, Harvard University, Cambridge, Massachusetts; Idaho State Historical Society, Boise; Washington State University, Pullman; and Whitman College, Walla Walla, Washington.

PREFACE.

In presenting to the public the Journal of a Tour beyond the Rocky Mountains, the only apology, necessary to offer, is the hope of promoting a more extensive and particular knowledge, than has hitherto been furnished, of the condition of that important section of our country. The author's mode of traveling furnished many opportunities for observation, being conducted with leisure, through one of the most interesting portions of the wide territories of the west. It is believed that no defects exist in the work, irreconcilable with a strict adherence to facts, and this scrupulous regard to truth is the principal merit claimed for the volume. The most of what is narrated came under the author's personal observation, and whatever is stated which did not, was obtained from gentlemen connected with the Hudson Bay Company, whose reputation for honesty and candor, as well as capability of judging intelligently, is well established. This source of information was available by collecting and comparing the statements of different individuals, retaining what corresponded with his own observation, or was well supported by evidence. The belief is cherished, that the following work contains a greater amount of statistical information in regard to the country, and important facts, than is to be found in any production furnished by the press. Having gone over a greater extent of territory than any traveler who had preceded, and with the express object of exploring the condition of the aboriginal population, this position cannot be considered as assumed. Messrs. Lewis and Clarke passed the Rocky Mountains under a governmental appointment to explore the country, more than thirty years since, and their published narrative carries with it evidence of candor and intelligence, and contains much valuable information; yet their opportunities for observation were somewhat limited. They passed over the great chain of mountains from the head waters of the Missouri between the 45° and 46° of north latitude, and came upon the head waters of the Cooscootskee, and followed that river to its junction with the Lewis or Snake river, and then proceeded by water to the Pacific ocean at the mouth of the Columbia river, wintered upon the south side of the bay, and early the following spring returned to the mountains by the same route which they pursued on their outward journey. All other persons who have published any history of their travels beyond the mountains, were persons engaged in the fur trade, and many of their observations upon different sections of the country are just, but they are deficient in statistical information, and their productions are mostly confined to personal ad-

ventures, anecdotes of battles with Blackfeet or Crow Indians, starvation, and hair-breadth escapes.   Justice to the
public requires fidelity in the historian and traveler.   It is
not our business to originate facts, but to record them.   The
license given to poets, or writers of romance, cannot be
tolerated here, and no flights of a lively imagination, or
graphic powers in relating passing occurrences, can atone
for impressions which are not in accordance with truth.

While it was a leading object to become acquainted with
the situation of the remote Indian tribes, and their disposition in regard to teachers of Christianity, yet a careful attention was given to the geography of the country, with its
productions; the climate and seasons, animals, lakes, rivers,
and smaller fountains ; forests and prairies, mountains and
valleys, its mineral and geological structure, and all the various aspects of its physical condition.   The country here
described is *sui generis ;* every thing is formed on a large
scale.   Its lofty and perpetual snow-topped mountains rising
20,000 feet or more above the ocean, the trees of the forest,
the widely extended prairies, plants of enormous growth, and
the results of volcanic agency which are met with in almost
every direction, render the whole an ever increasing scene
of interest to the traveler; and if any statements appear
large, it is because the facts are so in themselves.

It has been an object in writing this volume to compress
as much as possible the amount of information, instead of

unnecessarily extending it, and the hope is indulged, that while these facts are perused, the desire may be awakened if it do not already exist, to benefit the original, the rightful owners, and with the exception of a few thousand fur traders scattered in every direction over this territory, the sole occupants of this wide field of uncultivated nature.

The map which accompanies the work has been prepared with much labor and care; and though some minute parts are omitted, it will be found far more accurate than any which has before been published. In addition to my own surveys, I have availed myself of those of gentlemen connected with the Hudson Bay Company, in parts which I did not visit, and am especially indebted to Vancouver and the labors of other explorers for much that I have delineated of the North-West coast of the Pacific ocean, and the Islands.

PREFACE TO THE SECOND EDITION.

THE interest the public have taken in this work, evinced by the many highly commendatory reviews and notices, which have appeared in numerous periodicals, religious, scientific, and political, both in this country and in Europe, together with the sale of the first edition, has influenced the author to publish a second edition. Many persons, whose judgment, extensive knowledge, and piety, entitle them to be held in high estimation, have encouraged him to believe that this work has been interesting to men of science, useful in advancing general knowledge, and promoting the spirit of missions, and what is not the least to be valued, a sympathy for the long neglected Indians of Oregon.

As it was an object in preparing the first edition to compress as great an amount of information as possible in the compass of a duodecimo volume, so in this—the same object has been pursued, and while some parts have been enlarged, others have been abridged. The whole work has been attentively revised and corrected. It is hoped that it will contribute its influence, however small it may be, in aiding the cause of human welfare. I shall be pardoned if I assert the sentiment, that the acquisition of all knowledge should be made subservient to this important use, and that the gold from any region, if it cannot be refined in this crucible, is of no real value, and whatever will not directly or indirectly, nearly or remotely, concur in this great end, must at length endure the ultimate fate of that "knowledge which shall vanish away."

———————

PREVIOUS editions having been so well received, a third is now published, having undergone a careful revision, and some parts have been re-written, and additions have been made. It is hoped that it will be found not the less worthy of public favor.

ITHACA, 1842.

PARKER'S TOUR.

CHAPTER I.

The Tour commenced by way of Buffalo, Erie and Pittsburgh—passage to Cincinnati in the steam-boat Ohioan—the steam-boat takes fire—Cincinnati—Falls of the Ohio—the Ohio river—Ohio and Kentucky—confluence of the Ohio and Mississippi rivers—Point Girardou—beautiful appearance of fire on the prairie—St. Genevieve, old custom—Herculaneum—gambling on board the steamboats—St. Louis—Dr. M. Whitman—Mr. Fontenelle.

THE wide extent of country beyond the Mississippi and the Rocky Mountains, with its inhabitants and physical condition, has been a subject of interesting enquiry for the last thirty years. Many things, relating to the possession of the country, its future probable importance in a political view, its population and trade, have occupied much attention. The Christian public have not been inattentive to the interests, moral and religious, of those whom the God of providence has placed in these remote regions, and who are without the blessings of civilization and Christianity. The American Board of Commissioners for Foreign Missions appointed an exploring mission to that country, to ascertain by personal observation, the condition and character of the Indian nations and tribes, and the facilities for introducing the gospel and civilization among them.

That difficulties and dangers would be incident to a journey through a country of such extent, uninhabited except by wandering bands of Indians, where no provisions could be obtained besides uncertain game, could not be doubted. It was not a consciousness of undaunted courage, or indifference to suffering, or the love of romance, which fixed my purpose ; but it was the importance of the object. Although it was painful to bid adieu to family and friends, unapprised of the events of the future, yet committing all to the guidance and protection of an all-wise Providence, the enterprise was undertaken, without reluctance, on the 14th of March, 1835. Pursuing the journey by the way of Buffalo and Erie, I arrived at Pittsburgh on the twenty-fifth. The intervening distance to St. Louis, through the great valley of the west, had lost much of its novelty, having previously passed over it, and long since has it ceased to excite that degree of interest in the community, with which it was regarded before the numerous descriptions of the tourist and traveler had rendered its general features familiar. Only a passing notice, therefore, will be given.

Leaving Pittsburgh, which, from its multiplied manufactories, may be styled the Birmingham of America, I took passage in the steam-boat Ohioan, for Cincinnati, four hundred and fifty miles distant, by the river. The scenery of the Ohio, as it pursues its meandering course to the Mississippi, presents a most beautiful variety of forests, and cultivated fields, and flourishing villages. On the 28th, we arrived at Cincinnati. The steam-boat on that day was discovered to be on fire in the hold, in which were a large quantity of combustible goods. This created great alarm. A very strong head wind blew the fire from the furnace down the hatchway, which, after removing some goods, had been carelessly left open. The captain immediately rounded the boat to the shore, and no sooner was it gained, than there was a general rush for safety. Some of the passengers threw out their baggage, and many leaped from the upper deck to the land. The fire, however, was subdued, and with considerable difficulty we disengaged the boat from its grounded position, and from the trees among which it was entangled, and we were again under way.

Cincinnati is a large city for a country so new, and from its mature appearance would hardly be thought to have been the growth of only half a century. Its population, composed of emigrants from New England, the middle, and some of the southern states, and from various parts of Europe, is consequently not very homogeneous in its character. Its schools and institutions of literature, promise much for the great interests of science and religion in this interesting section of our growing country.

Here I exchanged my situation on board the Ohioan, for the Chien, Captain Reynolds, for St. Louis, which, by water is six hundred and ninety miles from Cincinnati. On the 30th, we passed Louisville, near which are the falls of the Ohio, twenty-two feet in height, and passable by boats only in high water, about two months in a year. To save the expense and delay of portage around the falls, a canal has been constructed on the south side of the river, two miles in length, fifty feet wide, and forty feet deep.

The water being high, we passed over the falls. It was a sublime scene. The water about Louisville moves slowly and smoothly; but as you approach the falls, it increases in velocity and power. You soon find yourself in an irresistible current; and you are anxious to know whether your pilots are well skilled in their profession. You look at them to see if they betray any fear ; you find, that while their attention is fixed, their countenances are serene. Your fears give way to emotions of the sublime. The boat shoots forward with amazing force and velocity, and very soon you find yourself gliding along in the wide-spread calm below.

The Ohio is a noble river, affording in its whole course romantic and beautiful prospects. It flows in a smooth and easy current, and is diversified on every side with rich bottom land, rolling hills, and precipitous bluffs. These hills and bluffs, in many places, rise abruptly from the shore of the river, in other places they recede some miles, but in every part are in view ; and so varied is the scenery, that there is no weariness caused by monotony. No where has the hand of industry been wanting to add interest in passing through this part of the great western valley. Farms, and towns, and villages, exhibit the advantage that has been taken of the exuberance of the soil. The many swift-moving, panting steam-boats show that industry furnishes the means of wide-extended and profitable commerce. The striking difference in the taste and habits of the people inhabiting the two sides of the river, was here very apparent. Upon the Ohio side, the farms and neatly painted dwellings are in the New England style, while on the Kentucky side, scattered here and there, you see the large log houses of the planters in a grade of architecture considerably above the log cabins of their slaves, by which they are surrounded, yet log houses still. These are built two stories high, with a wide airy hall through the centre, one of the lower rooms being the parlor, and the other serves the several purposes of a nursery, sleeping, and eating room. Open, frank hospitality characterizes the Kentuckian, which is pleasing to a stranger. I offered a lady in one of these mansions some tracts, which she at first declined with the enquiry, "Do you think we are heathen?" "No, madam; but tracts contain much that is interesting to all classes of people, and after they are read, can be circulated among those who may not be well supplied with books." I saw but very few houses of worship, except in villages.

On the first of April we passed out of the waters of the Ohio into those of the Mississippi. The Ohio spreads out into a narrow sea and meets the Mississippi in the same form. Both appear to expand themselves into their most majestic forms, as though each was making an effort to claim the superiority; and when joined, they move on with united grandeur. We should expect, at the confluence of these two rivers, to find a business-going village, but instead of such a place, there is only a whiskey-selling tavern, surrounded by a few miserable huts.

To-day, a boy ten or twelve years old, playing about the machinery of the boat, was caught in it by the leg, and had he not been immediately seized and extricated by two men standing by, must have been drawn wholly in and crushed to pieces. The bones were not broken, but the calf of the leg was distressingly mangled. There being no surgeon on board I officiated in dressing his wounds.

Passed, on the second, Point Girardou, fifty miles above the mouth of the Ohio. It is pleasantly situated upon a bluff on the west side of the Mississippi. It has a fine prospect of the river, and might, under the hand of industry, become a desirable place; but the French Catholics are not an enterprising people, and it has the appearance of decay. We moved but slowly against the wind and current.

The fires of the prairies coming over the bluffs, presented a very pleasing scene this evening. These bluffs are two hundred feet high, and extend one or two miles along the river. At a considerable distance they appeared like an illuminated city, but as we approached and had a nearer view, the illusion was dissipated. The fires had advanced nearly over the bluffs, and curtained them with a moderately ascending blaze, drawn up on the bluffs and let down in festoons in the ravines ; and the counterpart reflected from the smooth waters of the broad Mississippi, added much to the beauty and grandeur of the prospect.

A short stay was made on the third, at the landing of St. Genevieve. The village is situated a mile back from the river on the west side, and is inhabited almost entirely by French, who are slow to depart from the customs and manners established by their forefathers, who have long since passed away. To adopt new improvements would be a step next to giving up their catholic religion and turning infidel. It is amusing to see the manner they yoke their oxen, and to learn the reason they assign for so doing. The yoke is composed of a straight piece of wood, fastened to the back side of the horns by straps of leather. They say, that in this way, they save the whole power of the animal ; but that the yoke, bowed to the neck, and drawn back to the shoulder, loses the power of the head and neck. Their reasoning may satisfy themselves, but would not the thorough-going New England farmer.

To-day Herculaneum appeared in sight, which is situated on the west side of the river, thirty-five miles below St. Louis. It is almost surrounded by high precipitous hills, having only a narrow space for a village. There are several shot-towers, placed on the brink of high bluffs, in which con-

siderable business is done.   Large quantities of lead, brought
from the mines, are sold and carried to distant markets.

In travelling upon these waters, it is painful to see how
few books of any value there are on board the steam-boats.
Some novels are found, but the most of them are of a licen-
tious character.   Thousands of those who navigate these
rivers are going to the judgment regardless of the interests
of their souls, and most of them are destitute of the Bible.
It gave great offence to many, that we should have religious worship in the ladies' cabin, as we did by invitation.
Complaints of obtrusion were made—"Obtruding religion
—no place for such things."   But profanity and gambling
are no obtrusion; they are always in time and always in
place.   Christians must keep religion out of sight and hearing, but the wicked may be as open and obtrusive as they
please.   Gambling is practised on board the steam-boats
upon these waters to a very great extent, and is a favorite
amusement with those whose minds are not sufficiently cultivated to find satisfaction in reading, or intelligent conversation.   The number of black-legs who make gambling
their business is great, and they are adepts in their profession, as their success depends very much upon their skill
in deception, and in decoying the inexperienced.

On the evening of the fourth, we arrived at St. Louis.
This is a flourishing business place, situated on the west
side of the Mississippi, two hundred miles above the mouth
of the Ohio, and twenty miles below the mouth of the Missouri, and in its local position resembles Albany, N. Y.
The ground ascends for about a half mile from the river,
and then spreads out into a widely extended plain, partly
covered with shrubbery, back of which are open prairies.

In the parts of the town built by the French, the streets

are narrow. This may have been done to accommodate their propensity to be sociable, by enabling them to converse from the windows across the streets. The French population, with few exceptions, are Roman Catholics, noted for their indolence and dissipation. Gambling is their favourite amusement; and they have houses devoted to this object, with signs up, like those of whiskey venders. As gambling does not increase wealth, there are but few rich, enterprising men among the French population. Drunkenness is not common, and the temperance cause is doing much to remove what exists. Eastern enterprise and influence is gaining ground since the town has been brought under the laws of the United States; and a new impulse is given to business. This is the central place in the west for the fur trade, which is carried on by the American Fur Company to a considerable extent; and also much business is done in lead, which is obtained at Galena. A great number of steam-boats and other water craft, of various descriptions and destinations, are seen here at all seasons of the year. Adventurers, of almost every description of character and nation, collect here, such as trappers, hunters, miners, and emigrants, as a starting point from whence to go into the still far west, many of whom seek a miserable fortune among the Rocky Mountains. The local situation of this town is such, that it will undoubtedly continue to be one of the first places for trade in the great valley of the Mississippi. There are five houses of worship, four Protestant and one Roman Catholic. The Catholic cathedral is built of a firm light brown sandstone, and is a large expensive building. The Protestant influence is increasing, and there are here many active, devoted Christians, who exert a salutary influence upon the town and vicinity around. The population is fifteen thousand.

Doctor Marcus Whitman had already arrived here, who is appointed by the American Board of Commissioners for Foreign Missions to be my associate. He came through the central parts of Ohio, Indiana and Illinois, and arrived a few days before me. On the 7th, we had an interview with Mr. Fontenelle, who takes charge of the caravan sent out by the American Fur Company. The caravan proceeds a very little beyond the Rocky Mountains, for the purpose of carrying out goods for the Indian trade, and supplies for their men who are engaged in hunting and trapping; and returns with the furs which they have taken during the year. There are about three hundred men constantly employed in and about the mountains, and more than sixty who constitute the caravan. With a much less number it would be unsafe to perform this journey, as there are hostile tribes of Indians on the way, viz: the Arickaras, the Crows, and Blackfeet. Having obtained permission of the principal agents of the company, Mr. Fontenelle kindly offered to accommodate us with such advantages as may be afforded in his caravan. Finding it necessary to leave this place to-day for Liberty, which is one of the most western towns in the United States, we were very busily employed in making preparation for the journey, and in calling upon and bidding farewell to Christian friends. A fire last night destroyed a very large livery stable, in which we lost a horse, saddle, and bridle. The old cathedral, which was used for a store-house, was also burnt, together with a very large quantity of crockery which it contained.

CHAPTER II.

AT five o'clock, P. M. we went on board the steam-boat
St. Charles, Capt. Shellcross, and ascended the river twenty
miles ; anchored at the confluence of the Missouri and
Mississippi, and lay by for the night, as it was dangerous to
proceed, on account of the many snags and sand bars in
the Missouri.

On the eighth, proceeding up the Missouri by rather slow
progress, the first stop was made at St. Charles, which is
twenty miles above the confluence of this river with the
Mississippi, and the same distance north-west from St. Louis.
This is a pleasantly situated village, upon the north side
of the river. The country around is interesting, and the
soil of superior quality. An enterprising Christian population would make this one of the most desirable places in
the west. Soon after we left the shore, a boy six years of
age, fell overboard, but, from the swiftness of the current,
and as the boat was under full way, there was no opportunity to save him. He was seen floating a short time, but
before the yawl could be loosed from its fastening, and

manned, he sunk, and was seen no more. His mother, a widow, and her family, were removing from Kentucky to Franklin, Mo. The mother and the children lamented greatly and loudly.

Near the middle of the day, on the ninth, we struck a snag or rock, so deep beneath the turbid water, that we could not determine which it was, and it became necessary to repair one of the wheels of the boat, which was much injured. This afforded an opportunity to go on shore. Several of my fellow voyagers and myself ascended one of those high bluffs, which frequently skirt this river. This was accomplished by climbing on our hands and feet up an elevation of several hundred feet. Here we had a delightful view of the surrounding country, with its intermingled prairie and wood land, its cultivated spots, and its hills and dales. But in attempting to return, a new difficulty interposed. I said we ascended on our hands and feet—could we return in the same way? We were compelled, by descending backwards, to use much caution, and letting ourselves down by the grass, or sometimes a shrub or tree, and assisting each other, we came safely to the shore. We also visited a place, some distance below this, where Lewis and Clark encamped three days, the state of the river being such that they could not ascend with their batteaux. Many wild turkeys were seen along upon the uninhabited shores. On the tenth, our boat discharged a part of her cargo at Portland, a small newly built village. A fellow passenger, a merchant of this place, on landing, immediately put in requisition some thirty colored men, women, and children, who readily, without the aid of horses or carts, transferred his merchandise to its destination.

The boat stopped on the 11th, at Jefferson city, the cap-

ital of the state, situated on the south side of the river, upon
a high eminence, a little above the Osage river.   It has a
great name for so small a place.   The state house is of a
size which would be decent for a small academy ; and the
governor's house would do very well for a common farmer's
house in the country, but not such as we should expect
for a governor in *Jefferson City*.   But the state of Missouri
is comparatively new, and this place may in time support
its name.

Sabbath, the 12th, I remained in my state room, and endeavored to observe the day according to the commandment.

On Monday we passed Boonsville and Franklin, small
villages, which have a country of rich land around them,
and when it is brought under good cultivation, they must
rise in importance.   The scenery up this river is sufficiently
diversified to excite interest and to charm.   The trees along
the shores are mostly oak and cotton-wood, with some hac-
berry and buckeye, and it is interesting to see how easily
and how deep they take root in the free rich soil along the
river.   Frequently, where the banks are washing away, the
roots of the trees are exposed to full view, and generally
there is only a large central root descending ten or twelve
feet, with small ones branching out, presenting the appearance of an inverted cone.   The river makes nothing of
washing away, and forming islands.   Sand bars and snags
are so common, that, becoming accustomed to them, we
hardly think of danger.

We found the steam-boat Siam, on 14th, Captain L., at
Chariton, on board of which the St. Charles put her freight
and passengers, and returned ; both boats having so far
discharged their freight, that one could proceed with the
remainder.   When under way, the boat run upon a sand

bar, which gave it a sudden whirl about, apparently threat-
ening a disaster, but the quicksand of which the bar was
composed, soon washed away, and we went ahead again.
Running aground in this river is a very different thing from
what it would be in most waters; for the bars are so generally formed of quicksand, that in most instances the current
around the boat sets all clear.

Soon after getting under way, on the 16th, we ran upon
a bar, where we were detained two and a half hours, and
so frequently were we upon these obstructions, that we made
only five miles before one o'clock, P. M. Called at Lexington, a village pleasantly situated one mile back from the
landing, and surrounded by a fine country. We made only
about fifteen miles headway to-day, which is so slow, that it
would have been far more pleasant traveling by land; and
to have been free from imprisonment with shockingly profane swearers and gamblers, most of whom are intemperate.

It was necessary to spend the nineteenth, another Sabbath,
on board the steam-boat. How great a contrast to the sa-
credness of the day when it is enjoyed in the Christian family circle; or in the sanctuary where God is worshiped in
the great congregation; or in the quiet, unobtrusive sabbath
school, where attentive minds sit down to study the word of
God, that they may practice its precepts, and where the
teachers are heard explaining and enforcing divine truth
upon the young and tender conscience.

As we passed along, I saw many children standing on the
banks of the river, and thought how benevolent persons at
the east had desired their religious instruction, and how
much had been done for the enterprise; but it had failed to
reach these. I also reflected on the examples of infidelity
and vice around them, by which they are educated for de-

struction, and endeavored to ask the Great Benefactor of all to do that for them which it was not in my power to do. I contrasted in my mind the difference between kindred souls in sweet communion in the service of God to-day, and the unrestrained wickedness of ungodly men, which my eyes and ears were witnessing, and said, when will the kingdoms of this world become the kingdoms of our Lord and his Christ.

About the middle of the day, the captain and his men appeared to be given up to blind infatuation. The Siam was a new, well-built boat, had four boilers, and it was her first season. They appeared to regard no bounds in raising and applying steam. Such was the power under which the boat labored, that she more than trembled. For a long time I expected some disaster, and looked at the captain to see if I could discover any apprehensions of danger. There was no want of evidence that there was a free use of ardent spirits. Soon the disaster came, though less extensive than I had feared; the main shaft, which was large and made of iron, broke, and farther progress was impossible.

Monday, 20th. The day was spent in endeavoring to find some remedy for the disaster, but all to no purpose. It only remained to discharge her cargo upon the wilderness shore, let her passengers take care of themselves, and return with one wheel, like a crippled winged fowl. Two miles above us lay the steam-boat Nelson, upon a sand bar high and dry. She ran aground upon the Sabbath, and being left by a freshet in the river, is waiting for another, to be liberated. Our captain remarked at dinner to-day, that most of the accidents which happen to steam-boats take place on the Sabbath; and that he did not believe it would be long before they would not run on that day. We engaged a man to take us in a wagon to Liberty, and towards evening went out into a small neighborhood of Mormons, where we lodged. They had fled from Jackson county, which they call their promised land, and to which they say they shall return. They are a poor deluded people, and when they speak of their persecutions, they seem not to possess the spirit our Saviour, who, when he was reviled, reviled not again, and when he suffered, threatened not.

We rode on the 21st, twelve miles to Liberty, through a very pleasant and fertile country, thinly inhabited, well supplied with woods, and sufficiently undulating and hilly to render it healthy. It was at that opening season of the year, when nature, arousing itself from the sleep of winter, appears with renovated beauty. Not only man, but flowers, and trees, and birds, seemed to enjoy the season and the scene. I was much charmed with the wood duck, (A. Sponsa) which here were numerous; the variety of its colors was adapted to the beauty of the scenery which surrounded us. And the sprightly deer did not seem to accelerate its movements so much from fear, as from love of flight.

Liberty is a small village, situated three miles north of the river, and is the county town of Clay. It has a courthouse of brick—several stores, which do considerable business, a rope-walk, and a number of decent dwelling houses.

Continued in this place about three weeks, waiting for the caravan to get in readiness. At this place it forms—men, horses and mules, and wagons, are collected and put in readiness; and from this place commences the long journey for the west. While we remained here, we had an opportunity to collect much information from those who have been to and beyond the Rocky Mountains, in regard to the country, mode of traveling, and concerning the various Indian tribes on the way. Captain Ford, and Lieutenant Stein from Fort

Leavenworth, were also here. They are both professors of religion, and appear to be well acquainted with the Indian country. Lieut. S. has been much among the Indians, was out with the dragoons the last year—and was among the Pawnee Picts. He gives a very favorable account of them, and thinks the way is open to establish a mission among them with fair prospects of success. He also thinks the way is prepared, or is preparing, for a mission among the Camanches, who heretofore have been hostile, but now wish for peace and trade with the Americans. I saw also a Mr. Vaughn of this place, a Baptist professor, who has made two trips to Santa Fe, and has resided two years in that place. He gives a very interesting description of the Navahoes, a tribe who number about two thousand warriors. Their country lies between the Rio Del Norte and the eastern branches of Rio Colorado. They carry on agriculture to a very considerable extent ; have large herds of cattle and horses, and flocks of sheep ; and have many domestic manufactures and houses of good construction. They are friendly to the Americans, but not to the Spaniards. Mr. V. thinks they would readily receive Protestant missionaries, and would prefer them to Roman Catholics, because of their hostility to the Spaniards. He also speaks well of the Paches, or Apaches, a small tribe on the Del Norte towards old Mexico. These have been at war three years with the Spaniards.

Saturday, May 9th, rode twenty-six miles to Cantonment Leavenworth, which is situated on the west side of the Missouri river, nearly twenty miles out of the United States. The way is through a fertile section of country, part of the distance is an open prairie, other parts are handsomely wooded, and all well adapted to cultivation. I had an introduc-

tion to several of the officers, and made my home at Lieut.
S's, an agreeable and religious family.

I preached three times on the Sabbath, and most of the
people of the garrison assembled, and gave good attention.
There is a very considerable number of professors of religion attached to this station, but they have no chaplain
to teach and lead them in their devotions, which is a deficiency in our military establishments.   Colonel Dodge and
some of the other officers appear disposed to maintain good
order, and I should think they exert a salutary influence.
I had an opportunity, before I returned to Liberty, to take
a view of the fort and the adjacent country.   The buildings
of the fort are situated within an enclosure around a large,
beautiful square, which is covered with grass, and adorned
with shade trees.   The whole is on an elevation of a few
hundred feet, and has an interesting prospect of the majestic
river flowing on silently below.   The fertile country around
presents a wide and fine prospect, and when settled by an
industrious population, will equal the most favored parts of
the earth.

Liberty, and the surrounding country, is inhabited by
people of considerable enterprise, and when it shall be
brought under Christian influence, there will be but few
places more inviting.   There is but one Presbyterian minister in this county, a man of talents and very respectable
attainments, who is exerting a good influence.   The Bap-
tists in this section of country are unlike those of the east.
They are opposed to the benevolent operations of the day.
Elder H. the pastor of the church in this place, invited Rev.
Mr. Merril, a Baptist missionary, located among the Otoe
Indians of the Platte, and myself, to preach for him the
first Sabbath after our arrival.   His people objected, ap-

prehensive that Mr. Merril would say something about the
cause of temperance, or missionary efforts, and Elder H.
had to withdraw his invitation.   They profess to act from
Christian principles in refusing to give their minister any
thing for support, lest they should make him a hireling.

It is amusing to observe the provincialisms which are
common in this part of the country.   If a person intends to
commence a journey some time in the month, for instance,
in May ; he says, " I am going in all the month of May."
For a large assembly of people, they say, " a smart sprinkle
of people."   The word " balance," comes into almost every
transaction—" will you not have a dessert for the balance
of your dinner ?"—" to make out the *balance* of his night's
rest, he slept until eight in the morning."   If your baggage
is to be carried, it will be asked, " shall I *tote* your *plunder ?*"
This use of the word plunder is said to have originated in
the early predatory habits of the borderers.   They also
speak of a " mighty pleasant day"—" a mighty beautiful
flower"—" *mighty weak.*"   A gentleman, with whom I formed some acquaintance, invited me, when I should make " an
outing" for exercise, to call at his house ; for his family
would be " mighty glad" to see me.

During our continuance at this place, we were hospitably
entertained at the house of J. B. Esq., one of the judges of
the county court.   We were under many obligations to him
and Mrs. B. not only for their liberality, but also for the
privilege of retirement in so kind and intelligent a family.
Nor would we be unmindful of the hospitality shown us by
Rev. Mr. and Mrs. Y.

May 15th, all things being in readiness, we commenced
our journey for Council Bluffs, directing our course north-
west.   We did not get to-day beyond the boundaries of the

United States, and for the last time, for a long period to come, I lodged in the house of a civilized family.

The next day, we traveled twenty miles, which brought us beyond the limits of civilization, and into the Indian country, and encamped on a prairie surrounded with wood. The sensations excited by the circumstances of our situation were peculiar, and such as I had not before felt; in a wilderness, inhabited by unseen savages and wild beasts, engaged in setting our tent, preparing supper with only a few articles of furniture, the ground for our chairs, table, and bed. But all was conducted in good style; for I would not dispense with attention to decencies, because beyond the boundaries of civilization; and having adjusted every thing in good order, and offered up our evening devotions, we retired ro rest. But how to adjust all the anxieties and feelings of the mind, so as to obtain the desired repose, was a more difficult task.

On the 17th, I crossed over the east, or little Platte, which is a very considerable river, and spent the Sabbath with Mr. Gilmore, a Methodist professor, and governmental blacksmith for the Iowa Indians. Saw many Indians of the Iowa, Sioux, and Fox tribes. Among these a Fox Indian and his wife were noble-looking persons, having their faces painted with unmixed vermilion; the former entirely, and the latter in stripes. They felt too important to be seen noticing what was transpiring around, and seemed to think themselves the only objects worthy of notice.

Here is an excellent, fertile tract of country, and nothing discouraging for a missionary station, except the contaminating influence of vicious white men. The natives wish to cultivate their land, probably more from necessity than on any other account; for their game is mostly gone. One

of them came to Mr. Gilmore to get some ploughs, and remarked, "it is hard work to dig up our ground for corn by
hand." The Sioux here are only a small band, who would
not join Black Hawk in his war against the United States,
and who are now afraid to return to their own country.
Their condition is becoming more and more wretched; for
while they have not the knowledge, the means, nor much
of the inclination necessary to cultivate their lands advantageously, they have an insatiable thirst for ardent spirits;
and there are too many unprincipled men on our frontiers,
who, for the sake of gain, will supply them with the means
of drunkenness and destruction.

Leaving Mr. G., gratefully remembering his hospitality,
we rode on Monday, 18th, twelve miles to Blacksnake Hills.
At this place Mr. Rubedoux has a trading post, and an uncommonly fine farming establishment on the Missouri river.
His buildings are on a small elevation of land, having a
delightful prospect in front of more than a thousand acres
of open bottom land, lying along down the river; and hills
on the north and east partially covered with woods. What
has nature not wrought without the labor of man? The
herds of cattle, and other domestic animals, have as wide
a range as they choose, and fences are necessary only to
secure fields for cultivation.

The Indians here have a new mode of disposing of their
dead. A scaffold is raised about eight feet high, upon which
the dead are placed in rudely constructed coffins overspread
with skins.

Having obtained a supply of milk, I encamped out, pre-
ferring the field to the house, where I might have been sub-
jected to many kinds of annoyances.

For several days nothing special occurred. On the 22d,

we crossed the Nodaway river with a raft; the construction of which, and transporting our baggage, occupied most of the day. To construct a raft, a number of dry logs are collected, and secured together, side by side, with barks stripped from elm trees; some few men swim across the river, taking with them one end of a rope, while the other end is fastened to the raft; it is then shoved off, the men upon the other side of the river pulling upon the rope. The raft is generally drifted considerably down stream, before it is brought to land upon the opposite shore. In this manner they crossed and re-crossed, until the baggage was carried over. Then follows the swimming over the horses, which is attended with noise enough—hallooing of men, snorting of the horses, and throwing sticks and stones to prevent them, after having gone part the way over, from returning.

We saw many elk, but they were too wary to be approached, and too fleet to be chased, and our hunters were not sufficiently successful to obtain any. They are very large, and when their horns are on, have a very majestic appearance. We frequently found their horns on the prairie, some of which were four feet long, with large wide-spreading branches.

Sabbath, the twenty-fourth, passing over a brook near which we had encamped the evening before, my companion and myself remained for the day, while the caravan went on. The movements of the caravan are so slow, that we felt confident we could overtake them without any difficulty, and as there was no danger from the hostile Indians, we considered it our duty to rest on this holy day. The day was very warm for May, the thermometer standing, at two in the afternoon, at 88°.

The next day we overtook the caravan before night, and crossed the south branch of the Neshnabotana on a raft. Some of the men of the caravan, if not all, were much displeased, because we did not travel with them on the Sabbath. To express their displeasure, they cut some of the barks, with which the raft they had made was bound together, and set it adrift. Providentially it did not drift far before it lodged against a tree, and, without much loss of time, we repaired it and passed over.

On the twenty-sixth, came to the main branch of the Neshnabotana, and commenced making a raft, the finishing of which and crossing took most of the following day. The soil of this part of the country is rich, and the grass for our horses excellent ; but there are none here to till the ground, nor to gather in the ten thousand tons of hay, which might be made from the spontaneous growth. This part of the country does not yet answer the end for which it was created. The time will come, when a dense population will cover this country, who will render the sacrifice of prayer and praise to our God.

On the 28th, we rode eleven miles, and came to the north branch of the above mentioned river. After we had constructed a raft, we had a very difficult time of crossing. The water was continually and rapidly rising, and before we finished crossing, the banks were overflowed to considerable depth ; and the alluvial soil was rendered too soft to sustain our horses, and they sunk so deep that we could not proceed. After searching for a long time, a place was found sufficiently hard to bear up our animals when unloaded. We had to carry our baggage upon our shoulders about fifteen rods, part of the way in water mid deep, going forward and returning until all was carried to better ground; and then we had to ride a mile to the dry prairie in water one and two feet deep. We rejoiced to find ourselves once more on firm footing. Encamped by a stream of clear water, which is rare in this part of the country, and especially at this season of the year. The waters of all this portion of country, especially of the Missouri river and its large tributaries, are very turbid, owing to the nature of the soil over which they pass. A pail full of water, standing half an hour at the seasons of freshets, will deposit three-eighths of an inch of sediment; and yet the water, when settled, appears to be of good quality.

Our mode of living, from day to day, had already necessarily become uniform. Dry bread and bacon constituted our breakfast, dinner, and supper. The bacon we cooked, when we could obtain wood for fire; but when "out of sight of land," that is, when nothing but green grass could be seen, we eat our bacon without cooking. A very few of the simplest articles of furniture were sufficient for our culinary purposes. The real wants of life are few, artificial ones are numerous.

30th. Drew near to Council Bluffs, and passed down from the high rolling prairie, through a vale two or three miles long, and a half mile wide, into the rich alluvial, and widely extended valley of the Missouri, through a section of country of uncommonly interesting scenery. The mounds, which some have called the work of unknown generations of men, were scattered here in all varieties of forms and magnitudes; and thousands in number, and perhaps I may say ten thousands. Some of these mounds were conical, some eliptical, some square, and others parallelograms. One group of these attracted my attention more than any others. They were twelve in number, of conical form, with their bases joined, and twenty or thirty feet high. They formed about two-thirds of a circle, with an area of two hundred feet in diameter. If these were isolated, who would not say they are artificial ? But when they are only a group of ten thousand others, which have as much the appearance of being artificial, who will presume to say they are the work of man ? But if they are the work of art, and attest the number, the genius, and perseverance of departed nations, whose works have survived the lapse of ages, their history is shrouded in darkness. " The mind seeks in vain for some clue to assist it in unraveling the mystery. Was their industry stimulated by the desire to protect themselves against inroads of invaders, or were they themselves the aggressors ?" " Are they the monuments of western Pharaohs, and do they conceal treasures which may yet be brought to light ?" There is nothing plainer than that they were never designed as works of defense. But some, while they admit they were not designed for offensive or defensive operations of belligerent powers, supposed they were erected as " mausoleums, and that the difference in their size was intended to convey an idea of the difference in the relative importance of those whose bones they cover." If this theory is true, the La Trappe on the Mississippi, which I had an opportunity of examining on my northern tour, which is as much as one hundred and fifty feet high, and covering about six acres, must inclose mighty bones, or the bones of a mighty monarch. I would not be understood to dissent from the belief, that there are artificial mounds in the great valley of the west, but I believe there is a great mistake upon this subject. It is said, by those who advocate the belief, that they are the work of ancient nations, that they present plain evidence of this, from the fact that they contain human bones, articles of pottery, and the like, which evince that they were constructed for burying places of the dead. That some of them have been used for burying places is undoubtedly true ; but may it not be questionable whether they·were constructed, or only *selected* for burying places. Besides, if these mounds were works of human art, I confess myself wholly at a loss to discover the traces of *design*, which are always characteristic of every human effort. The absence of every other vestige of a race extinct, such as monuments, walls, cities, or ruins of any description, lead us to believe, that such a people must have lived only to burrow in the earth, as these mounds alone are all the traces they have left of their existence. Depopulate any portion of the world, with which we are acquainted, and, save the savages who roam the desert or the prairie, many centuries must elapse, before their monuments would entirely cease to exist. No one, who has ever seen the immense number of mounds scattered through the valley of the Mississippi, will ever be so credulous as to believe, that a five hundredth part of them are the work of man.

We crossed the Maragine river, which, though very deep,· was not so wide but that we constructed a bridge over it. Proceeding many miles through the rich bottom lands of the Missouri, we crossed this noble river over against Bellevue, in a large canoe, and swam our horses and mules across, which, on account of the width of the river and the strength of the current, required much effort. I went to the agency house, where I was happy to find brethren Dunbar and Allis, missionaries to the Pawnees, under the direction of the American Board of Commissioners for Foreign Missions. There is a Baptist mission here, composed of Rev. Moses Merrill and wife, Miss Brown, and a Christian Indian woman, a descendant of Rev. D. Brainard's Indians. They are appointed by the Baptist Board to labor among the Otoe Indians, about twenty-five miles from this place, on the river Platte. These Indians are away from their intended residence about half the time, on hunting excursions.

A little more than a half mile below the agency, the American Fur Company have a fort, and, in connexion, they have a farming establishment and large numbers of cattle and horses, and a horse power mill for grinding corn.

CHAPTER III..

Continuance at Council Bluffs—interesting scenery—Indian curiosity
—information obtained about several Indian tribes—Spasmodio
Cholera—an Indian chief killed—leave Bellevue for the Black Hills
—storm of rain—heavy thunder storm—Elkhorn river, the country
around—Loups fork of the Platte—manner of encamping—Big Ax,
Pawnee chief—Indian feasting—fourth of July—Messrs. Dunbar
and Allis—thunder storm—Indian Ornaments—effects of drunkenness—bite of a rattle-snake—buffalo seen—prairie horse-fly—forks
of the Platte—want of wood—swiftness of antelopes—climate—thousands of buffalo—badgers—prairie dog—interesting bluffs—old castle—the chimney, or beacon—an alarm—Ogallallah Indians, their
lodges—Black Hills.

CONTINUED in this place three weeks, waiting the movements of the caravan, who made slow progress in preparing
their packages for the mountains. During our continuance
here, I frequently walked over the hills bordering upon the
west of the valley of the Missouri, to enjoy the pure air of
the rolling prairies, and to view the magnificent prospects
unfolded in the vale below. From the summit of those pro-
minences, the valley of the Missouri may be traced until
lost in its far winding course among the bluffs. Three miles
below, is seen the Papillon, a considerable stream from the
north-west, winding its way round to the east, and uniting
with the Missouri, six miles above the confluence of the
Platte coming from the west. These flow through a rich
alluvial plain, opening to the south and south-west as far
as the eye can reach. Upon these meadows are seen feeding some few hundreds of horses and mules, and a herd of

cattle ; and some fields of corn which diversify the scenery.
The north is covered with woods, which are not less valuable than the rich vales.   But few places can present a prospect more interesting, and when a civilized population shall add the fruits of their industry, but few can be more desirable.

In respect to efforts for the religious instruction and conversion of the Indians, I am convinced, from all I can learn of their native character, that the first impressions which the missionary makes upon them, are altogether important in their bearings on successful labors afterwards.   In things about which they are conversant, they are men ; but about other things, they are children ; and like children, the announcement of a new subject awakens their attention, their curiosity, and their energies ; and it has been remarked by a Methodist missionary who has labored among the Indians, that many seemed to embrace the gospel on its first being offered, and that those among the adults, who failed to do so, were rarely converted.   If, from any motives, or from any cause, instruction is delayed, and their expectations are disappointed, they relapse into their native apathy, from which it is difficult to arouse them.

We had an opportunity, whilst we continued in this place, to collect much information about the Indians in the Sioux country, from Maj. P. the agent appointed by government to the Yanktons, a band of the Sioux.   He appears to be not only intelligent and candid, but also well disposed towards Indian improvement.   The following is the substance of the information which he gave us in regard to several tribes to the north and north-west of this place : that the Omahaws are situated upon the Missouri, about one hundred and fifty miles above this place, and number about two thousand. They have been well disposed towards the whites, but, owing to their intercourse with traders and trappers, and abuses which they have received from them, they are becoming more vicious in their habits, and less friendly. Yet, kind treatment would conciliate their favor, so that there would be no reason to fear but that a mission might be established among them with fair prospects of success.

The Yanktons are an interesting band of the Sioux, of about two thousand people. Their village is to be located on the Vermilion river, where it unites with the Missouri from the north. Maj. P. thinks this will be a very eligible place for a missionary station, and says he will do all in his power to aid such an enterprise.

The Ponca Indians, on the south side of the Missouri, at the confluence of the *L'eau qui coure*, number six or eight hundred, and speak the same language as the Omahaws.

The region of country, from the mouth of the Big Sioux river and that on the south of the *L'eau qui coure*, as high as the country of the Mandan Indians, may be classed under the general head of the Sioux country ; and is inhabited by the following bands of Sioux, viz : the Yanktons, already mentioned, Santas, Yanktonas, Tetons, Ogallallahs, Siones, and the Hankpapes, who course east and west from the Mississippi to the Black Hills, and sometimes as far south as the river Platte. The real number of the several bands cannot be correctly ascertained, but probably it is from forty to sixty thousand. Their habits are wandering, and they rely exclusively upon the chase for subsistence. Their principal trade is in buffalo robes. The traders have for many years maintained a friendly intercourse with them, and generally speaking, they are much attached to white men.

The Mandans are a much more stationary people than almost any other tribe in this whole region of country, and the opportunity to establish missionaries among them is good; but on account of repeated ill treatment, which they have experienced, they are beginning to grow suspicious, and are losing confidence in white men.

Our stay in this place had been protracted much beyond our expectations. Two weeks after our arrival the spasmodic cholera broke out with a great degree of malignity. The weather was very warm, and there were showers from day to day. The intemperate habits of the men, and their manner of living, probably had a tendency to induce the disease. Three of the company died; and several others barely survived, through the blessing of God upon the assiduous attentions of Doct. Whitman, my associate, and the free use of powerful medicines. And, had it not been for his successful practice, the men would have dispersed, and the caravan would have failed of going to the place of rendezvous. This was plainly seen and frankly acknowledged. This alarming disease was the means of effecting our departure sooner that it otherwise would have taken place. It was necessary to hasten to the higher prairies, as the only prospect of escaping the farther ravages of the disease. Not a single new case occurred after we recommenced our journey. This afflictive scourge, so far as it respected Dr. W. and myself, was providential. The assistance we rendered the sick, and the medical skill of the Doctor, converted those into permanent friends, who had so disliked the restraints which our presence imposed upon them, that, as they afterwards confessed, they had plotted our death, and intended on the first convenient occasion to put their purpose in execution.

Whilst at Bellevue, a man by the name of Garrio, a half-blood Indian chief of the Arickara nation, was shot under very aggravated circumstances. Garrio and his family were residing in a log cabin on the Papillon river. Six or seven men, half intoxicated, went down to his house in the night, called him up, took him away a half mile, and shot him with six balls, scalped him, and left him unburied. The reason they assigned for doing so, was, that he was a bad man, and had killed white men. If he was guilty, who authorized them to take his life? The Arickara nation will remember this, and probably take revenge on some innocent persons. This, I apprehend, is the way Indian wars are often produced. While we charge the Indians with inveterate ferociousness and inhuman brutality, we forget the too numerous wrongs and outrages committed upon them, which incite them to revenge. They cannot apprehend and do justice to such offenders. Or if they could, would it not be published as a gross Indian murder and aggression, and a war of extermination be commenced against them. When Indian offences are proclaimed, we hear only one side of the story, and the other will not be heard until the last great day.

Monday, June 22d. After so long delay, we re-commenced our journey for the "far west." The Black Hills are to be our next stopping place. The caravan started yesterday. We passed over a rich extensive prairie, but so poorly watered, that we did not find a stream through the whole day. In the afternoon we had to ride in a heavy, cold rain, in consequence of which I became much chilled. Overtook the caravan, and encamped before night on a high prairie, where we could find but little wood, and it was difficult to make a fire. We had some coarse bread made of corn, and some bacon for supper. The change from the comforts to the bare necessaries of life was trying; but when I had wrapped myself in my blankets and laid down upon the ground to repose for the night, I felt thankful to God for his goodness.

Being now beyond all white inhabitants, in an Indian country, and not knowing what the eventful future may unfold, I thought I could give up all my private interests for the good of the perishing heathen, if I could be instrumental of their temporal and eternal welfare. Come life or death, I thought I could say, "thy will be done." Felt strong confidence, that God would protect and provide for us, and derived great consolation from the promise, "Lo, I am with you always." The very pelting of the storm upon our tent had something in it soothing, and calculated to awaken the feeling that God was near.

On the 23d, the storm still continued, and we did not remove our encampment.

Towards noon on the 24th, went forward on our way and crossed the Papillon river, which occasioned much delay to get the baggage, wagons, and animals over. We did not find a suitable place for encamping where we could be accommodated with wood and water until about sunset; and before we could pitch our tent, a thunder storm, which had been gathering for a long time, came down upon us with great violence, accompanied with wind and hail. The animals of the caravan fled in different directions, some packed and some unpacked. I had only time to unpack my mule and let him go, and it was with much difficulty I could hold my horse, which had become almost frantic under the beating hail, nor did I escape without some contusions. The lightning was very frequent, and the thunder was almost one continual roar. After a while the fury of the storm abated, and in the dark we pitched our tent and got our baggage into it, but were not able to make a fire. We took such supper as we could provide with our coarse bread and bacon, without light and without fire, and laid ourselves down to rest. During the night there were several showers which created rivulets, some of which found their way under our tent. Towards morning we slept, and arose somewhat refreshed.

The morning of the 25th was very pleasant, and afforded a good opportunity to dry our baggage, and for the caravan to collect together their packs of goods, which were scattered over the prairie. After having spent the forenoon in drying and adjusting them, we went forward and arrived at the Elkhorn, a very considerable river. For conveyance over this river, we constructed a boat of a wagon body, so covered with undressed skins as to make it nearly water tight. The method was very good, and we commenced crossing, but night came on before we finished, and therefore we encamped on the east side. The country here is excellent, and tolerably supplied with wood.

On the 26th, continued carrying over our baggage, and finished crossing at half after twelve, after which we traveled ten miles up the Elkhorn, and stopped for the night.

On the 27th, arose very early and pursued our journey, and made good progress until three, P. M. when we met Messrs. Campbell and Sublette with a small caravan, returning from the Black Hills. When mountain traders meet under such circumstances there must be mutual exchanges of friendship, more ceremonious and complicated than can be gone through with in the passing " how do you do." The two caravans encamped, in due form, and at a respectful distance from each other.

Sabbath, 28th. The caravans continued here through the day. This gave us an opportunity to rest, and to attend to devotional exercises in our tent.

On the 29th, passed over and traveled a good distance up Shell creek. As a traveler, I should be guilty of neglect of duty, if I should not give a description of this section of country, belonging to the Otoes on the east, and the Pawnees on the west. For about twenty-five miles since we crossed the Elkhorn, between this river and the Platte, which are here about ten miles apart, there is not a single hill. It is rich bottom land, covered with a luxuriant growth of grass. No country could be more inviting to the farmer, with only one exception, the want of wood land. The latitude is sufficiently high to be healthy ; and as the climate grows warmer as we travel west, until we approach the snow-topped mountains, there is a degree of mildness, not experienced east of the Alleghany mountains. The time will come, and probably is not far distant, when this country will be covered with a dense population. The earth was created for the habitation of man, and for a theatre, on which God will manifest his perfections in his moral government among his moral creatures, and therefore the earth, according to divine prediction, shall be given to the people of God. Although infidels may sneer, and scoffers mock, yet God will accomplish his designs, and fulfil every promise contained in his word. Then this amazing extent of most fertile land will not continue to be the wandering ground of a few thousand Indians, with only a *very few* acres under cultivation ; nor will millions of tons of grass grow up to rot upon the ground or to be burned up with the fire enkindled to sweep over the prairie, to disincumber it of its spontaneous burden. The herds of buffalo which once fattened upon these meadows are gone ; and the deer which once cropped the grass have disappeared ; and the antelopes have fled away ; and shall solitude reign here till the end of time ? No : here shall be heard the din of business, and the church-going bell shall sound far and wide. The question is, by whom shall this region of country be inhabited ? It is plain that the Indians under their present circumstances will never multiply and fill this land. They must be brought under the influence of civilization and Christianity, or they will continue to melt away, until nothing will remain of them but relics found in museums, and some historical records. Philanthropy and the mercy of God plead in their behalf.

We were awakened on the 30th, at the first breaking of the day, by the usual call, "out, out ; gear up your mules." We traveled until one o'clock, P. M. more than eight hours, when we halted and breakfasted. We went again on our way, and came to the Loups fork of the Platte, and stopped for the night. Most of the country over which we traveled to-day was a rolling prairie. There is nothing in this section of country to interest the geologist. I did not see a single stone, after passing the Papillon to this place, excepting a few small ones in the place where we crossed that stream, and which on that account is called Rockford. It is one of the peculiarities of the dialect of the people in the westernmost states, to call small stones rocks. And therefore they speak of throwing a rock at a bird, or at a man. There are no forests in these western regions. The meadows spread out almost without bounds. There are only here and there some clumps of trees ; and the rivers and smaller streams are skirted with cotton wood, elms and willows. Whatever propriety there once was, there is none now, in calling the Indians, children of the forest.

The thermometer stood to-day, at noon, at 81°.

Wednesday, July 1st. I rested the last night as quietly as I should have done in a civilized country, and upon a good bed, and was cheerful in committing myself to God, to awake in this, or in the eternal world, as he shall direct.

We have a small tent made of coarse cotton cloth, forming a cone. After setting this, we stow away our baggage so as to leave a space in the centre for our lodgings. My bed is made by first spreading down a buffalo skin, upon this a bear skin, then two or three Mackinaw blankets, and my portmanteau constitutes my pillow.

We proceeded to-day a few miles up the Loups fork, and unexpectedly found a good fording place, where we crossed the river, which in this place is nearly a mile wide. After going a few miles up the river, we halted for the night. The manner of our encamping, is to form a large hollow square, encompassing an area of about an acre, having the river on one side ; three wagons forming a part of another side, coming down to the river ; and three more in the same manner on the opposite side ; and the packages so arranged in parcels, about three rods apart, as to fill up the rear, and the sides not occupied by the wagons. The horses and mules, near the middle of the day, are turned out under guard, to feed for two hours ; and the same again towards night, until after sunset, when they are taken up and brought into the hollow square, and fastened with ropes twelve feet long, to pickets driven firmly into the ground. The men are divided into small companies, stationed at the several parcels of goods and wagons, where they wrap themselves in their blankets and rest for the night ; the whole however are formed into six divisions to keep guard, relieving each other every two hours. This is to prevent hostile

Indians from falling upon us by surprise, or coming into the camp by stealth and taking away either horses or packages of goods. We were permitted, by favor, to pitch our tent next to the river, half way between the two wings, which made our situation a little more retired.

Nothing of special interest occurred on the second. On the third, we passed the villages of the Tapage and Republican Pawnee Indians. These Indians have dwellings which appear substantial and somewhat adapted to comfort. Many of the Pawnee Loups came to us, and received us with great civility and kindness. Big Ax, their second chief, had charge of this party. He is a man of dignified appearance, and his countenance is expressive of intelligence and benevolence. He is very friendly to white men. These Indians were going out upon their summer hunt, by the same route we were pursuing, and were not willing we should go on before them, lest we should frighten away the buffalo.

They manifested their friendship by inviting us to feasts; and as we may attend half a dozen in a day without being surfeited, an explanation may not be out of place. Big Ax gave the first invitation; and as it is not customary for those who provide the feast to sit down with their guests, he and his associates sat in dignified silence on one side of the lodge, while those of us who partook of the feast, occupied the centre. The daughters of Big Ax served us on the occasion, and bountifully helped us to boiled corn and beans. Such are their customs, that to avoid giving offence, we must eat all that is set before us, or take it away, and Mr. Fontenelle took what remained. In the evening we were invited to two others. The first consisted of boiled corn and dried pumpkins, and the other of boiled buffalo meat. We also gave the principal chiefs a feast, setting before them all the variety which our bacon and coarse bread could furnish, having it in our power to add a dish of coffee, of which luxury we partook for this once on our whole journey.

Amidst the uniformity of prairie scenery, there is yet some variety. It was curious to mark the alterations which time and flood have made in the channel of this river. Formerly, perhaps not a few centuries ago, the river ran a hundred feet higher than at present, and it is probably owing to the yielding nature of the soil that its waters are so very turbid. The water of the Loups fork, however, comparatively speaking, is quite clear. This section of country offers an interesting field for botanical research. Since crossing the Elkhorn, I have noticed nine different species of grass, most of which are entirely new. The flowering plants are very numerous and beautiful, and especially the rose, which is found of almost every hue. Thermometer, at noon, 90°.

July 4th. This is a day of great noise and bustle in the States. Orators speak of the deeds and achievements of our forefathers: their audiences catch the spirit of patriotism. Not so with our company. Having almost expatriated themselves, they had forgotten their nation's birth-day; and knowing that their days of indulgence would be seasons of reveling, I forbore to remind them of it. How suitable would be a rational religious expression of gratitude to Heaven, instead of the confusion and riot, which are the common demonstrations of joy on such occasions. Thermometer 96° at noon.

On the fifth, which was the Sabbath, the caravan went forward a few miles and then encamped. The Indians were constantly calling at our tent through the day. It was painful to witness their poor degraded condition, ignorant of God and salvation, and, for want of a knowledge of their language, to be unable to point them to the Savior, or teach them their obligations to their Maker, and their duty to turn to him with their whole heart. I hope and pray that the Pawnee mission may prosper; that the disposition which Messrs. Dunbar and Allis manifest to go with the Indians and live as they live, may be followed up, until their teaching and influence are felt, and the Indians shall locate themselves upon their lands, under the influence of Christianity and civilization. The mode which Messrs. D. and A. have adopted of going with the Indians where they go, appears to be the right one, and must be generally adopted to bring the numerous wandering nations and tribes to the knowledge of Christ.

It is all important that the missionary be able to speak to the heathen in the language wherein they were born. It is also important that the Indians settle down and cultivate the soil; but how can they be induced to do this before they are taught? Do any say, by an interpreter? An interpreter may be employed for awhile, but the missionary must become, as soon as possible, his own interpreter. And why can he not learn the Indian language as well as the trader and hunter? He can, if he will exercise as much self-denial.

On the sixth, we left the Loups fork, very early in the morning, in company with the Pawnees, and directed our course south-west for the Platte river. Towards evening, we had a thunder storm with heavy rains, which continued through most of the night; but, protected by our tent, we slept so soundly, that our meat was stolen from us; and in our circumstances, though only about six pounds, it was a sensible loss.

After we came to the Platte, we pursued our way up the river, which is broad, but not very deep, as its name indicates. The country begins to diminish in its fertility, but still is very good. We were prevented from making the progress we might have done, if the Indians would have permitted us to go on and leave them. The men of the caravan began to complain of the delay, and had reason to do so, having nothing to eat but boiled corn, and no way to obtain any thing more before finding buffalo.

The intellectual powers of these Indians are very good, but need cultivation. They are fond of ornaments, and not having the means of gratifying their vanity as civilized people have, they resort to almost any thing to decorate their persons; such as porcupine quills, beads, wreaths of grass and flowers, brass rings upon their wrists, birds' feathers, and claws of wild beasts; the claws of a grizzly bear are an ornament of the first order, and the tails of white wolves are in high estimation. But their most universal and particular ornament is painting their faces with vermilion.

These heathen, like all others, are ignorant of the benign influence of the gospel, and therefore, while they have many interesting traits of character, are cruel to their old men and women. The women are compelled to do all the work— the men only hunt and go to war. Having but few horses, when they journey, they place burdens upon the old men and women, and even upon the blind and lame—and their dogs. I did not see among these Indians a single person having any natural deformity, nor any one who appeared to be deficient in common sense.

July 9th. To-day Big Ax came to my tent and sat by me a long time. Never did I so much wish to converse with any man and tell him about the Savior, and, from the expression of his countenance, I thought he desired to be instructed. But the gift of tongues was not imparted to me, and we could only converse with the language of signs, which is far more intelligible than I had anticipated.

Capt. Fontenelle, by a large present, purchased of the Indians the privilege of going on to-morrow without them. Our men could hardly have been kept in subordination, if they had not consented.

Towards the night of the 10th, we had an uncommon storm of thunder, hail, rain, and wind. The horses and mules could not be controlled, and turned and fled in all directions before the storm. The whole caravan was scattered over the prairie; but when the storm abated, they were again collected without much difficulty, and nothing was lost. If any hostile band of Indians had been about us, it would have been easy for them to have made us a prey. But the Lord not only rode upon the storm, but was also near for our defence. The scene was alarming, and yet grand and truly sublime.

Sabbath, 12th. We are in a land of dangers, but God is our preserver, and how desirable it is, that his mercies should be had in grateful remembrance, and that the portion of time, which he has set apart as holy, should be observed as such. The caravan travelled a part of the day, but were under the necessity of stopping in consequence of rain, which wet their packages. It is worthy of notice, that there have been various providences, which have thus far prevented them from traveling much upon the Sabbath. But this day has been one of great confusion and wickedness. In consequence of the men being drenched with rain, whiskey was dealt out freely, to keep them from taking cold. Most of them became much excited, and one, who took an active part in killing

Garrio, stabbed a man, with full intent to have pierced his heart ; but the knife, by striking a rib, turned aside and only made a deep flesh wound.

I think I know the feelings of David, when he expressed a strong desire after the sanctuary of God, and to dwell in his tabernacle.

July 13th. We are not traveling through forests, nor a solitary desert, but through almost boundless meadows, that have the appearance of being under good cultivation. We see no fields of grain, secured from the beasts of the earth by fences, nor habitations of civilized men, but meadows adorned with a great variety of plants, some of which appear to be gregarious. Often some acres are diversified with great variety of colors and species.

There are two species of plants which are said to be a sovereign remedy against the poison of the rattle-snake, the virtues of one of which we had an opportunity of testing. One of our men was bitten in the foot, and before we knew it the poison had so far progressed, that both the foot and leg had become much inflamed and very painful. One of these plants was applied to the parts affected, and at once the man was convalescent, and in a few hours was well. The leaves of the plant resemble those of the blue flag, except that they are serrated. The healing properties are contained in the roots, which are bruised and applied to the affected parts. Rattle-snakes are not numerous. These and other reptiles are prevented from multiplying, by the fires which every year run over the prairies.

On the 14th, the announcement of buffalo spread cheerfulness and animation through the whole caravan, and to men whose very life depended on the circumstance, it was no indifferent event. From the immense herds of these wild animals, dispersed over these beautiful fields of nature, we were to derive our subsistence. Although several were seen to-day, yet our hunters were not successful in obtaining many.

I had heard of the prairie horse-fly, but was not aware that it would be so very annoying and even tormenting to our horses. Its bite is like the thrust of the point of a lancet, and when the fly is surfeited, or is brushed off, the blood immediately gushes out. When the caravan is in close company, there being about two hundred horses and mules, the number of the flies are so divided that they are more tolerable; but when for any purpose a horse is separated from the company, he is severely bitten by them. On one occasion, when I rode forward to find a crossing place over a deep muddy stream of water, they came around my horse in such swarms that he became frantic, and I was obliged to return in full speed. I have no doubt that a horse left alone in the season of these flies would be killed by them.

The next day, we journeyed as usual, and about noon arrived at the Forks of the Platte. We saw a large herd of buffalo, from which we obtained a good supply of excellent meat. These animals, with their shaggy shoulders, neck, and heads, make a very majestic appearance, and if their natures were unknown, would be terrific. But they are timid and inoffensive, showing no disposition to injure any person, except in self-defense, when wounded and closely pursued. Their strength is great; and, although they look clumsy, they run very swiftly. It requires a horse of more than ordinary speed, to outrun them for any considerable time.

The section of country about the Forks of the Platte is very pleasant, without any high mountains in sight; but at a distance beyond the widely extended rich bottom lands, bluffs of various forms present a picturesque scenery. The entire absence of forests in a large space of country around, is a deficiency which cannot be easily supplied; but probably forest trees might be cultivated to advantage. Is it not highly probable that mineral coal will be found here as well as upon the prairies in the western states? We found no wood yesterday, nor to-day, and probably shall not for some days to come; and therefore we have been under the necessity of making our fires with the dry dung of the buffalo. The most thoroughly weather-beaten is selected, and proves to be a better substitute for common fuel than we had anticipated. Although we are now where we had fears of finding the Arickara Indians, the death of whose chief has been mentioned, and who have been residing near this place for several months past, yet we have seen no Indians since we left the Pawnees. It is supposed they have gone far up the south Fork of the Platte, to avoid the United States dragoons, under the command of Col. Dodge, who are on their way to call them to account for their conduct towards white men, and to form with them a treaty of peace. But they intend to keep out of the way of the dragoons, and therefore we hope to pass unmolested.

We took our course up the north-west Fork of the Platte, and towards night encamped upon its bank in our usual form, using particular caution to be prepared for an attack of the Arickaras, should any of their war parties be about us. Every man was required to see that his rifle was in good order, and to have a good supply of powder and balls. We all slept with our clothes on, so that, if called by the sentinel's fire, we might in less than a moment be ready for action; but the night passed away in quietude, and at the first breaking of the day we were awakened with the customary call of the guide.

Saw, on the 16th, the buffalo in greater numbers, and nearer than previously. They are less shy than those we first found. They are more majestic than the elk, but less beautiful. The antelopes, some of which we have seen for several days past, are becoming very numerous, and their speed exceeds that of any animal I have ever seen. Our hounds can do nothing in giving them the chase; for the dogs are so soon left far in the rear, that they do not follow more than ten or twenty rods, before they return, looking ashamed of their defeat. Our hunters occasionally take some by coming upon them by stealth. When they are surprised, they start forward a very small space, then turn, and with high lifted heads, stare for a few seconds at the object which has alarmed them, and then, with a half whistling snuff, bound off, seeming to be as much upon wings as upon feet. They resemble the goat, but are far more beautiful. Though they are of different colors, yet they are generally red, and have a large, fine, prominent eye. Their flesh is good for food, and about equal to venison.

July 17th. We did not go on our way as early this morning as usual, having been detained by breaking an axle-tree of one of our wagons. The country is becoming more hilly, and the bluffs in some places come down to the river. Herds of buffalo are seen in almost every direction, and they are so numerous, that our animals find scanty pasture. The thermometer stood at noon at 88°. Encamped a little below Cedar bluffs, so called from the few cedars scattered over them, which promise a better supply of fuel.

Commenced our journey on the 18th, at our usual early hour, to travel on until near noon before breakfast. From the change of vegetation of various kinds, and birds, &c. it is evident we are ascending into higher regions of country, and an atmosphere more resembling that of the New England States. As we advance, the flowering plants are becoming less numerous; and although the middle of the day is very warm, yet the nights and mornings are more cool. The ascent is so gradual, that the change is not perceptible. Rocks begin to appear, and still we are far from the Rocky Mountains. Limestone of light brown color is found in the bluffs, laying in horizontal strata, which might be easily worked and to any extent. Very small black gnats, hardly discernible by the naked eye, have been numerous and very annoying, and for several days we rode with silk handkerchiefs closely tied over our faces to protect us from their poisonous bite.

July 20th. Thousands of buffalo were seen to-day, and our men amused themselves with chasing and shooting at them; but it was well for the buffalo that they made poor shots. I can hardly reconcile it with a good conscience, to trifle with the life even of the most insignificant animals, yet, for once, I felt myself powerfully inclined to try my horse in the chase. The noble creature enjoyed the sport, and would have rushed fearlessly into the midst of them, had I not held him in check. At that time, not being sufficiently acquainted with this species of amusement, and intending to make sure of my victim, I dismounted in order to take a more steady aim than I could have otherwise done; and by so doing, as our guide afterwards informed me, placed myself in imminent danger; for the animal, if wounded, often turns upon his antagonist to retaliate his injuries. Fortunately, though I wounded one, he did not rise upon me, and I returned to the caravan unconscious of danger.

Badgers inhabit this part of the country, and from the many holes, which they dig in the ground for their dwellings, they must be very numerous, though we have seen only a few, and have killed but one. They keep near their burrows, and run into them on the least approach of danger. The badger is of the genus *ursus*, about the size of the marmot, or what is often called the woodchuck, of a silvery gray color, with short legs, and its whole aspect is interesting. I did not have an opportunity to learn many of its habits. A small animal called the prairie dog, abounds in this section of country. It takes its name, not from its appearance, but from its barking, which is like that of a very small dog. It is of a brown color, and its fur is of superior fineness. It is very shy and difficult to be taken. Was it not for this last circumstance, I should think it might be an important article of traffic.

We passed, on the 21st, many uncommonly interesting bluffs composed of indurated clay ; many of them very high, with perpendicular sides, and of almost every imaginable form. Some appeared like strong fortifications with high citadels ; some like stately edifices with lofty towers. I had never before seen any thing like them of clay formation. And what adds to their beauty is, that the clay of which they are composed, is nearly white. Such is the smoothness and whiteness of the perpendicular sides and offsets ; and such the regularity of their straight and curved lines, that one can hardly believe that they are not the work of art.

It was a very warm day. The thermometer stood at noon, at 90°, and at five o'clock, P. M. at 100°. There were no prairie winds as usual. Almost every day winds blow over the prairies like sea breezes, or trade winds. They generally commence about eight in the morning, and continue through the day. These winds render the traveling comfortable, although the thermometer may range high.

We encamped to-day in the neighborhood of a great natural curiosity, which, for the sake of a name, I shall call the old castle. It is situated upon the south side of the Platte, on a plain, some miles distant from any elevated land, and covers more than an acre of ground, and is more than fifty feet high. It has, at the distance of the width of the river, all the appearance of an old enormous building, somewhat dilapidated ; but still you see the standing walls, the roof, the turrets, embrasures, the dome, and almost the very windows ; and large guard-houses, standing some rods in front of the main building. You unconsciously look around for the enclosures, but they are all swept away by the lapse of time—for the inhabitants, but they have disappeared ; all is silent and solitary. Although you correct your imagination, and call to remembrance, that you are beholding the work of nature, yet, before you are aware, the illusion takes you again, and your curiosity is excited to know who built this fabric, and what have become of the by-gone generations. I found it impossible to divest myself of such impressions. The longer and the more minutely I examined it, the more I saw to admire ; and it reminded me of those descriptions of power and grandeur in ruins, of which we read of ancient times and nations.

Encamped at noon of the 22d, near another of nature's wonders. It has been called the chimney ; but I should say, it ought to be called beacon hill, from its resemblance to what was beacon hill in Boston. Being anxious to have a near view, although in a land of dangers, I concluded to take an assistant and pass over the river to it. The river where we crossed was about a mile wide, shallow and full of quicksand, but we passed it without any difficulties. We rode about three miles over a level plain, and came to the base. This distance from the other side of the river did not appear more than a mile, so deceptive are distances over plains without any landmarks. This beacon hill has a conical formed base of about half a mile in circumference, and one hundred and fifty feet in height; and above this a perpendicular column, twelve feet square, and eighty feet high; making the whole height about two hundred and thirty feet. We left our horses at the base, and ascended to the perpendicular. It is formed of indurated clay or marl, and in some parts is petrified. It is of a light chocolate, or rufous colour, in some parts white. Near the top were some handsome stalactites, at which my assistant shot, and broke off some pieces, of which I have taken a small specimen. We descended, and having finished my survey, had just mounted our horses, when we saw two bands of buffalo, six or eight hundred in number, coming full speed towards us, taking their course down the river. We knew somebody must be pursuing them, and as, from indications for two days past, we had suspected Indians near, we thought it would be the safest for us to make and secure a speedy retreat to the caravan, and set off in haste for the river, which at the nearest point was two miles distant. Very soon we saw a man on horseback coming full speed towards us—he stopped and gave a signal for others behind him to hasten on, and at once we saw a band of men coming full rush. We put our horses to their utmost speed, and when we thought our retreat to the river fully secured, we stopped and took an observation with a large spy-glass, which we had taken the precaution to have with us, and found they were white men, who had come from a fort of the American Fur Company at the Black Hills, to meet the caravan. Mr. Fontenelle, the commander of the caravan, saw the movement, was alarmed for our safety, and came out in all haste, with a number of armed men to our assistance. But all resulted in friends meeting friends. There were some Ogallallah Indians near us, who came to our camp in the evening. Thermometer 90°.

On the 23d, after traveling a few miles, we encamped near Scott's bluffs. These are the termination of a high range of land running from south to north. They are very near the river, high and abrupt, and what is worthy of notice, there is a pass through the range a short distance back from the river, the width of a common road, with perpendicular sides two or three hundred feet high. It appears as though a part of the bluffs had been cut off, and moved a few rods to the north. Instead of journeying, the naturalist would desire weeks to examine the interesting scenery of this section of country, and the more minute his examination the more would he find to gratify his curiosity.

This whole country appears to abound in magnesia, so that epsom salts are found in almost every part; in some places in large quantities in a crystalized state. Our horses and mules were disposed to make these a substitute for common salt. Thermometer to-day stood at 90°.

While we were encamped at noon of the 24th, and our horses and mules were turned out under guard, and we were preparing our breakfast, or what should be dinner, we were alarmed with the call, " secure your animals! secure your animals!" I looked around to discover the cause of the alarm, and saw, at about a mile and a half distance, some thirty or forty Indians coming on horseback at full speed. We had not more than half secured our animals and prepared for defence, when the Indians were close upon us; whether friends or foes we could not tell, until they were nearly within rifle shot, when, according to the customary expression of friendship, they fired their guns into the air, and then rushed into our camp, and exchanged salutations of peace. They were Ogallallahs, headed by eight of their chiefs, clad in their war habiliments, and presenting somewhat of a terrific appearance. The chiefs dined with us, and were very talkative among themselves ; for, not having any good interpreter, we could not join in conversation with them. Every thing, however, went on pleasantly, and to mutual satisfaction. They told us their whole village was only a few hours travel ahead of us, going to the Black Hills for the purpose of trading.

On the 25th, the heat was very oppressive in the middle of the day, there not being as much wind as usual. Thermometer 92°. Towards evening, we came to the main village of the Ogallallahs, consisting of more than two thousand persons. These villages are not stationary, but move from place to place, as inclination or convenience may dictate. Their lodges are comfortable, and easily transported. They are constructed of eight or ten poles about eighteen feet long, set up in a circular form, the small ends fastened together, making an apex, and the large ends are spread out so as to enclose an area of about twenty feet in diameter. The whole is covered with their coarse skins, which are elk, or buffalo, taken when they are not good for robes. A fire is made in the centre, a hole being left in the top of the lodge for the smoke to pass out. All that they have for household furniture, clothing, and skins for beds, is deposited around according to their ideas of propriety and convenience. Generally not more than one family occupies a lodge. These are the finest looking Indians I have ever seen. The men are generally tall and well proportioned ;

the women are trim, and less pendulous than is common among Indian women, and all were well dressed and cleanly. They came around us in multitudes, and manifested great curiosity to see whatever we had. I did not know why, but my boots were particularly examined ; probably they had never seen any before, as moccasons are worn, not only by Indians, but also by traders and hunters.

Sabbath, 26th. The caravan moved on a little way to the crossing place of the Platte, near Larama's fork in the Black Hills, and encamped for the day. This gave us an opportunity for reading and devotion. Some of the Ogallallahs came to my tent while I was reading the Bible, and observed me attentively, as though enquiring the reason why I was differently employed from others. I endeavored to make them understand by the language of signs, that I was reading the book of God, which teaches us how to worship him. After spending some time in teaching them to read, and how God is to be worshiped, I sung a hymn, which greatly interested them. They took me by the hand, and the expression of their countenance seemed to say, we want to know what all this means. My spirit was pained within me, and I anxiously desired to understand their language, that I might tell them about Christ, the only Savior. The enquiry arose forcibly in my mind, why will not some of the many Christian young men of the east, exercise so much self-denial, as to come and teach them the way of salvation ? In such a labor what Christian would not glory ? And if there should be any tribulations attendant on the enterprise, would they not, like St. Paul, glory in tribulations ?

At evening, we passed over the Platte, and went a mile and a half up to the fort of the Black Hills, and encamped near the fort in our usual form.

CHAPTER IV.

Black Hills—day of indulgence—buffalo dance—the desire of Indians
for instruction—met the chiefs in council—re-commenced our journey for rendezvous—anthracite coal—species of wormwood—Red
Bute—traces of grizzly bears—geology—Rock Independence—
Rocky Mountains—perpetual snow—valley through the mountains
—"thunder spirits" gone—an alarm—waters of the Colorado.

THE Black Hills do not derive their name from any thing
peculiar in the color of the soil and rocks of which they are
composed, but are so called from being covered with shrubby
cedars, which give them a dark appearance when seen at
a distance.   The alluvial soil upon the rivers and in the
valleys is very good, but upon the higher lands and hills,
it is thin and rather barren, and in many parts full of stones,
which are worn smooth by the action of water, and are of
various kinds and forms.   One spur of the Rocky Mountains is seen from this place, which is forty or fifty miles
distant, and is probably five thousand feet high.

At this place the caravan halted, and according to immemorial usage, the men were allowed a " day of indulgence,"
as it is called, in which they drink ardent spirits as much as
they please, and conduct as they choose.   Not unfrequently
the day terminates with a catastrophe of some kind, and
to-day one of the company shot another with the full intention to have killed him.   The ball entered the back, and
came out at the side.   The wounded man exclaimed, " I am
a dead man ;" but after a pause, said, " No, I am not hurt."
The other immediately seized a rifle to finish the work, but

was prevented by the bystanders, who wrested it from him
and discharged it into the air.

July 28th. The day of indulgence being past, a quiet
day succeeded. The exhilaration was followed by conse-
quent relaxation, and the tide of spirits which arose so high
yesterday, ebbed to-day proportionally low. The men were
seen lounging about in listless idleness, and could scarcely
be roused to the business of making repairs and arrangements for the long journey yet before us. The Indians
were active, and manifested a disposition to be sociable and
kind, and also to open a trade with us in various articles,
such as moccasons, belts, and dressed skins; and desired
in return, knives, awls, combs, vermilion, &c.

Although the nights were cool, yet the thermometer stood
in the middle of the day at 98°, but the heat was relieved
by the usual prairie winds.

On the 29th, the Ogallallah Indians who accompanied us,
had a buffalo and a dog dance, the real object of which I
could not satisfactorily ascertain. Whether it was from
some superstitious notion that their success in hunting depended on these rites, or whether the custom originated in
the gratitude of their hearts for past successes, or more probably as an amusement, or neither, I cannot tell. I witnessed the first mentioned ceremony, and was content to
dispense with the latter. In the buffalo dance, a large
number of young men, dressed with the skins of the neck
and head of buffalos with their horns on, moved round in a
dancing march. They shook their heads, imitated the low
bellowing of the buffalo, wheeled, and jumped. At the same
time men and women sung a song, accompanied with the
beating of a sort of drum. I cannot say I was much amused to
see how well they could imitate brute beasts, while ignorant

of God and salvation. The impressive enquiry was constantly on my mind, what will become of their immortal spirits ? Rational men imitating beasts, and old gray-headed men marshaling the dance ! and enlightened white men encouraging it by giving them intoxicating spirits, as a reward for their good performance. I soon retired, and was pleased to find that only a small number of the Indians took any part in the dance.

An Indian whom I attempted to teach last Sabbath, came to me again to-day, and manifested that he wished me to instruct him. I endeavored to communicate to his mind some ideas of God, and sang the hymn, " Watchman, tell us of the night." He and those with him, shook hands with me as a token of their satisfaction, and left me. He soon returned, however, bringing others, that they too, might hear what he had heard with so much apparent pleasure, and they again shook hands with me. This was several times repeated. These Indians appear not only friendly to white men, but kind in their intercourse with each other, and in no instance did I witness any quarrels among them. Their minds are uncommonly gifted and noble, their persons are finely formed, and many of them are truly " nature's grenadiers." The women are graceful, and their voices are soft and expressive. I was agreeably surprised to see tall young chiefs, well dressed in their own mode, walking arm in arm with their ladies. This is what I had not expected to see among those whom we term " savages." It is true that they are heathen, in all the guilt of sin and destitute of the knowledge of God, and the hopes of the gospel, but in politeness and decency, as well as in many other respects, they are very unlike the frontier Indians, who have been corrupted and degra-

ded by their acquaintance with ardent spirits, and wicked
white men.

On the 30th, we met in council with the chiefs of this
tribe, to lay before them the object of our tour, and to know
if they would wish to have missionaries sent among them
to teach them to read and write, and especially how to
worship God.   They expressed much satisfaction with the
proposal, and said they would do all they could to make
their condition comfortable.   There can be no doubt, that
this community of the Sioux would be a promising field for
laborers.   They are inquisitive, and their language is distinct and sonorous.

On the 31st, thermometer stood at 81°.

August 1st.   At half past eight in the morning, we re-
commenced our journey, and the next point to which we
direct our course is across the Rocky Mountains, where
the general rendezvous will be held.   Our wagons were
left at the fort of the Black Hills, and all our goods were
packed upon mules.   Several of our company went out into
various parts of this country to hunt and trap, but as many
more joined us for the mountains, so that our number is not
diminished.   Mr. Fontenelle stopped at the fort, and Mr.
Fitz Patrick took his place in charge of the caravan.   We
had received during our journey to this place, many kind
attentions from Mr. F. as well as the privilege of traveling
under his protection, for which we offered him a remunera-
tion, but he declined it, saying, "If any one is indebted,
it is myself, for you have saved my life, and the lives of my
men."   We shall gratefully remember their kindness.

Sabbath, 2nd.   I enjoyed some opportunities for devotional exercises, but felt the loss of the privileges of God's
house.

We found on the 3d but very little grass for our horses and mules, owing to three causes ; the sterility of the soil, the proximity of the snow-topped mountains, and the grazing of numerous herds of buffalos and antelopes. To save distance in following the bends of the river, we passed to-day over rough and somewhat dangerous precipices. I had found, before I arrived at the Black Hills, some loose specimens of anthracite coal on the banks of streams, but to-day I found a regular "*cropping out*" of coal, the same to all appearances as I have seen in the coal basins of Pennsylvania. The existence of a coal basin here is also confirmed by indications of iron ore. Certainly an invaluable substance, should it prove abundant, to the future inhabitants of a country so destitute of other fuel. This was the first discovery of coal in this region. A range of mountains, a spur of which is seen from Larama's fork in the Black Hills, runs parallel with the river, ten or fifteen miles distant, and some of the peaks are very high.

August 4th. The country was more level and fertile. I discovered more anthracite, indicating large quantities ; also, in one place, yellow sand stone of remarkably fine texture. It undoubtedly would answer an excellent purpose for polishing metals. A species of wormwood grows in great quantities in this region, where the soil is gravelly and barren. Some of it grows eight or ten feet high, and four or five inches in diameter, and is an obstruction to traveling. It is generally called wild sage. Scarcely any animal will taste it unless compelled by extreme hunger. The prairie hen, however, crops the buds or leaves, which renders it flesh bitter and unpalatable for food. I saw some granite to-day of a dark gray color, like the granite in parts of the Atlantic states. What I had seen before in boulders was of the red cast, like that which is found about Lake Superior.

On the 5th, we arose at the first breaking of the day and proceeded on our route, making forced marches through this barren region. Encamped towards night at a place called the Red Bute, which is a high bluff of land, resembling red ochre in color, but composed of clay somewhat indurated. This is a central place for Indians traveling east or west, north or south. Here the north-west branch of the Platte, along which we have been traveling, comes from a southern direction, the head of which is about one hundred and fifty miles distant. From the Red Bute we pass over to the Sweetwater, a branch of the Platte, which comes from the west. We saw to-day tracks of grizzly bears, which were perfectly fresh, and were indicative of their formidable size and strength. One with two large cubs passed out of some gooseberry and currant bushes near the river, as we proceeded around to an open spot of ground for an encamping place. Lieut. S. of the dragoons, a man of undoubted veracity, told me he saw several buffalos passing near some bushes, where a grizzly bear lay concealed, and the bear with one stroke tore three ribs from a buffalo and laid it dead. It has been said, if you meet one of these bears, you must either kill him, or be killed ; but this is not true, unless you come upon them suddenly, or wound them. If you let them pass off unmolested, they will, in most cases, withdraw, showing that the fear of man is upon them as well as upon other beasts.

August 6th. The geology of these regions is becoming more interesting, as we approach the mountains. I saw to-day, not only granite *in situ*, but also a quantity of the most beautiful serpentine I ever beheld. It was semi-transparent and of a deep green hue, very much resembling specimens of emerald which I saw in the mineralogical cabinet at New Haven. I regretted the necessity which a long journey, yet before me, imposed of passing by opportunities for making collections.

Passed Rock Independence, on the 7th. This is the first massive rock of that stupendous chain of mountains, which divides North America, and forms, together with its barrens on each side, a natural division. This rock takes its name from the circumstance of a company of fur traders suspending their journey, and here observing, in due form, the anniversary of our national freedom. It is an immensely huge rock of solid granite, entirely bare and covering several acres. Advancing a little distance, we came to a stream of no inconsiderable size, which has its origin in the mountains, and to which the name of Sweetwater has been given on account of its purity. We followed up the course of this river for several days. In one place it passes a small branch of the mountains, through a narrow chasm only thirty or forty feet wide, and more than three hundred feet high. The caravan passed around the point of this mountain, and to obtain a better prospect of this natural curiosity, I left them and rode to it. A deep-toned roar is heard as the river dashes its way through the rocky passage. The sight is soon intercepted by its winding course, and the darkness caused by the narrowness and deepness of the avenue.

Passed to-day, several small lakes of crystalized epsom salt, from which the water in the drouth of summer is evaporated. I rode into one of them to examine the quality and depth, but finding my horse sinking as in quicksand, I was glad to make a safe retreat. Whatever may be beneath, whether salt in a less solid state than on the surface, or quicksand, yet large quantities of good quality might be easily collected.

The mountains are indeed *rocky mountains*. They are rocks heaped upon rocks, with no vegetation, excepting a few cedars growing out of the crevices near their base. Their tops are covered with perpetual snow, which are seen on our left and before us. As we advanced, the atmosphere was increasingly more chilling through the night and most of the day, excepting the middle, which to-day was very warm ; the thermometer standing at 84°.

Sabbath, 9th. I endeavored to supply the absence of the privileges of the sanctuary and its ordinances, as well as I could by reading, and recalling to mind portions of the scriptures, hymns, and the doctrines of our excellent, but neglected catechism. One needs to be on heathen ground to realize the solitariness of absence from the social worship, where

> " The cheerful songs and solemn vows
> Make their communion sweet."

On the 10th, cold winds were felt from the snow-topped mountains to an uncomfortable degree. The passage through these mountains is in a valley, so gradual in the ascent and descent, that I should not have known that we were passing them, had it not been that as we advanced the atmosphere gradually became cooler, and at length we saw the perpetual snows upon our right hand and upon our left, elevated many thousand feet above us—in some places ten thousand. The highest part of these mountains are found by measurement, to be eighteen thousand feet above the level of the sea. This valley was not discovered until some years since. Mr. Hunt and his party, more than twenty

years ago, went near but did not find it, though in search
of some favorable passage.   It varies in width from three
to fifteen miles ; and following its course, the distance
through the mountains is about eighty miles, or four days'
journey.   Though there are some elevations and depressions in this valley, yet comparatively speaking, it is level.
There would be no difficulty in the way of constructing a
rail road from the Atlantic to the Pacific ocean ; and probably the time may not be very far distant, when trips will
be made across the continent, as they have been made to
the Niagara Falls, to see nature's wonders.   In passing the
Black Hills and the Rocky Mountains we heard none of those
" successive reports resembling the discharge of several
pieces of artillery," mentioned by some authors as *common*
" in the most calm and serene weather, at all times of the
day or night :" nor did we witness " lightning and thunder,
pealing from clouds gathering round the summits of the hills"
or mountains.   " The thunder spirits, who fabricate storms
and tempests," appear to have closed their labors, and the
Indian tribes no longer " hang offerings on the trees to pro-
pitiate the invisible lords of the mountains."

The geology presents some variety ; for while the main
ridge of the mountains is granite, yet to-day parallel ridges
of red secondary Sandstone have abounded.   They appear
to have been affected by heat ; and some elevating force
has broken them into dyke-like ridges at different distances
from each other, running from east north-east to west south-
west.   The strata are mostly vertical, but some have a
slight dip to the south.

We had an alarm, while we were encamped for noon,
and the men were called to arms.   They all rushed forth
full of courage, rather stimulated than appalled by danger.

Only one Indian made his appearance upon the hill, at the foot of which we were encamped. This was taken as an indication that others were near, which was the fact; but he and they retreated.

August 11th. The last night was very cold—we had a heavy frost with ice. A little before sunrise, the thermometer stood at 24°. Our early morning ride was not very comfortable for myself, and less so for some of our men who were not furnished with over-coats. Our horses and mules began to show that constant labor, without sufficient food, was not favorable to strength, and some of them failed. To-day we came to the Big Sandy river, one of the upper branches of the Colorado, which empties into the gulf of California. Along its banks are some Norway and pitch pine, and a very few small white pines, and clumps of common poplar. In some of the low vales, there were beautiful little fresh roses, which bloomed amidst the desolations around. " How ornamental are the works of nature ! She seems to decorate them all, as if each spot was a garden, in which God might perchance walk, as once in Eden."

CHAPTER V.

Arrive at rendezvous—trappers and hunters—four Indian nations—
Flatheads and Nez Perces, no reason why so called—surgical operations—an interview with the Flathead and Nez Percé chiefs—
their anxiety for religious instruction—return of Doct. Whitman—
Shoshones and Utaws—mountain life.

AFTER stopping for the night upon the New Fork, a
branch of Green river, we arose on the 12th, at the first
breaking of the day, and continued our forced marches. Although we were emerging from the mountains, yet peaks
covered with perpetual snow were seen in almost every direction, and the temperature of the air was uncomfortably
cold. I found to-day some beautiful calcedony, of which
I took a specimen, and also green stone, quartz, and trap
in large quantities. In the afternoon, we came to the Green
river, a branch of the Colorado, in latitude 42°, where the
caravan hold their rendezvous. This is in a widely extended
valley, which is pleasant, with a soil sufficiently fertile for
cultivation, if the climate was not so cold. Like the country we have passed through, it is almost entirely prairie,
with some woods skirting the streams of water.

The American Fur Company have between two and three
hundred men constantly in and about the mountains, engaged in trading, hunting and trapping. These all assemble
at rendezvous upon the arrival of the caravan, bring in their
furs, and take new supplies for the coming year, of clothing,
ammunition, and goods for trade with the Indians. But few of

these men ever return to their country and friends. Most of them are constantly in debt to the company, and are unwilling to return without a fortune ; and year after year passes away, while they are hoping in vain for better success.

Here were assembled many Indians belonging to four different nations ; the Utaws, Shoshones, Nez Percés, and Flatheads, who were waiting for the caravan, to exchange furs, horses, and dressed skins, for various articles of merchandise. I was disappointed to see nothing peculiar in the Flathead Indians to give them their name. Who gave them this name, or for what reason, is not known. Some suppose it was given them in derision for not flattening their heads, as the Chenooks and some other nations do, near the shores of the Pacific. It may be so, but how will those who indulge this imagination, account for the Nez Percés being so called, since they do not pierce their noses ? This name could not be given them in derision, because those near the Pacific, who flatten their heads, also pierce their noses. That those names have been given by white men, is evident, since they do not call each other by the names which signify either flat head or pierced nose.

While we continued in this place, Doct. Whitman was called to perform some very important surgical operations. He extracted an iron arrow, three inches long, from the back of Capt. Bridger, which was received in a skirmish, three years before, with the Blackfeet Indians. It was a difficult operation, because the arrow was hooked at the point by striking a large bone, and a cartilaginous substance had grown around it. The Doctor pursued the operation with great self-possession and perseverance ; and his patient manifested equal firmness. The Indians looked on meanwhile, with countenances indicating wonder, and in their own peculiar manner expressed great astonishment when it was extracted. The Doctor also extracted another arrow from the shoulder of one of the hunters, which had been there two years and a half. His reputation becoming favorably established, calls for medical and surgical aid were almost incessant.

After spending a few days in collecting and digesting information in regard to this country and the condition of the people, we had an interesting interview with the chiefs of the Nez Percés and Flatheads, and laid before them the object of our appointment, and explained to them the benevolent desires of Christians concerning them. We then enquired whether they wished to have teachers come among them and instruct them in the knowledge of God, his worship, and the way to be saved; and what they would do to aid them in their labors. The oldest chief of the Flatheads arose, and said, " he was old, and did not expect to know much more ; he was deaf, and could not hear, but his heart was made glad, very glad, to see what he had never seen before, a man near to God," (meaning a minister of the gospel.) Next arose Insala, the most influential chief among the Flathead nation, and said, " he had heard, a man near to God was coming to visit them, and he, with some of his people, together with some white men, went out three days' journey to meet him, but missed us. A war party of Crow Indians came upon them, and took away some of their horses, and one from him which he greatly loved, but now he forgets all, his heart is made so glad to see a man near to God." There was a short battle, but no lives were lost.

The first chief of the Nez Percés, Tai-quin-su-watish, arose, and said, " he had heard from white men a little about God, which had only gone into his ears ; he wished to know enough to have it go down into his heart, to influence his life, and to teach his people." Others spoke to the same import, and they all made as many promises as we could desire.

The Nez Percés and Flathead Indians present a promising field for missionary labor, which is white for the harvest, and the indications of divine providence in regard to it are plain, by their *anxiety* to obtain Christian knowledge. Taking the various circumstances under deliberate and prayerful consideration, in regard to these Indians, we came to the conclusion, that, though many other important stations might be found, this would be one. So desirable did this object appear, that Dr. Whitman proposed to return with the caravan, and obtain associates to come out with him the next year, with the then returning caravan, and establish a mission among these people, and by so doing, save at least a year, in bringing the gospel among them. In view of the importance of the object, I readily consented to the proposal, and to go alone with the Indians the remainder of my exploring tour. Dr. Whitman, on further consideration, felt some misgivings about leaving me, lest, if any calamity should befall me, he should be blamed by the Christian public. It was my desire that no disquietude should be felt for me, for we could not go safely together without divine protection, and with it I was secure in any situation. This confidence inspired me with all the courage I needed, and composed my mind in regard to coming dangers, as it had sustained me under those that were past.

Met with the chiefs again by appointment, and I stated to them the contemplated return of Doctor Whitman. They were much pleased, and promised to assist me, and to send a convoy with me from their country to Fort Walla Walla, on the Columbia river. They selected one of their principal young men for my particular assistant, as long as I should have need of him, who was called Kentuc; and I engaged a *voyageur*, who understood English, and also the Nez Percé language sufficiently well to interpret common business, and some of the plain truths of our holy religion, to go with me while I should continue with these tribes.

We did not call together the chiefs of the Shoshones and Utaws, to propose the subject of missions among them, lest we should excite expectations which would not soon be fulfilled. We were the more cautious upon this subject, because it is difficult to make an Indian understand the difference between a proposal and a promise. The Shoshones are a very numerous nation, and appear friendly. They are probably the most destitute of the necessaries of life of any Indians west of the mountains. Their country lies south-west of the south-east branch of the Columbia, and is said to be the most barren of any part of the country in these western regions. They are often called Snakes and Root Diggers, from being driven to these resorts to sustain life ; and parts of the year they suffer greatly from hunger and cold. They are more squalid than any Indians I have seen ; but their poverty does not lessen their need of salvation through Christ. The Utaws are decent in appearance, and their country, which is toward Santa Fe, is said to be tolerably good.

A few days after our arrival at the place of rendezvous, and when all the mountain men had assembled, another day of indulgence was granted to them, in which all restraint was laid aside. These days are the climax of the hunter's happiness. I will relate an occurrence which took place near evening, as a specimen of mountain life. A hunter, who goes technically by the name of the great bully of the mountains, mounted his horse with a loaded rifle, and challenged any Frenchman, American, Spaniard, or Dutchman, to fight him in single combat. Kit Carson, an American, told him if he wished to die, he would accept the challenge. Shunar defied him. C. mounted his horse, and with a loaded pistol, rushed into close contact, and both almost at the same instant fired. C's ball entered S's hand, came out at the wrist, and passed through the arm above the elbow. Shunar's ball passed over the head of Carson; and while he went for another pistol, Shunar begged that his life might be spared. Such scenes, sometimes from passion, and sometimes for amusement, make the pastime of their wild and wandering life. They appear to have sought for a place where, as they would say, human nature is not oppressed by the tyranny of religion, and pleasure is not awed by the frown of virtue. The fruits are visible in all the varied forms to which human nature, without the restraints of civil government, and cultivated and polished society, may be supposed to yield. In the absence of all those motives, which they would feel in moral and religious society, refinement, pride, a sense of the worth of character, and even conscience, give place to unrestrained dissoluteness. Their toils and privations are so great, that they more readily compensate themselves by plunging into such excesses, as in their mistaken judgment of things, seem most adapted to give them pleasure. They disdain the common-place phrases of profanity which prevail among the impious vulgar in civilized countries, and have many set phrases, which they appear to have manufactured among themselves, and which, in their imprecations, they bring into almost every sentence and on all occasions. By varying the tones of their voices, they make them expressive of joy, hope, grief, and anger.

In their broils among themselves, which do not happen every day, they would not be ungenerous. They would see "fair play," and would "spare the last eye;" and would not tolerate murder, unless drunkenness or great provocation could be pleaded in extenuation.

Their demoralizing influence with the Indians has been lamentable, and they have practiced impositions upon them, in all the ways that sinful propensities dictate. It is said they have sold them packs of cards at high prices, calling them the Bible; and have told them, if they should refuse to give white men wives, God would be angry with them and punish them eternally: and on almost any occasion when their wishes have been resisted, they have threatened them with the wrath of God. If these things are true in many instances, yet from personal observation, I should believe, their more common mode of accomplishing their wishes has been by flattery and presents; for the most of them squander away their wages in ornaments for their women and children.

The Indians, with whom I was to travel, having appointed the 21st to commence the journey for their country, a few days were occupied in writing to my family, the American Board of Commissioners for Foreign Missions, and other friends; and also in making preparations for my journey to Walla Walla. While we continued in this place, though in the middle of the day it was warm, yet the nights were frosty, and ice was frequently formed.

CHAPTER VI.

Part with my associate—arrive at head waters of the Columbia—kind-
    ness of the Indians—narrow defile—geology—Jackson's Hole—wild
    flax—trappers go out on a hunt—mountain prospect—Trois Tetons
    —danger from affrighted buffalo—Pierre's Hole—Volcanic chasm—
    children on horseback—interesting worship with the Indians—bu-
    rial of a child—scarcity of food—a timely supply—Salmon river—
    expected battle—geological observations—scene of mourning.

AUGUST 21st, commenced our journey in company with
Capt. Bridger, who goes with about fifty men, six or eight
days' journey on our route.   Instead of going down on the
south-west side of Lewis' river, we concluded to take our
course northerly for the Trois Tetons, which are three very
high mountains, covered with perpetual snow, separated
from the main chain of the Rocky Mountains, and are seen
at a very great distance ; and from thence to Salmon river.
Went only about three miles from the place of rendezvous,
and encamped.

On the 22d, I parted with Doct. Whitman, who returned
with the caravan to the United States.   My anxious desire
was, that the Lord would go with him and make his way
prosperous, and make him steadfast to the object of his return, until it should be accomplished ; and that, with next
year's caravan, he might come with associates into this
promising field, and with them reap a plentiful harvest.
To-day we traveled twenty miles, through a somewhat barren country, and down several steep descents, and arrived
at what is called Jackson's Hole, and encamped upon a

small stream of water, one of the upper branches of the Columbia river. It was interesting to find myself, for the first time, upon the waters of this noble river. The Indians were very attentive to all my wants—took the entire care of my packed animals, cooking, &c. They preserve particular order in their movements. The first chief leads the way, the next chiefs follow, then the common men, and after these the women and children. The place assigned me was with the first chief.

Found some buffalo to-day, of which our men killed a small number. These furnished a timely supply, as our provisions were becoming scarce. The principal chief of the Flatheads kindly furnished me with a horse to relieve mine.

Sabbath, 23d. Had an opportunity for rest and devotional exercises. In the afternoon we had public worship with those of the company who understood English. The men conducted with great propriety, and listened with attention. I did not feel any disposition to upbraid them for their sins, but endeavored affectionately to show them, that they are unfit for heaven, and that they could not be happy in the employments of that holy place, unless they should first experience a great moral change of heart by the grace of God, since the only source of happiness in heaven consists in serving and glorifying God forever. The place of our encampment was such as would naturally fill the mind with solemnity—just above a very deep and narrow defile which we had to pass, called by the hunters Kenyan. So high were the mountains, that some of them were tipped with perpetual snow, and so narrow the passage, that twilight shades obscured the view. The distance through must occupy more than a half day's journey.

Arose very early on the 24th, and commenced our way through the narrow defile, frequently crossing and re-crossing a large stream of water which flows into the Snake river. The scenery was wild and in many parts sublime—mountains of rock, almost perpendicular, shooting their heads up into the regions of perpetual snow, and in one place projecting over our path, if a zigzag trail can be called a path. Often we had to pass over the sides of mountains, which inclined at an angle of 45° toward the stream of water below, and down which packed mules have fallen, and been dashed upon the rocks. I endeavored to guide my Indian horse so cautiously that he became unmanageable, being resolved to have his own method of choosing the way. I was under the necessity of dismounting and making the best of my way. But on farther acquaintance with Indian horses, I learned that their dashing mode of going ahead, even in dangerous places, was preferable to the most cautious management of the American.

For some miles there was Sandstone in ridges at equal distances of six or eight rods apart, and from six to ten feet wide, rising a little above the surface of the earth, running from south-east to north-west; laying in strata dipping to the west at an angle of 60°. At some distance I observed a mountain of red earth of similar character, excepting that the strata dipped to the east at an angle of 40°. In one place where the strata of rocks and earth were in waves nearly horizontal, a section a few rods wide, of a wedge form, had its waving strata in a perpendicular position, as though the mountain had been rent asunder, and the chasm filled with the perpendicular wedge. A great diversity of the strata of rocks and earth prevailed in every part. Towards the last of the way through this narrow defile, we came to what appeared to be magnesian limestone, stratified, of a brown color, and very hard. As we passed on we saw dark brown gypsum, like that found in the western part of the state of New York. Here for some distance I was much annoyed with the strong scent of sulphureted hydrogen, and soon saw at the foot of the mountain under the bed of gypsum a large sulphur spring, which sent up more than thirty gallons of water per minute. Around this spring were large quantities of incrusted sulphur, and so strongly is the water saturated, that it colors the water of the river, on the side next to the spring, a greenish yellow, for more than a mile below.

We passed more forests to-day, than since we left Rock Independence; among which is Norway pine, balsam fir, double spruce, and common poplar—some low cedar and flowering raspberry, and various species of shrubbery which are not found in the United States. The Indians were very kind, and seemed to vie with each other to see who could do the most for my comfort, so that they more than anticipated my wants. Two little girls brought me a quart of strawberries, a rare dish for this season of the year. And an Indian brought me some service berries, which are large, purple, and oblong, of a pleasantly sweet taste, similar to whortleberries. We encamped upon a fertile plain, surrounded by mountains, where three years before three men were killed by a small war party of Blackfeet Indians. There were seven of the hunters, and when they saw the Blackfeet, they all fled in different directions, and by so doing emboldened the Indians to the pursuit. Had they stood firm and combined, it is probable they would have escaped unhurt.

We traveled four hours on the 25th, to another branch of Lewis' or Snake river, and encamped in a large pleasant

valley, commonly called Jackson's large hole. It is fertile
and well watered with a branch of Lewis' river coming from
the south-east, and another of some magnitude, coming from
the north-east, which is the outlet of Jackson's lake, a body
of water laying back of the Trois Tetons. There are also
many very large springs of water of uncommon clearness,
which issue from the base of the surrounding mountains.
This valley is well supplied with grass of excellent quality,
which was very grateful to our horses and mules, and the
avidity with which they helped themselves seemed to say,
they would be remunerated for past deprivations.

Flax is a spontaneous production of this country. In
every thing, except that it is perennial, it resembles the flax
which is cultivated in the United States—the stalk, the boll,
the seed, the blue flower closed in the day time and open in
the evening and morning. The Indians use it for making
fishing nets. Fields of this flax might be mowed like grass;
for the roots are too large and run too deep into the earth,
to be pulled like ours—and an advantage, which this would
have, is, that there would be a saving of ploughing and sowing.
Is it not worthy the experiment of our agricultural societies?

Kentuc, my Indian, brought me to-day some very good
currants, which were delicious in this land. There are
several species, yellow, pale red, and black. The yellow
and pale red were the best flavored.

We continued in this encampment three days, to give our
animals an opportunity to recruit, and for Captain Bridger
to fit and send out several of his men into the mountains to
hunt and trap. When I reflected upon the probability, that
most of these men would never return to their friends, but
would find their graves in the mountains, my heart was
pained for them, and especially at their thoughtlessness

about the great things of the eternal world: I gave each of
them a few tracts, for which they appeared grateful, and
said they would be company for them in their lonely hours ;
and as they rode away, I could only pray for their safety
and salvation.

During our continuance here, I took an Indian for an assistant, and ascended one of the highest mountains in the
vicinity, to view the surrounding country. The prospect
was as extensive as the eye could reach, diversified with
mountains, hills, plains, and valleys. Most of the mountains
were covered with woods ; but the plains and valleys were
covered with grass, presenting less of bright green, however,
than might be expected where the summer is favored with
dews and rains. But the whole was a scene of perfect en-
chantment. About sixty miles to the east the Rocky mountains lay stretched through the whole extent of vision, spread
out like luminous clouds in the horizon ; their summits so
elevated, that no soil ever rises to sully the pure whiteness
of their everlasting snows, and tinged and mellowed with a
golden hue by the rays of the sun. Not very far to the
north, the Trois Tetons, a cluster of high pointed mountains,
covered with perpetual snow, rising ten thousand feet almost
perpendicularly, were distinctly visible, with two others of
the same form but of less magnitude. Only three of the
cluster are so high as to be seen at a very *great* distance.
Here I spent much time in looking over the widely extended
and varied scenery, sometimes filled with emotions of the
sublime, in beholding the towering mountains ; sometimes
with pleasure in tracing the windings of the streams in the
vale below ; and these sensations frequently gave place to
astonishment, in viewing the courses in which the rivers flow
on their way, unobstructed by mountain barriers. After

some hours occupied in this excursion, I descended to the encampment much gratified with what I had seen of the works of God. The soil in this valley and upon the hills, is black and rich, and the time will come, when the solitude which now prevails will be lost in the lowing of herds and bleating of flocks, and the plough will cleave the clods of these hills and vales; and from many altars will ascend the incense of prayer and praise. After I returned, Tai-quin-su-wa-tish took me to his company of horses and gave me one in token of his friendship, and probably not without the motive to enlist me in his favor. The horse was finely made, and of the beautiful color of intermixed cream and white.

On the 28th, we pursued our journey and passed over a mountain so high, that banks of snow were but a short distance from our trail. When we had ascended two-thirds of the way, a number of buffalo, which were pursued by our Indians, came rushing down the side of the mountain through the midst of our company. One ran over a horse, on the back of which was a child, and threw the child far down the descent, but providentially it was not materially injured. Another ran over a packed horse, and wounded it deeply in the shoulder. The buffalo are naturally timid, yet when they have laid their course, and being affrighted are running at full speed, it is seldom they change their direction, whatever obstacles may be in their way.

I noticed nothing particularly new in geology, excepting upon the highest parts of these mountains, granite of very light color. Our descent was through woods more dense than those on the other side, and the most dense of any forests since we left the waters of the Missouri. Many parts of the descent were of almost impassable steepness; and part of the way down a rough deep ravine, a stream of water commences, and increasing from springs and rivulets to considerable magnitude, winds its way through the valley of Pierre's Hole; in the upper part of which we made our encampment among willows, in the prairie vale.

On the 29th, removed our encampment, and traveled five hours along this valley to the place, where two years before, two fur companies held their rendezvous. Pierre's Hole is an extensive level country, of rich soil, well watered with branches of Lewis' river, and is less frosty than any part we have passed this side the rocky chain of mountains. The valley is well covered with grass, but like most other places is deficient in woodland, having only a scanty supply of cotton-wood and willows scattered along the streams. It extends around to the north-west, as far as the eye can reach. We expected to have found buffalo here, but saw none. As parties of Blackfeet warriors often range this way, it was probable they had lately been here and frightened them away. Between this and our last encampment, I was shown the place where the men of the fur companies, at the time of their rendezvous two years before, had a battle with the Blackfeet Indians. Of the Blackfeet party there were about sixty men, and more than the same number of women and children; of the white men in the valley, there were some few hundred who could be called into action. From the information given me, it appeared that these Indians were on their way through this valley, and unexpectedly met about forty hunters and trappers going out from rendezvous to the south-west on their fall and winter hunt. The Indians manifested an unwillingness to fight, and presented tokens of peace; but they were not reciprocated. Those who came forward to stipulate terms of peace were fired upon and killed. When the Indians saw their danger, they fled to the cotton-wood trees and willows which were scattered along the stream of water, and, taking advantage of some fallen trees, constructed as good defenses as time and circumstances would permit. They were poorly provided with guns, and were still more destitute of ammunition. The trappers keeping out of reach of their arrows, and being well armed with the best rifles, made the contest unequal; and still more unequal, when, by an express sent to rendezvous, they were reinforced by veterans in mountain life. The hunters, keeping at a safe distance, in the course of a few hours killed several of the Indians, and almost all their horses, which, in their situation, could not be protected, while they themselves suffered but small loss. Those killed, on both sides, have been differently stated, but, considering the numbers engaged, and the length of time the skirmishing continued, it could not have been a bloody battle; and not much to the honor of civilized Americans. The excuse made for forcing the Blackfeet into battle is, that if they had come upon a small party of trappers, they would have butchered them and seized upon the plunder. If heathen Blackfeet would have done so, civilized white men should not. What a noble opportunity was here afforded for our American citizens to have set an example of humanity.

When night approached, the hunters retired to their encampment at the place of rendezvous, and the Indians made their escape. Thus the famous battle of Pierre's Hole began and ended.*

---

* Since my return, I have seen an account of this battle, written by a graphic hand, in all the fascinating style of romance, representing the Indians as having entrenched themselves in a swamp, so densely wooded as to be almost impenetrable; and there they kept the trap-

I attended worship this evening with the chiefs, and as many as could assemble in one of their lodges, and explained to them the ten commandments—and after showing them their sin in their transgression of God's holy law, pointed them to the Savior, and endeavored to make them understand the way of salvation. My method of instructing them was to give the first chief the first commandment, by repeating it, until he could repeat it; and the second commandment to another chief in the same way, and so on through the ten, with directions for them to retain what was given to each, and to teach their people; and the same manner was pursued with other parts of divine truth; informing them, that at our next assembling, I shall examine them to see if they rightly understood, and retained what I committed to each. And on examination, in no case did I find more than one material mistake. I also found that they took much pains to communicate instruction to each other.

---

pers at bay, until they were reinforced from rendezvous. When the Blackfeet saw the whole valley alive with horsemen rushing to the field of action, they withdrew into the dark tangled wood. When the leaders of the several hunting parties came into the field, they urged their men to enter the swamp, but they hung back in awe of the dismal horrors of the place, regarding it impenetrable and full of danger. But the leaders would not be turned from their purpose—made their wills—appointed their executors—grasped their rifles, and urged their way through the woods. A brisk fire was opened, and the Blackfeet were completely overmatched, but would not leave their fort, nor offer to surrender. The numerous veteran mountaineers, well equipped, did not storm the breastwork, even when the Blackfeet had spent their powder and balls, but only kept up the bloody battle by occasional firing during the day. The Blackfeet in the night effected their retreat; and the brave mountaineers assembled their forces in the morning, and entered the fort *without opposition.*

With those who have seen the field of battle, the glowing description, drawn out in long detail, loses its interest; for although I saw it, yet I did not see dense woods, nor a swamp of any magnitude any where near.

In this place I parted with Captain Bridger and his party, who went north-east into the mountains to their hunting ground, which the Blackfeet claim, and for which they will contend. The first chief of the Flatheads and his family, with a few of his people, went with Captain Bridger, that they might continue within the range of buffalo through the coming winter.

The Nez Percés, and the Flatheads, with whom I go, take a north-west direction for Salmon river, beyond which is their country. Our encampment for the Sabbath was well chosen for safety against any war parties of Blackfeet Indians, near a small stream of water running through a volcanic chasm, one hundred feet deep, and in most places perpendicular. We were on the west side of the chasm, with a narrow strip of wood on every other side. Here was a passage made for the *water* by *fire*. The courses, which are formed for the rivers, as forcibly prove the creating and directing hand of God, as the design manifested in the organic part of creation ; and I would as unwillingly account for the positions of mountains, and valleys, and the channels of rivers, by natural phenomena, without including the power and design of God, as for the formation of plants and animals. It is true, there is more minute and curious organization in the one than in the other, but in both the wisdom and power of God are manifest.

This day of rest, to a weary traveler, is peculiarly refreshing, and it seemed as though the Sabbath was designed especially for persons in such circumstances. It was, to my mind, a type of the final rest of the spirit when it shall return to God, after the toils of its present brief existence are done. I read with new satisfaction, the Epistle to the Hebrews, and committed again myself and family, the church and world of mankind, to God. It was pleasant to reflect on the promises, that the kingdoms of this world shall become the kingdoms of the Lord and of his Christ, and he shall reign forever; and that the time will come, when all shall know the Lord, and God shall be merciful to their unrighteousness, and their sins and iniquities he will remember no more.

Monday, 31st. While the Indians were packing and preparing to leave this encampment, I went and examined the volcanic chasm. It is many miles in length, and narrow, considering its depth; formed of basaltic columns in many places, and in others of amygdaloid. I found many large and fine specimens of pure obsidian, or volcanic glass— much lava and vitrified stones. I took some small specimens. In the vicinity around, there was clinkstone in great abundance, which, when struck by the horses hoofs, gave a metallic sound. The soil is black, and appears to be formed of decomposed lava, and is covered with a nutritious grass.

The Indians are very kind to each other, and if one meets with any disaster, the others will wait and assist him. Their horses often turn their packs, and run, plunge and kick, until they free themselves from their burdens. Yesterday a horse turned his saddle under him upon which a child was fastened, and started to run, but those near hovered at once around with their horses so as to enclose him, and the child was extricated without injury. When I saw the condition of the child, I had no expectation that it could be saved alive. This was the second case of the kind which had occurred since I had been traveling with these Indians. They are so well supplied with horses that every man, woman, and child, are mounted on horseback, and all their possessions are packed upon horses. Small children, not more than three years old, are mounted alone, and generally upon colts. They are lashed upon the saddle to keep them from falling, when they sleep, which they often do when they become fatigued. Then they recline upon the horses shoulders; and when they awake, lay hold of their whip, which is fastened to the wrist of their right hand, and apply it smartly to their horses; and it is astonishing to see how these little creatures will guide and run them. Children which are still younger, are put into an encasement made with a board at the back and a wicker work around the other parts, covered with cloth inside and out, or, more generally, with dressed skins; and are carried upon the mothers' back, or suspended from a high knob upon the fore part of their saddles.

As we recede from the mountains the climate becomes warmer. We encamped upon another tributary of the Columbia. Tai-quin-su-wa-tish, the principal chief of the Nez Percés, came to me and requested me to meet in his lodge a number of his people who had separated, husbands from their wives, and wives from their husbands, and explain to them what God had said upon the subject. I readily consented, and was the more pleased with the proposal as it was without any suggestion from myself, but the result of his own reflections after what I had before said in explaining the ten commandments. When they were assembled, I read to them about the relative duties of husbands and wives, and of parents and children. I commented upon the subject, and told them that when they marry it must be for life. All but two agreed to go back to their former husbands and wives. It was interesting to see that they are ready to practice instructions as soon as received. The chief said they desired me to instruct them in all that God has said ; for they wish to do right. After I left them, they stayed a long time in the lodge of the chief, which was near my tent, and I heard them conversing on the subject until I went to sleep, which was at a late hour. They all shook hands with me when I left them, and said my words were "*tois*" (good.)

Tuesday, September 1st. We pursued our journey to-day only about four hours. Crossed Henry's Fork, another branch of Lewis' river, which is itself a river of some magnitude, about twenty rods wide in this place, and fordable only when the water is low. After proceeding a few miles down on the north side, we encamped at an early hour in a spot upon the bank of the river, surrounded by cotton-wood with a dense growth of shrubbery. Our fears of meeting a war party of Blackfeet Indians, were increased by seeing three Indians pass who were strangers to us. Some of the chiefs went through our encampment and harangued the people, the object of which was to be prepared for defending themselves against an attack, should any enemies appear. We were preserved in safety through the night, and arose on the morning of the second and went on our way, and performed a journey of twenty-two miles over a barren section of country. The surface is composed of quartose sand, intermixed with disintegrated amygdaloid, basalt, and obsidian. In some places were large excavations, plainly indicative of ancient volcanoes, which had spread out their melted contents in a level plain of hard lava, or amygdaloid, without forming cones. In other places there were conical rocks of different magnitudes at the base, and of different height—none perhaps over the diameter of three rods at the base and sixty feet high. They were universally divided in the centre, as though an explosion had taken place after they were hardened. At some distance from us were several hills, rising in high cones some hundred feet—two of them I should judge to be not far from three thousand feet high. I did not have an opportunity of examining their geological formation.

We arrived at evening at a small branch of the Salmon river, which was the first water we had found through the day, and upon which was good grass for our horses. Here Kentuc, my Indian, caught some excellent trout, which was a very grateful change of food.

Our progress during the next day was through a barren tract, as yesterday, where there is no vegetation except wormwood, which grows very large. A sluggish stream bordered with willows, afforded us some conveniences for stopping at night. Thermometer, at noon, 65°.

We traveled on the fourth, five hours, and encamped by a stream of water, in Coté's defile, which comes out of the mountains and is lost in the barren plains below. Coté's defile passes through a range of high mountains, some of the tops of which are covered with snow. Most of the day was uncomfortably cold with snow-squalls. Thermometer, at noon, 54°.

Friday, 4th. To-day I received a letter from Fort Hall, containing an invitation from Mr. A. Baker to spend the winter with him ; but the object for which I have passed the Rocky Mountains required me to pursue my tour, and if possible to reach the Pacific Ocean, and to return to Fort Vancouver before winter. We providentially learned that a large band of Nez Percés was a few miles below us, and would come to us to-morrow. We had become almost destitute of provisions, but to-day killed a few buffalo.

The morning of the 5th was very cold. We continued in our encampment, to give the band of Nez Percés an opportunity to join us, and about the middle of the day they came ; the principal chief marching in front with his aid, carrying an American flag by his side. They all sung a march, while a few beat a sort of drum. As they drew near they displayed columns, and made quite an imposing appearance. The women and children followed in the rear. Tai-quin-su-wâ-tish, and other chiefs, arranged their people in the same order and went out to meet them ; and when we had approached within ten rods of each other, all halted, and a salute was fired, in which I had to take the lead. They then dismounted, and both bands formed into single file, and meeting, shook hands with me and each other in token of friendship, and to express their joy to see one come among them to teach them respecting God and salvation. The principal chief of the other band who is called Charlie, and is the first chief of the Nez Percé nation, is a good looking man, his countenance rather stern, intelligent, and expressive of much decision of character. I never saw joy expressed in a more dignified manner, than when he took me firmly by the hand and welcomed me.

In the afternoon I took Kentuc and rode five miles to see a prominence of interesting appearance. It is detached from the main mountain, stands on a plain upon the east side of Cote's defile, is about a half mile in circumference at the base, and rises up abruptly, having most of its west side perpendicular. It is more than two hundred feet high, has a level horizontal summit of eighty rods long, north and south, and twenty rods wide. It furnishes plain evidence of having been fused and thrown up by subterranean fires.

In the evening I met the chiefs, and as many as could

assemble in the lodge, and explained to those whom I had not seen before, the object of my mission.   Charlie, the first chief, arose and spoke with much good sense for some time —mentioned his ignorance, his desire to know more about God, and his gladness of heart to see one who can teach him ; and said, " I have been like a little child, uneasy, feeling about in the dark after something, not knowing what ; but now I hope to learn something which will be substantial, and which will help me to teach my people to do right."   I told them to-morrow would be the Sabbath ; and explained to them the nature of the institution, and their obligation to remember and keep it holy.   They expressed their desire to obey, and said they would not remove camp, but attend to the worship of God.   Providentially there came to us this afternoon a good interpreter from Fort Hall, so that to-morrow I can preach to the people.

Sabbath, 6th.   Early this morning one of the oldest chiefs went about among the people, and with a loud voice explained to them the instructions given last evening ; told them it was the Sabbath, and they must prepare for public worship.   About eight in the morning, some of the chiefs came to me and asked where they should assemble.   I enquired if they could not be accommodated under the shade of the willows, which skirted the stream of water on which we were encamped.   They thought on account of their numbers they could not.   I then enquired if they could not take the poles of some of their lodges and construct a shade ; and without any other directions they went and made preparation, and before eleven o'clock came and said they were ready for worship.   I found them all assembled, men, women, and children, between four and five hundred, in what I would call a sanctuary of God, constructed with their lodges, nearly one hundred feet long and about twenty feet wide ; and all were arranged in rows, through the length of the building upon their knees, with a narrow space in the middle, lengthwise, resembling an aisle. The whole area within was carpeted with their dressed skins, and they were all in their best attire. The chiefs were arranged in a semicircle at the end which I was to occupy. I could not have believed they had the means, or could have known how to erect so convenient and so decent a place for worship, and especially as it was the first time they had had public worship. The whole sight affected me, and filled me with admiration ; and I felt as though it was the house of God and the gate of heaven.

They all continued in a kneeling position during singing and prayer, and when I closed prayer with Amen, they all said what was equivalent in their language, to Amen. And when I commenced sermon, they seated themselves back upon their heels. I stated to them the original condition of man when first created, his fall, and the ruined and sinful condition of all mankind ; the law of God, and that all are transgressors of this law and as such are exposed to the wrath of God, both in this life and the life to come ; and then told them of the mercy of God in giving his Son to die for us, and of the love of the Savior, and that though he desires our salvation, he will not save us unless we hate sin and put our trust in him, and love and obey him with all our heart. I also endeavored to show them the necessity of renovation of heart by the power and grace of the Holy Spirit. Told them they must pray to God for the forgiveness of their sins and for salvation. They gave the utmost attention, and entire stillness prevailed, excepting, when some truth arrested their minds forcibly, a little humming sound passed through the whole assembly, occupying two or three seconds.

I never spoke to a more interesting assembly, and would not have changed my audience for any other upon earth ; and I felt that it was worth a journey across the Rocky Mountains, to enjoy this one opportunity with these heathen who are so anxious to obtain a knowledge of God. I hope, that in the last day it will be found that good was done in the name of Jesus. If Christians could have witnessed this day's service, it would have enlisted their sympathies, and they would be willing to do something adequate to the conversion of these perishing souls.

An Indian boy about sixteen years old, who belonged to the band which joined us yesterday, died this morning. He was speechless when he was brought here. We attended his funeral in the afternoon. They buried him in a very decent manner, without any heathen rites, excepting that they buried with him all his clothes and blankets. I addressed the people at the grave upon the subject of the resurrection and of the judgment. This was entirely new to them and very interesting. Tai-quin-su-wà-tish came to my tent towards evening, and said, what I had said was "*tois*," it was spiritual, and now he knew more about God. So deep was the interest awakened by the few ideas their benighted minds had obtained of this most precious truth of our religion, that they came to my tent after I had retired to rest, and awakened me, to go and converse still farther with them on the subject.

Monday, 7th. We traveled five hours to-day. The Indians make slow progress in traveling with their village ; for it takes them a long time to pack and unpack, to set up and take down their lodges. This is, however, of little consequence to them ; for wherever they are, it is their home.

They are very kind, and manifest their kindness in anticipating all, and more than all, my wants, which they have the power to supply. They consult me upon all their important business, and are ready to follow my counsels. They are attentive to furnish little comforts. If the sun shines with much warmth into my tent, they will cut green bushes and set them up for shade. A few days since, we encamped where there were some fragrant plants of a species of mint, and the wife of Tai-quin-su-wâ-tish, with a few other women, collected a quantity, and strewed them in my tent.

We passed to-day mountains of volcanic rocks and over a more rich, black soil, where we found a good supply of grass for our horses at night.

Our route, on the 8th, was continued as usual. My health hitherto, since I commenced my journey, has been uninterruptedly good, until to-day I suffered a slight attack of inflammation of the lungs, in consequence of a cold.

The Indian mode of living is very precarious, and yet they are seldom anxious about the future. When they have a plenty, they are not sparing ; and when they are in want, they do not complain. The Indians at this time were almost destitute of provisions, and we were approaching the Salmon river mountains, to pass over which occupies between twelve and fifteen days, and where there are no buffalo and scarcely any other game. I felt a prayerful concern for them, that God would send a supply before we should get beyond the range of buffalo, and was confident that we should experience the truth of His word, that he provides for all their meat in due season ; and as the cattle upon the thousand hills are his, so he would not withhold his providential care from us.

We continued to pass basaltic mountains; and also passed some very white marl clay, which the Indians use for cleansing their robes and other garments made of dressed skins.

Their mode of doing this is to make the clay into a paste, and rub it upon the garments, and when it becomes dry rub it off, which process leaves the garment soft, clean, and white. We encamped to-day where they had before made an encampment, a little below a steep bank. Near night I was alarmed by shouts of Indians and a general rush up the bank. I hastened up and saw great numbers running towards our camp. It proved to be a foot race, such as they frequently exercise themselves in, for the purpose of improving their agility.

September 9th, I was more unwell. To-day we unexpectedly saw before us a large band of buffalo, and halted to make preparation for the chase. The young men and all the good hunters prepared themselves, selected the swiftest horses, examined the few guns they had, and took a supply of arrows with their bows. Our condition was such, that it seemed our lives almost depended upon their success. And while they were preparing, I could not but offer prayer to God, that he would in mercy give them judgment, skill, and success. They advanced towards the herd of buffalo with great caution, lest they should frighten them before they could make a near approach; and also to reserve the power of their horses for the chase, when it should be necessary to bring it into full requisition. When the buffalo took the alarm and fled, the rush was made, each Indian selecting for himself a cow with which he happened to come into the nearest contact. All were in swift motion, scouring the valley—a cloud of dust began to arise—the firing of guns and the shooting of arrows followed in close succession—soon here and there buffalo were seen prostrated ; and the women, who followed close in the rear, began the work of securing the valuable acquisition ; and the men were away again in pursuit of the fleeing herd. Those in the chase, when they came abreast of the buffalo and at the distance of two rods, shoot and wheel, expecting the wounded animal to turn upon them. The horses appeared to understand the way to avoid danger. As soon as the wounded animal flies again, the chase is renewed, and such is the alternate wheeling and chasing until the buffalo sinks beneath its wounds. They obtained between fifty and sixty.

I was interested to see how expertly the Indians used the bow and arrow, and how well the women followed up the chase, and performed their part in dressing the buffalo which were slain. After traveling six hours to-day, we encamped on the eastern branch of Salmon river, where it is of considerable magnitude. The pain in my breast changed and seated in my head, on the right side.

On the 10th, my health was no better, and I was obliged to resort to medicine. I could say with the Psalmist, "I laid me down and slept ; for thou art with me." We did not remove to-day, for it was necessary for the Indians to dry their meat by a process which is called "jerking." The meat is cut into pieces, an inch thick, and spread out on a fixture made with stakes, upon which are laid poles, and upon these cross sticks ; and then a moderate fire is placed beneath, which partly smokes, cooks, and dries it, until it is so well freed from moisture, that it can be packed, and

will keep without injury almost any length of time. Here
we made preparation for the remainder of my journey to
Walla Walla, which will probably occupy about twenty
days.

September 11th. To-day most of the Nez Percés and
Flatheads left us to continue within the range of buffalo,
that they might secure a larger store of provisions before
winter, leaving, however, about one hundred and fifty to go
with me towards Walla Walla. Before they left us, I experienced another token of their regard in a very valuable
present of twenty fine buffalo tongues, which are a great
delicacy, together with a large quantity of dried meat. I
reciprocated their kindness by making such presents as were
in my power to bestow—among which was a britania cup,
to the first chief, which he highly valued. And I gave him
some writing paper, requesting him to present it to the missionaries whom I had encouraged him to expect next year.

After traveling three hours, we encamped upon the same
branch of the Salmon river, to give the Indians an opportunity to dry their meat more thoroughly.

We continued our journey, on the 12th, down the eastern
branch of Salmon river. The valley through which this
river runs is generally fertile, and varies from one to three
or four miles in width, but as we advanced toward the Salmon river mountains, the mountains upon each side increased in height and converged towards each other. They
presented some noble prospects. It is a custom with Indians
to send out numbers of their best hunters and warriors, in
different directions, to reconnoiter, and especially when they
are apprehensive that enemies may be near. We had evidence, from tracks recently made, that Indians of some other
nation, or tribe, were about us; and therefore more than

usual numbers of our men were flanking, and ahead. On the banks of the river down which we were traveling, there was a dense growth of willows extending, however, only a few rods into the bottom-lands. About two in the afternoon, we were all very much alarmed to see our men, who were out as hunters and guards upon the hills, running their horses full speed, in an oblique direction towards us. Two of them were our principal chiefs. We knew that they had discov-ered something more than ordinary, but what we could not conjecture. Being in a country where war parties of Black-feet Indians often range, our thoughts were turned upon dan-ger; and soon our fears were increased by seeing on the sides of the mountains at our left, clouds of dust arise, and in the obscure distance, men descending as swiftly as their horses could run. They were so far off that we could not deter-mine who they were. At the same time our two chiefs on the hills halted and made signals which we did not under-stand. In addition to this, some of the Indians said they saw Blackfeet Indians in the willows, not far off, between us and the chiefs; and our belief that it was so, was confirm-ed, when two deer rushed from the willows towards us, and when they saw us, instead of returning, only declined a lit-tle to the left, and passed before us. These enquiries arose in my mind—Why have the chiefs halted? Do they see enemies between us and themselves? Are their signals to give us warning of danger? What so frightened the deer that they rushed out towards us? We had all halted, and made what preparation we could for battle. As we did not know in what part of the willows to make the attack, we were waiting for our enemies to commence the fire, and were expecting every instant to have their balls poured in upon us. It was a moment of awful suspense. We sent out a few men, upon an eminence to our right, to see what they could discover, and they soon returned without having seen any enemies. The two chiefs upon the hills, who were now joined by those who rushed down the mountains, and who proved to be some of our own men, applied their whips to their horses, and in full speed came to us; and Charlie, the first chief, rode up to me, and smiling, reached out his hand and said, " *cocoil cocoil*," (buffalo, buffalo.) Thus ended the battle; and the remainder of the day was spent in killing and dressing buffalo, which was far more pleasant than fighting Blackfeet Indians. This made a desirable addition to their stock of provisions. We encamped in this place, which supplied a plenty of good grass for our horses, and where there was no want of fuel.

The inflammation in my head still continued with throbbing, pain, and fever—my pulse one hundred a minute. Bled myself again and took medicine. Thermometer, at noon, 73°.

Sabbath, 13th. My health no better, and my strength was failing. I felt that all was right, and that I needed this trial to lead me to an examination of my spiritual condition, my motives in engaging in this mission, and whether I could give up all for Christ to promote his kingdom in the world. I thought I could surrender all into the hands of God, my soul to my Redeemer, and my body to be buried by these Indians in this desert land. I felt as though it was desirable to finish my tour, and return and make my report, and urge the sending of missionaries into this field, which is white for the harvest; and again to meet my family and friends; but still I wished not to have any will of my own, but say, the will of the Lord be done. These Indians persevere in their kindness, and are very respectful, and ready to obey as fast as I can impart instruction; and they say that what I tell them is different from any thing they have ever heard, being spiritual, and that they wish to have *Sueapo* (American) teachers. If the American churches will not send them teachers, criminality must rest upon them for disobedience to Christ's authority. Are there any heathen more anxious than these to be taught the way of salvation, where there are so few obstacles to the introduction of the gospel? Here are no idols, no sacrifices, no power of caste to combat; nor, as yet, the destructive influence which exists upon the frontiers.

September 14th. Re-commenced our journey, and proceeded five hours down the river, and stopped a few miles above the main branch of Salmon river, which comes from the south, and has its source in two small lakes in the mountains north of Henry's fork.

For some distance on our way, on the 15th, the mountains came down near the river, rendering the valley through which it runs, narrow. Some of these mountnins terminate in high bluffs, which in many places present uncommonly interesting strata. The lowest stratum was white marly earth, about twenty feet in depth, nearly horizontal, and somewhat indurated; upon this a green stratum of about four feet in thickness; next a stratum of brown of about ten feet; upon this a stratum of red about the same depth of the green; over this a mould of decomposed lava. This marly earth slightly effervesces with acid. The rocks in most places are basalt—in some places very fine granular quartz. Noticing some unusual appearances near the foot of the mountains, on the left, I rode to the place, and found a cluster of volcanic eruptions, which, though ancient, appeared more recent than any I had previously seen. A little

way down the descent into one of the craters, I found a petrified stump, standing in its natural position ; its roots and
the grain of the wood entire.   I think it was cedar, and
about eighteen inches in diameter.   This stood undoubtedly,
upon what was the natural surface of the earth, and the
mound above and around was thrown up by volcanic fires.
While time is mouldering the lava into dust, the wind is
scattering it over the country around, to renew the soil
which was destroyed by the great conflagration, which once
fused this whole region of the setting sun.   This petrified
stump, found in this position, proves that this country, which
is now so destitute of wood, was once supplied if not covered
with forests.   From various sources of evidence, it is plain
that these prairie regions were formerly better supplied with
wood than at present, and also that the present supply is
constantly diminishing.

We passed, to-day, a place where two years ago thirty
Nez Percé young men, who were killed by the Blackfeet,
were buried.   They were all active young men, going out
upon some expedition, the nature of which I could not learn.
They had gone but a little distance from the village, which
encamped here, when passing through a very narrow defile
on a small stream of water, walled up on both sides with
perpendicular rocks, the Blackfeet Indians, who had way-
laid them, attacked them from before and behind, and killed
all but one, who mounted a horse belonging to the Blackfeet, and rushed through the opposing enemy.   After the
Blackfeet Indians had retired from the place of slaughter,
the Nez Percés brought away the dead bodies and buried
them in this place.   According to their mode, they buried
with them their clothes, blankets, and buffalo robes, in graves
about three feet deep, putting five or six bodies in a grave.

Some time after this, the Blackfeet Indians came and dug them up, and made plunder of their blankets and whatever they thought worth taking. The Nez Percés, some time afterward, came this way and collected their bones and buried them again. The graves in which they were first buried were open when we passed, and fragments of garments were lying about. Here my Indians halted, and mourned in silence over their murdered sons and brothers. The whole scene was affecting, and I could not but long for the time to come when they shall settle down in a Christian community, and cease from their dangerous wanderings; and the gospel shall be sent to the Blackfeet Indians, that they may imbibe its spirit of peace on earth and good will toward men. After some time spent in reflections and solemn mourning, we left the place and proceeded down the river, and encamped near Bonneville's Fort, which he has abandoned, and which is situated in a small pleasant valley. This place would be favorable for fur business, was it not on the ground where conflicting tribes often meet.

CHAPTER VII.

Salmon river—mineral salt—chimneys—forest trees, new species of
pine—geology—sulphur lake—a rare animal—new species of squirrels and pheasants—came to the Lewis branch of the Columbia—ferryman—Basaltic formation—fine climate—arrive at Walla Walla.

SALMON river is a beautiful transparent stream, and takes
its name from the immense number of salmon found in its
waters. The shores are covered with pebbles of primitive
formation.

I took an observation of latitude, and found it 44° 41′.

September 16th. Passing a mile down the river, we
came to a location of mineral salt. It crops out of the
mountain near its base, on the south side of the river. On
account of the impaired state of my health, and having no facilities for exploring the mine, I was under the necessity of
passing it with an examination of such specimens only as
the Indians procured. The salt is pure and white, containing less of the water of crystalization than our common
salt. I took a quantity to replenish my nearly exhausted
store. That the mine may be extensive is probable from
the circumstance, that the geological formations around are
like those about the mines in Poland, and besides it is in the
vicinity of the great Salt Lake, whose waters are so strongly
saturated that crystals form upon the shores.

After passing down the river two hours in a north-west
direction, we entered into the mountains, leaving Salmon
river. The river literally passed into the mountains; for

the opening in the perpendicular rocks, two or three hundred feet high, through these mountains several thousand
feet high, was wide enough only for the river to find a passage. It flowed into the dark chasm, and we saw it no
more. During the two hours ride, before we entered the
mountains, the scenery was grand. While there was some
level bottom-land along the river, in every direction mountains were rising above mountains, and peaks above peaks,
up to the regions of perpetual snow. These mountains are
not so much in chains, as of conical forms, with bases in
most instances small in proportion to their height. So
much sublimity and grandeur, combined with so much variety, is rarely presented to view. Horizontal strata, with
interchanges of white, green, red, and brown, were similar
to those seen yesterday ; and in one place, for more than a
mile, a vertical front was presented, facing the south-west, of
one hundred and fifty, and two hundred feet high, resting upon a base of conglomerated rock. The stones of which it is
composed are round, of primitive origin, cemented with
marly clay, and of the various colors already mentioned.
The opposite side of the river is studded with dark basalt.

After leaving Salmon river we traversed a dreary, narrow, and winding course for several hours, until an open
space spread out before us. Here I beheld what appeared
at a distance like a village of thirty or forty houses which
the fire had desolated, leaving the decayed, broken, and
tottering chimneys yet standing. On a nearer approach
they proved to be masses of slaty rock, ten, twenty, and
even forty feet in height. The firm and impenetrable texture of their material preserves them from being crumbled
to a level with the earth around them.

From this place we turned more westerly, and passed a

high mountain, parts of which are very steep, and encamped in a valley by a stream of crystal water.

On the 17th, we pursued our journey over high mountains, which, in some places were intersected by deep ravines, very difficult to be passed. Encamped in a grove of large Norway pines.

September 18th. The villages of Indians make slow progress in traveling, and being desirous to expedite my journey to some of the posts of the Hudson Bay Company, I took ten Indians and went forward, leaving the remainder to follow at their leisure. We passed over a mountain six thousand feet high, occupying more than half a day to arrive at the summit. These mountains are covered with woods, excepting small portions, which are open and furnish grass for our horses. The woods are composed mainly of fir, spruce, Norway pine, and a new species of pine. The leaves of this new species resemble those of pitch pine, growing in bunches at the ends of the limbs, but are shorter and smaller ; the bark and the body of the tree resemble the tamarack ; the wood is firm and *very* elastic. On account of this last and peculiar property, I have called it the elastic pine. It grows very tall and straight, and without branches except near the top. These pines would undoubtedly make excellent masts and spars for shipping. On experiments which I made, I found it difficult to break sticks an inch in diameter. After passing part of the way down this mountain, we stopped for the night.

We arose early on the 19th, and commenced our day's labor, and by diligence went more than twice the distance than when we were with the village. We were much annoyed by trees that had fallen across the trail. Encamped upon the south-east side of a high mountain, where there was a large opening, a spring of water, and a good supply of grass for our horses.

Sabbath, 20th. We continued in the same encampment. I expressed my wish to the chief, that the day should be spent religiously, and that he should communicate to his men, as well as he was able, the scripture truths he had learned. This was faithfully done on his part, and he prayed with them with much apparent devotion. I was interested to see how readily they were disposed to obey to the extent of their knowledge, and I was affected with the thought that so few were willing to come and teach these benighted minds. After they had closed their worship, I sang a hymn and prayed, and conversed with them.

The inflammation in my head continuing, I bled myself copiously, which reduced my pulse for awhile, but increased my weakness, so that I could walk only a few rods without much fatigue.

Sometimes, amidst all the evidences of God's mercy to me, I found my heart sinking in despondency, and was ready to say, I shall perish in these wild, cold mountains. It seemed, that such was my loss of strength, and I was becoming so emaciated, that I could not endure the fatigue of traveling eight days longer over these mountains, which are on an average about six thousand feet high ; and as they range north and south, with only very narrow valleys between, and our course was only a little north of west, we were constantly ascending and descending ; and we could not discontinue our journey for the want of provisions. The thought that I must fail of accomplishing the object of my mission, and close my life without a sympathising friend with whom I could converse and pray ; and be buried in these solitary mountains, filled me with a gloom which I knew was wrong. My judgment was clear, but I could not make it influence the feelings of my heart. At night I sometimes thought a pillow desirable, upon which to lay my aching, throbbing head, but my portmanteau was a very good substitute, and I rested quietly upon the ground, and every morning arose refreshed by sleep.

Monday, 21st. At an early hour we resumed our journey, and our horses being recruited with the rest and good fare they had yesterday, made a long day's journey. I had noticed the mountain over which we passed to-day, which is about seven thousand feet high, two days before we arrived at the top ; and queried in my mind whether Charlie, my guide, would not depart in this instance from the common custom of the Indians, which is to pass over the highest parts of mountains, and to descend into the lowest valleys.

But we passed the highest point, excepting one peak, which is nearly perpendicular, and rises like an immense castle or pyramid. It is composed of basalt ; and around it volcanic rocks lie scattered in great profusion. At the base there are also excavations, around and below which there is a large quantity of lava. This is a granite mountain, most of which is in its natural state. The way by which I calculated the height of these mountains is, that some of them are tipped with perpetual snow ; and as eight thousand feet, in latitude 42°, is the region of perpetual snow, there can be no doubt, as these do not vary greatly from each other, that they average six thousand feet.

I was much interested with a curiosity upon this mountain, which was two granite rocks, each weighing many tons, placed one upon the other, like the parts of an hour glass. It was wonderful, how nicely the uppermost one

was balanced upon the other. It would seem that a puff
of wind would blow it off its centre. Charlie, the chief,
seeing me one day examining minerals, with a magnifying
glass, said, "these white men know every thing. They
know what rocks are made of, they know how to make iron,
and how to make watches, and how to make the needle always point to the north." They had seen a compass before, and when I showed them mine, they said, "that would
keep me from getting lost." A waterfall was seen descending down a high point of this mountain, which, by its
continual foaming, looked like a white belt girding its side.

Left our encampment, on the 22d, at an early hour and
continued our mountainous journey. Parts of the way the
ascent and descent was at an angle of 45°, and in some
places even more steep ; sometimes on the verge of dizzy
precipices ; sometimes down shelves of rocks where my
Indian horse would jump from one to another, and in other
places would brace himself upon all fours and slide down.
I had become so weak that I could not walk on foot, but
was obliged to keep upon his back. Frequently between
the mountains there would be only space enough for a rushing stream of the purest water to find its way ; the bank on
one side of which would terminate the descent of one mountain, and the other bank commence the ascent of another.
The question often arose in my mind, can this section of
country ever be inhabited, unless these mountains shall be
brought low, and these valleys shall be exalted ? But
they may be designed to perpetuate a supply of wood for
the wide-spread prairies ; and they may contain mines of
treasures, which, when wrought, will need these forests for
fuel, and these rushing streams for water power. Roads
may be constructed running north and south, so that trans-.

portations may be made south to the Salmon river, and north to the Coos-coots-ke.*

After a fatiguing day's march, we encamped in a low stony place where there was but little grass, for the want of which some of our horses strayed away.   Our men killed a deer, which was a very agreeable exchange for dried buffalo.

The mountains, over which we made our way on the 23d, were of primitive formation, with the exception of some parts which were volcanic.   Granite and mica slate predomina-ted.   In one place there were immense quantities of granite, covering more than a hundred acres, in a broken state, as though prepared for making walls, mostly in cubic forms. In some places the change from granite, in its natural state, to amygdaloid, was so gradual, that it would be difficult to say where the one ended and the other began ; like the change from day to night.   While riding along upon a nar-row ridge of this mountain, I saw two small lakes a little down the sides ; one on the right hand, which appeared to be very black, and the other upon the left was very yellow with sulphur, issuing from a spring in the mountain side. These two lakes were directly opposite each other, and not far distant.   I should have examined them more minutely, had my strength permitted me to go down to them, and again ascend to where I must have left my horse.   There was also much in the scenery around to admire ; mountain rising above mountain, and precipice above precipice.

We spent the night in a valley, where there was a small meadow, well supplied with grass.   The woods around

---

* The name of this river in the journal of Clarke and Lewis, and in all other writings I have seen, is written Coos-coos-kee.   This signi-fies the water water.   But Coos-coots-ke signifies the little water. Coos, water ; coots, little ; ke, the.   The little river.

were very dense, composed mostly of the new species of pine, which here were very tall and straight, not however very large in diameter. The neighborhood of beaver was indicated by the mud dam, and by the barked willows on the stream. The Indians brought in a wolverine which they killed.

Took an early departure, on the 24th, from our encampment, and made good progress through the day. About the middle of the day, we came where we could look forward without the sight being obstructed by mountains, and it was pleasant to have a prospect opening into the wide world. We continued to descend, until we came into a valley of considerable extent, through which flows a large branch of the Coos-coots-ke. Found to-day a new species of elder, which grows five or six inches in diameter, and from ten to twenty feet high, bearing berries which are blue and pleasant to the taste. Kentuc caught some fine trout.

Here was a band of horses, belonging to the Nez Percés, which they left last spring. They were in fine order. It is remarkable that their horses do not wander far from where they are left, although there are no fences to inclose them. Here some of the Indians changed their horses and took fresh ones, relieving those which were worn down with journeying.

On the 25th, we pursued our course down this fertile valley, until one in the afternoon, when, contrary to my expectations, we left this branch of the Coos-coots-ke, which was too much of a northerly direction, and ascended another high mountain, densely covered with woods. Among the largest trees is a new species of fir, single leafed, the bark thick and rough like the bark of hemlock, but the balsam is the same as the common fir. I saw more birds in this val-

ley, than in all the country through which I had passed
west of the Rocky Mountains ; robins in great numbers,
the magpie, and with them a new species of bird about as
large as the magpie, its color uniformly a dull red, somewhat resembling chocolate. Thermometer stood at 54°.

On the 26th, we proceeded but about four hours on our
way, and encamped on the side of a mountain near its summit ; the distance to another suitable place for our horses
over Sabbath, being too great. Saw to-day a new species
of animal, such as I never saw before. It was about as
large as a martin, and probably of that genus. Its color
was a bright orange red, resembling a live coal of fire ; its fur
appeared to be fine ; its head round and large ; its eyes black,
prominent, and very piercing. I was forward of my Indians,
and when it saw me, it sprang about eight feet up a tree,
ran part of the way up, but appeared afraid to ascend higher.
Attempts were made to obtain it, but without success. An
Indian hit it with an arrow, but did not kill it, and it came
down and escaped. I saw in these mountains, a new variety of striped squirrel, only about half as large as those
found in the United States ; and another kind, in every respect resembling the red squirrel, but in color. It is nearly
black, excepting its under parts, which are rufous, or reddish yellow. Also a new species of pheasant, if it may be
called a pheasant. It is much smaller than the common
species ; somewhat lighter colored and more spotted ; its
habits are gregarious like the common quail. It was remarkably tame, as if unacquainted with enemies ; and
when assailed with stones by the Indians, appeared to be
amazed, and made scarcely any effort to escape. Its flesh
was very good, and furnished an additional supply to our
waning stock of provisions.

Sabbath, 27th. We continued in our encampment. My health was no better—sweat profusely last night, and yet the inflammation was increasing—took from my arm a pint of blood, which, while it weakened, gave me relief.

We had religious services both in the morning and afternoon of this day, as last Sabbath. Charlie prays every morning and evening with his men, and asks a blessing when they eat. In the afternoon, he, with Compo, my interpreter, came and sat by me, and said, " we are now near our country, and when we come into it, I wish you to look over it and see if it is good for missionaries to live in. I know but little about God—my people know but little—I wish my people to know more about God." He said he wished to talk with me much more, and was sorry I had not a better qualified interpreter.

Monday, 28th, my health was improved, and we made a long day's march and emerged from the mountains about two o'clock in the afternoon. Not finding water as we expected, wo woro obliged to travel on until near night, when we came to another branch of the Coos-coots-ke, at which we found several lodges of Nez Percé Indians. A salute was fired, and then we were welcomed with a ceremonious, but hearty shaking of hands. They feasted us with excellent dried salmon, for which I made them some small presents. I was rejoiced to find myself safely through the Salmon river mountains, and convalescent. These mountains were far more difficult to pass than the Rocky Mountains, as we could not take advantage of any valley, but one in which we journeyed only two-thirds of a day. Excepting in the middle of the days, the atmosphere was cold, and frequently ice was formed during the night. It was a favor that we had no snow, which often falls upon the tops of these mountains very early in the autumn; nor had we any storms, or unpleasant weather in our passage. Frequently heavy gales of winds sweep through these mountains, and prostrate parts of the forests ; but we had none to endanger us.

On the 29th, we proceeded down this branch more than half the day, and found the soil black and good, well covered with grass, but dried into hay by the summer drouth. Here, as on most prairies, there is much want of wood, there being but little besides what is found along the streams of water. This country continues to be volcanic, as is evinced by the abundance of lava and basalt. Came at noon to six lodges of Indians, who welcomed us with the same friendly expressions, as those did where we encamped last night. We left the branch of the Coos-coots-ke and ascended westerly to the upper prairies, which are as fertile as the lower, and do not suffer more with the drouth. After a long and fatiguing ride over these prairies, we descended into a deep gulf, almost enclosed with perpendicular walls of basalt ; in the bottom of which, we found a large spring of water, where we encamped.

Arose very early on the 30th, set forward, and made good progress, considering the exhausted state of our horses. Most of the streams were dried up, and one, which is generally large, and where we intended to have arrived last night, was wholly destitute of water and grass. Ascending out of this gulf, we found toward the summit of the high prairie, a good spring of water, with sufficiency of grass, where we refreshed ourselves at noon. The horses, contrary to my expectations, preferred the dried grass to the green. In the afternoon, we went through a section of country well supplied with woods, chiefly made up of yellow pine and white oak ; where much of the soil appeared to be very good. Towards night we came to a stream of water running west, where we encamped. Thermometer 82° at noon.

Thursday, October 1st. Arose early with substantially better health, for which I cannot be too thankful. After travelling a few miles, we came to several lodges of Nez Percés, who gave us their kind welcome, and seemed, as at the other lodges, much pleased to see their first chief. They manifested the same feelings on learning who I was, and the object of my coming into their country, as their countrymen did whom we met at the rendezvous. With these Indians, I left two of my horses, which were too much exhausted with the fatigues of our long journey to proceed any farther. I had fears that they would not endure the deprivations of the coming winter, without any shelter from the cold and storms, and with nothing to eat, except what they could find upon the prairies.

We arrived, two o'clock in the afternoon, at the Lewis branch of the Columbia river, near the confluence of the Coos-coots-ke. Though this is a large river, yet on account of the summer's drouth there is less water flowing down its channel than I anticipated.

A squalid looking Indian took us over the ferry in a canoe, which appeared as weather-beaten as himself, and reminded me of fabled Charon and his cerulean boat.

This country differs much from what I had expected; for while the soil is generally good, and furnishes a supply for grazing, yet there is such want of summer rains, that some kinds of grain cannot flourish, especially Indian corn. The crops sown in the fall of the year, or very early in the spring, would probably be so far advanced before the severity of the drouth, that they would do well. In general there is a great want of wood for building, fencing and fuel; but at the confluence of these rivers a supply may be brought down the Coos-coots-ke. This place combines many advantages for a missionary station.

I began to doubt the correctness of the statements of some travelers, in regard to the great numbers of wild horses, and the immense multitudes of wolves, which they say they saw this side the Rocky Mountains; for as yet I had seen no wild horses, and only a *very few* wolves. Encamped upon the west bank of Lewis river, or as it is more commonly called, the Snake river.

On the 2d, we arose early, but were detained some time, before all our horses could be found. We started about eight, and proceeded three hours down the river to a place where it takes a northerly bend, through a section of mountains which are difficult to be passed. Our direct course to Walla Walla being west north-west, we here left the river and followed a small stream up a valley nearly to its source. The section of country through which we journeyed to-day was mountainous. One part of the river along which we traveled was walled up with volcanic rocks. The lowest part was amygdaloid, about thirty feet high and very cellular, terminating in a narrow horizontal plain. Above this is superimposed columnar basalt; the columns of which are regular pentagons, varying from two to four feet in diameter, rising forty feet high, perpendicular excepting in one place, where they were a little inclined. Above this formation of columns there was a stratum of volcanic stones and disintegrated basalt, of some six or eight feet thickness, lying in a confused state. Then upon this another section of basalt and amygdaloid of fifty feet depth, and so on to the height of three hundred feet, nearly perpendicular.

The pentagons are as regularly formed, and have much the same appearance, as those composing the Giant's causeway in Ireland. From the best observations I could make, I was led to conclude that the different sections were raised, at different periods of time, by widely extended subterranean fires. The basalt in this place, and also in almost all other places, which I have yet seen, is of very dark color, containing augite, or black oxyd of iron ; and is what Clarke and Lewis, and those who have copied from them, have called black rocks.

Saturday, 3d. We took an early departure from our encampment. We had through the day, an uncommonly high wind from the west, a pleasant sun and serene atmosphere. We have had no rain since the 12th of July, while on the east side of the mountains, and not more than five cloudy days. The water this side the Rocky Mountains is excellent, and no country can possess a climate more conducive to health. After passing over a somewhat hilly country well covered with grass, we encamped for the night, and for the Sabbath, in a fertile vale upon an upper branch of the Walla Walla river. Here we found three lodges of Nez Percés who were out on a hunt for deer, and the women were gathering cammas roots. This root in some degree resembles in taste and nutritive properties the sweet potato, and constitutes a large item of food for the Indians throughout a considerable section of country, this side Salmon river and Salmon river mountains. The common tokens of friendship were interchanged, and they presented us a share of such food as they themselves had.

Sabbath, Oct. 4th. We had public worship, at which all the men, women and children of three lodges attended. What there was of a truly spiritual nature in our worship, was known to the Searcher of hearts, but there was the appearance of devotion, and good attention was paid to what was said. It is affecting to see the anxiety these Indians manifest to know what they must do to please God, and to obtain salvation.

Employed part of the day in reading Vincent's Explanation of the catechism. This is an excellent compendium of divinity, and is too much neglected in families and Sabbath Schools.

Decamped early, on the 5th, and pursued our journey down the Walla Walla river, through a beautiful valley of thirty miles in extent, parts of which are overgrown with the common trees and shrubs of such locations, interspersed with wild roses. The prairie hen, the avoset, the robin, and varieties of smaller birds, seem to have selected this as a favorite retreat ; while the animals, which we have been seeking for game, desert this delightful place and find their dwellings on more rugged tracts. This spot impressed me favorably as the situation for the missionaries who should succeed me, and in every thing but its populousness would furnish advantages beyond any I have as yet seen. Indians of different tribes border on, and around, this valley, and the location is therefore less central for any one of them. They might, however, be brought by degrees to collect and settle down around a mission station, when once it should be established.

October 6th. We arose early and commenced our journey with the animating hope of reaching Walla Walla, and of seeing civilized people before noon. Ascended the bluffs and passed over an undulating prairie of good soil, leaving Walla Walla river to our left. As we drew near the Columbia river the soil became more and more sandy. Before we arrived at the fort, my attention was arrested by seeing cows and other cattle, in fine order, feeding upon the bottom-land ; and the sight was not only novel, after having been so long from civilized life, but the more interesting because unexpected. As we came near the fort, the Indians fired their customary salute, and then rushed forward to the gate. Mr. P. C. Pambrun, the superintendent, met us, and gave me a kind welcome. I never felt more joy in entering a habitation of civilized men, whose language was not strange. I felt that I had cause of thankfulness, that God, in his great mercy, and by his watchful providence, had brought me in safety and with restored health to this place. Soon I was invited into another apartment to breakfast ; and it was truly pleasant again to sit in a *chair*, at a *table* spread with furniture, and such luxuries as bread and butter, sugar and milk, of which I had been deprived for about three months.

CHAPTER VIII.

Description of Walla Walla—the kind treatment of the Indians by the
Hudson Bay company—leave Walla Walla for fort Vancouver—loquacious orator—rapids—introduction to the Cayuse Indians—morning prospect—long rapids—Volcanic mountains—trial of Indian
generosity—arrival at the falls of the Columbia river—rousing effects of oratory—La Dalles—Boston trading company—remarkable
subsidence—Cascades—Chenooks are the Flatheads and Nez Percés
—dangerous rapids—Indian burying places—Pillar rock—interesting waterfall—sea fowl—arrive at fort Vancouver.

FORT Walla Walla is situated on the south side of the
Columbia river, ten miles below the confluence of the Columbia and Lewis' river, which last is commonly called,
by the people belonging the Hudson Bay Company, Nez
Percé river ; and one mile above the Walla Walla river,
in latitude 46° 2', longitude 119° 30'. Two miles below
the fort there is a range of mountains running north and
south, which, though not high, are yet of considerable magnitude ; and where the Columbia passes through, it is walled
up on both sides with basalt, in many places three hundred
feet perpendicular height. The soil, for considerable distance around, with the exception of some strips of bottom-
land, is sandy, and for the want of summer rains is not productive. This establishment is not only supplied with the
necessaries of life, but also with many of its conveniences.
They have cows, horses, hogs, fowls, &c. and cultivate
corn, potatoes, and a variety of garden vegetables ; and
might enlarge these and other productions to a great extent.

They also keep on hand dry goods and hardware, not only for their own convenience, but also for Indian trade. Most of the year they have a good supply of fish, and an abundance of salmon of the first quality.

I arrived here in six months and twenty-three days after leaving home—forty-five days from Rendezvous—and twenty from entering Salmon river mountains.

Wednesday, 7th. Continued in this place. Settled with my interpreter, gave presents to my Indians, and made arrangements for leaving to-morrow, in a canoe propelled by Indians belonging to the Walla Walla tribe, for Fort Vancouver, which is two hundred miles down the Columbia.

Thus I am putting myself, without fear, into the hands of Indians, where a few years ago an escort of fifty men was necessary for safety, and shall have to pass places which have been battle grounds between traders and Indians.

The gentlemen belonging to the Hudson Bay Company are worthy of commendation for their good treatment of the Indians, by which they have obtained their friendship and confidence, and also for the efforts, which some few of them have made to instruct those about them in the first principles of our holy religion; especially in regard to equity, humanity and morality. This company is of long standing, have become rich in the fur trade, and intend to perpetuate the business; therefore they consult the prosperity of the Indians as intimately connected with their own. I have not heard as yet of a single instance of any Indians being wantonly killed by any of the men belonging to this company. Nor have I heard any boasting among them of the satisfaction taken in killing or abusing Indians, that I have elsewhere heard.

Thursday, 8th. My three Walla Walla Indians having

got all things in readiness, mats, provisions, &c. furnished by the kindness of Mr. Pambrun, and he having given them their instructions, I went on board the canoe at nine o'clock in the morning, and having passed the usual salutations, we shoved off, and gently glided down the river, which here is three-fourths of a mile wide. I felt myself in a new situation—my horses dismissed—in a frail canoe upon the wide waters of the Columbia, subject to winds, and with rapids and falls on the way, and among stranger Indians, two hundred miles by water before I could expect to find any white men; to pass through several nations whose languages are entirely different; yet the change from horseback, for months over mountains and plains, through defiles and ravines, was anticipated with satisfaction.

My three Indians were well acquainted with the river and with the art of managing the canoe. One of them understood the Nez Percé language tolerably well, was very loquacious and vain, and wished to be thought a man of importance. He told me he was to do the talking, and the other two were to do as he should direct. On account of his important and loquacious habits, I called him my orator. One of the other two, who took the stern and steered the canoe, was a stout, brawny, savage looking man, excepting the expression of his countenance, which was indicative of intelligence and good nature. The third, who took the bow, was an able and well disposed young man. The channel through the volcanic mountain a little below the fort, is one of the wonders of nature; how it was formed through those immensely hard basaltic rocks to the depth of about three hundred feet, and for the distance of two or three miles, remains unexplained. But my attention was so much taken up with the boiling eddies and the varying currents, that I did not take those observations which under different circumstances might have been made, and which the scenery and phenomena demanded. In one place, as we passed out of the mountain channel, the river ran so rapidly over a rocky bed, and the water was so broken, that I thought it unsafe to continue in the canoe, and requested my Indians to put me ashore. My talking Indian said, "*tois*," (good.) I told him, *waiitu tois, kapseis*, not good, but bad. But still he said, *tois, tois*, and I concluded, that they would not decline putting me on shore, if there was any particular danger. The man at the stern put off into the middle of the river, where the water was the smoothest, but where the current was equally strong, and with his keen eye fixed upon the varying eddies, applied his brawny arms to the work; and whenever a change of his paddle from one side of the canoe was necessary, it was done in the twinkling of an eye. Any failure of right management would have been disastrous; but they kept the canoe in the right direction, and we shot down with such velocity, as, together with the breaking in of some water, to cause solicitude. But this served to make the smooth parts, when we arrived at them, more pleasant, and my mind more tranquil in regard to future dangers.

At two o'clock in the afternoon, we called at an encampment of Cayuse Indians of about a dozen lodges. My orator, when we had come within hearing, announced our approach and informed them who I was, and the object of my tour, and that they must prepare to receive me with all due respect—that I was not a trader, and that I had not come with goods, but to teach them how to worship God. They arranged themselves in single file, the chiefs and principal men forward, then the more common men, next the women, according to their rank, the wives of chiefs, the old women, the young—and then the children according to age. All things being made ready, the salute was fired, and I landed and shook hands with all, even the youngest children, many of whom, when they presented the hand, would turn away their faces through fear. I made them some presents, and bought of them some dried salmon and cranberries. These were the first cranberries I had seen west of the Rocky Mountains, and they were a grateful acid. The Indians expressed much satisfaction in seeing me, and in the object of my coming among them. I told them I could not explain to them what I wished, but they must meet me next spring at Walla Walla, where I should have an interpreter, and then I would tell them about God. After again shaking hands with them, we went on our way.

At five o'clock we landed upon the north shore, and encamped near a large number of Nez Percé Indians, who came about me with the tokens of friendship and kindness, which characterize their nation. Among their acts of kindness they brought me wood, which in this section of the country is scarce ; and gathered small bushes and grass to make my bed upon.

October 9th. Arose before day, and as soon as any light appeared, resumed our voyage down the river. The morning was pleasant, the country around open and diversified with rolling prairies and distant mountain tops mellowed with the opening beams of the rising sun. It was a time for pleasing contemplations, such as banished all feelings of solitude, although no sound broke upon the ear, but the regular timed strokes of the paddles of my Indians, who were urging forward the canoe with an accelerated velocity, greater than the current of the river would have carried us.

About the middle of the day, the silence was interrupted
by the roar of a distant rapid, the sound of which continued
to increase, until the white breaking water was presented
to view. For several miles the bed of the river was filled
with rocks, and several rocky islands and shoals, among
which the whirling and foaming water was forcing its way.
The only part of the river, which presented any appearance
of safety, was along near the south shore.   This had somewhat the appearance of a wake.   My Indians made no
movement for landing, but kept near the middle of the river.
On my expressing some apprehensions of danger, they pointed toward the wake and said, " *tois*."   I pointed forward
and toward the north shore, and said, *kapseis*, bad.   They
answered, " *ai, kapseis ;*" and with the language of signs
accompanying their words, told me they would keep the
canoe in the good water, and it would not fill, nor be drawn
into the breakers.   My confidence in their skill of management being well established, I made no objection to their
going forward, and in a very short time we had passed the
apparent danger, and were gliding along over the smooth
surface on the south side of a large island, about six miles
long.

During the day, the country around was comparatively
level, covered with a black soil, which appears to have been
formed by atmospheric agents decomposing the volcanic
substances, which so generally abound.   This section of
the country is well supplied with grass, which during the
summer drouth is converted into hay.   Who can calculate
the multitudes of cattle and sheep, which might be kept
here summer and winter, with no other labor than the care
of a few herdsmen and shepherds.   Encamped upon the
north side of the river among some sand hills, a little below

several lodges of the Walla Walla Indians, to whom I had the usual and formal introduction.

I was pleased to find Indians belonging to different tribes scattered all along this river, living in harmony without any feuds or jealousies. It speaks much in favor of their kind and peaceable dispositions.

On the 10th, we arose before day, after a night's comfortable rest, and by the first breaking light had our baggage on board and were under way. Towards the middle of the day, we came to a more mountainous tract of country, and at a place where the mountains crossed the river, there were very rocky rapids, but by winding our way among islands near the north shore, we made a safe descent. About noon a head wind, which commenced in the fore part of the day, had become fresh, and the waves began to multiply their white caps, so that it was dangerous navigation for our canoe, and we had to land and wait for a more favorable time. We encamped on the north side of the river under a very high and romantic basaltic mountain ; in some parts near us the rocky walls were more than two hundred feet in perpendicular height—in one place hanging over. In some places, and at different altitudes of this immense wall, there were cavities of considerable magnitude, and in others, wide and deep fissures ; through one of which passes the road traveled by pedestrians and those on horseback. This place is ten miles above the falls of the Columbia, which the Indians call the *tum tum ;* the same expression they use for the beating of the heart.

About a mile above us, were encamped some Walla Wallas, many of whom came to my tent and wished to enter into trade with me, offering beaver at a low price. I told them to trade was not my business, any farther than to buy salmon, &c. for food. My orator told me one of them was a *Meohot*, a chief, and would expect a present. As a trial of their disposition, I told him they had not brought me any wood for a fire, and I would not give them any thing until they showed their kindness. But he said I must make the chief a present and buy of them wood. I replied, *waiitu*, if he is a chief let him show the generosity of a chief. Very soon they brought wood, and a fire was made, which I followed with some presents.

Sabbath, 11th. Continued in the same encampment, and my heart's desire was much excited for the salvation of these poor heathen. There were a sufficient number here to have made a decent congregation if I had possessed any medium of communication. Their language differs from the Nez Percés, so that I could have no communication with them except through my orator, who asked me if he should teach these Indians what he had learned about God and his worship. I gave him permission, though I feared he was influenced more by love of distinction than any higher motive ; but still, if any true light should be imparted to them, I would rejoice in it.

I arose the latter part of the night of the 12th, and the weather being calm, and the moon shining pleasantly, we took our departure for the Falls, where we arrived some time before day. Above the Falls there is a large island, on the south side of which is a commodious bay, near which and upon the river De Shutes, which here unites with the Columbia, there is a village of the Fall Indians of about thirty lodges. Here we landed, and my talker raised his oratorical voice to such a note as aroused the whole village, calling upon the chiefs to arise, and with their people receive the personage with him in due form. It was but a

short time before their line was formed, the first chief leading the way, and others according to their rank and age
following, and the ceremony of shaking hands was performed ; and all retired to their lodges again.

There is a great want of neatness among Indians in general, but more especially among those on this river, who
live by fishing.

Here we left our canoe, and took horses and proceeded
by land, upon the south side of the river, by the Falls, and
down the La Dalles, six miles.   From the lower end of the
island where the rapids begin, to the perpendicular fall, is
about two miles ; and here the river contracts, when the
water is low, to a very narrow space, and with only a short
distance of swift water, it makes its plunge twenty feet perpendicular ; and then, after a short distance of rapids, dashing against the rocks, moves on in a narrow passage, filled
with rapids and eddies, among volcanic rocks, called the La
Dalles, four miles ; and then spreads out into a gentle broad
channel.   At the Falls and the La Dalles below, there are
several carrying places, where boats and canoes, as well as
baggage, have to be transported.   The geological formation along this distance is singular.   With the exception of
a few high hills and bluffs, the shore and lands around are
but little above the river in the freshet rise ; and yet the
channel of the river is through the hardest basalt and amygdaloid.   Has this channel worn this solid rock formation ?
If so, at what time ?   There is no appearance of the channel having worn perceptibly deeper, since these rocks, from
their melted state, spread out into their present condition,
which must have taken place centuries and centuries ago.
As I have no confidence in theories founded upon conjecture, nor in Indian traditions, I leave the subject for others to

tell us how these things took place. Former visiters, among whom I name Doct. Gardner, a learned English naturalist whom I saw at Oahu, Sand. Islands, expressed his entire inability satisfactorily to account for this peculiar phenomenon. Nor does the Indian tradition, that the *Great Wolf* made this, together with all the scenery that delighted my eye as I passed down the river, relieve the mind of its irrepressible curiosity. This is one of the best locations for salmon fishing, and great numbers of Indians collect in the season of taking them, which commences the last of April, or the first of May, and continues several months.

At the lower part of the La Dalles, I found Capt. Wyeth, from Boston, with a small company of men going up the river to Fort Hall. Capt. Wyeth, who is an intelligent and sociable man, had the charge of the business of a company formed in Boston, for salmon fishing on the Columbia, and for trade and trapping in the region of the mountains. The plan of the company was to send a ship annually around Cape Horn into Columbia river, to bring out goods for trade, and to take home the salmon and furs which should be obtained during the year. It was expected the profits on the salmon would defray all common expenses, and that the profits on the furs would be clear, and yield a handsome income. But thus far the enterprise has been attended with many disasters, and the loss of many lives—several of the men were drowned, and others killed by Indians.

Here I dismissed my Walla Walla Indians to return, and Tilkī, the first chief of the La Dalles Indians, engaged to furnish me with a canoe and men to carry me to Fort Vancouver. Encamped with Capt. Wyeth, and obtained from him a short vocabulary of the Chenook language, to enable me to do common business with the Indians residing along on the lower part of this river.

Tuesday, 13th.   I left at nine o'clock in the morning, in the canoe with three men furnished by Tilkī, and made good progress down the river, which flows in a wide and gentle current.   Many parts of the way, the river is walled up with high and perpendicular basalt.   At the La Dalles commences a wood country, which becomes more and more dense as we descend, and more broken with high hills and precipices.   I observed a remarkable phenomenon—trees standing in their natural position in the river, in many places where the water is twenty feet deep, and rising to high or freshet water mark, which is fifteen feet above the low water.   Above the freshet rise, the tops of the trees are decayed and gone.   I deferred forming an opinion in regard to the cause, until I should collect more data.   About the middle of the day a south wind began to blow, and continued to increase until it became necessary to go on shore and encamp, which we did about four in the afternoon.

On the 14th, we did not make much progress on account of wind and rain.   Encamped in a cavern under a large projecting rock, the upper part of which was formed of basalt, the lower of pudding stone.   Although this was at least six miles above the Cascades, yet the roar of the water could be distinctly heard.   The same phenomenon of trees continued.   I paid particular attention to the condition of the shores of the river and adjacent hills and mountains, to see if there were any escarpments presenting such condition, as would furnish evidence of their having descended by *landslips ;* but as there were no such appearances, and the condition of the trees was the same where there were no hills or mountains near, I was led to conjecture, that I

should find the river at the Cascades dammed up with volcanic productions; and I was induced to believe it would
be found so, from the fact, that the river, the whole distance
from the La Dalles, is wide and deep, and moves with a
sluggish current.

On the 15th, the wind and rain continuing through the
morning, I did not leave my encampment until noon, when
we set forward and arrived at the Cascades at two o'clock
in the afternoon. The trees, to-day, were still more numerous, in many places standing in deep water, and we had
to pick our way with the canoe in some places, as through
a forest. The water of the river is so clear, that I had an
opportunity of examining their position down to the spreading roots, and found them in the same condition as when
standing in the natural forest. As I approached the Cascades, instead of finding an embankment formed from volcanic eruptions, the shores above the falls were low, and the
velocity of the water began to accelerate two-thirds of a
mile above the main rapid. On a full examination, it is
plainly evident that here has been a *subsidence* of a tract of
land, more than twenty miles in length, and about a mile in
width. The trees standing in the water are found mostly
towards and near the north shore, and yet, from the depth
of the river and its sluggish movement, I should conclude
the subsidence affected the whole bed. That the trees are
not wholly decayed down to low water mark, proves that
the subsidence is comparatively, of recent date; and their
undisturbed, natural position, proves that it took place in a
tranquil manner, not by any tremendous convulsion of nature. The cause lies concealed, but the fact is plain.
That parts of forests may in this way submerge, is evident
from similar facts. The noted one on the eastern coast of

Yorkshire and Lincolnshire, England, is about fifteen feet below low water mark, extending eastward a considerable distance from the shore, of which stumps and roots are seen in their natural position. So manifest is the evidence of great changes having taken place by volcanic power, in these regions west of the Rocky Mountains, both by upheaving and subsidence, that we are led to enquire whether there are not now such agents in operation, and upon such materials, that the valleys shall be literally exalted; and the mountains be made low, and waters spring up in the deserts.

The Cascades, so called to distinguish them from the Falls, do not differ materially from them, except in the wild romantic scenery around. There is no perpendicular fall, but the water concentrates, from its wide spread form, to a very narrow compass, and then rushes with great impetuosity down an almost perpendicular precipice twenty or thirty feet, and continues in a foaming and whirling descent most of the way five miles farther, where it meets the tide waters from the Pacific ocean. Above the falls, in the river, there are many islands, but none of them are very large— some are only volcanic rocks. The country about the Cascades, and many miles below, is very mountainous, especially on the south side. The volcanic peaks are as diversified in their shapes as they are numerous, being conical, denticulated, and needle-pointed, rising from one to fifteen hundred feet. While imagination generally over-draws her pictures, nature here has furnished abundant scope for all her powers.

A little above the Cascades, upon the north shore, there is a small village of Chenooks. These Indians are the only real Flatheads and Nez Percés, or pierced noses, I have found. They both flatten their heads and pierce their noses. The flattening of their heads is not so great a deformity as is generally suppossed. From a little above the eyes to the apex or crown of the head, there is a depression, but not generally in adult persons very noticeable. The piercing of the nose is a greater deformity, and is done by inserting two small tapering white shells, about two inches long, through the lower part of the cartilaginous division of the nose. These shells are of the genus *dentalium*, they inhabit the Pacific shore, and are an article of traffic among the natives. I called at this village to obtain men to carry our canoe by the portage of the Cascades. They wished to engage in trade with me in several articles of small value, which I declined, informing them that my business was of a different nature. Whilst detained, the daughter of the chief, fancifully decked out in ornaments, and in all her pride and native haughtiness, walked to and fro to exhibit, to the best advantage, her fine, erect, and stately person.

After considerable delay, I obtained four Indians to carry the canoe about one hundred rods by the principal rapids, or falls, for which I gave each five charges of powder and balls ; and an additional reward to one to carry a part of my baggage a mile and a half past the most dangerous rapids, to a basin just below another rapid, formed by large rocks confining the river to a very narrow passage, and through which it rushes with great impetuosity. My Indians ran the canoe over this rapid. I was much concerned for their safety ; but they chose to do it. Two years before, the men of the Hudson Bay Company *cordelled* several batteaux down this rapid—part of the men going in the boats, and part on the shore *cordelling*. The rope of one broke, and the batteau, in spite of the efforts of the men in it, was hurried out into the surging and whirling waves among the rocks—capsized, and all were lost.

I walked about four miles, until I had passed all the rapids of any special danger. About three-fourths of a mile below the uppermost cascade, following an Indian path, I came to a pleasant rise of ground, upon which were several houses of a forsaken village, which were both larger and far better than any I had seen in any Indian country. They were about sixty feet long, and thirty-five wide, the framework very well constructed and covered with split planks and cedar bark. A little back of these houses a small beautiful lake spread itself out, on the surface of which some dozens of wild ducks were enjoying the quietness of its solitude. As I continued down the Indian path, at no great distance from the village, I came to several depositories of their dead. They were built of plank split from balsam fir and cedar, about eight feet long, six wide, and five high, and well covered. At one end is what may be called a door, upon which are paintings of various devices, which do not appear to be designed for any other purpose than for ornament. Some had painting upon the sides as well as upon the doors. I had with me two Indians who paid no particular attention to them, more than we should in passing a burying ground. They pointed me to them, and made a short, solemn pause, without any actions which would indicate their paying homage to the pictures or any other object. The number of these depositories I did not ascertain, as many of them were so far decayed, as to be hardly distinguishable ; but there were eight or ten in good condition. Below this we passed several houses of less magnitude than those above ; and while the floors of those were on a level with the surface of the ground, these were sunk about four feet below, and the walls rose only about three feet above the ground. It would seem that these were designed for winter habitations, but at this time their occupants were all absent. At the distance of four miles below the main cataract, the country, on the north side, spreads out into a level plain, which near the river is a prairie, a little distance back covered with dense forests ; while on the south side of the river it is very mountainous.

Toward the lower part of Brant island I re-embarked, and we proceeded a few miles farther and encamped below Pillar rock, over against an extraordinary cascade of water which descends the mountain from the south. Pillar rock is of basaltic formation, situated on the north side of the river, a few rods from the shore, on a narrow strip of rich bottom-land, wholly isolated, rising five hundred feet, on the river side perpendicular, and on the others nearly so. Upon all, except the river side, there are narrow offsets upon which grow some cedars, and also a few upon the highest point. The base in proportion to the height, is very small, giving the whole the appearance of an enormous pillar. This is one of the astonishing wonders of volcanic operations.

A cascade upon the south side of the river first strikes the view at an elevation of not less than a thousand feet ; and by several offsets the water descends in a white foaming sheet at an angle of sixty or eighty degrees, presenting the appearance of a belt laid upon the side of the mountain. In two places the descent is perpendicular, and the lowest probably not less than two hundred feet, and before the stream reaches the bottom, it is dissipated into spray and disappears, until you see it again collecting itself at the foot of the mountain, and after winding its way a short distance, it unites with the Columbia. The whole scene, combining the ruggedness and wildness of nature's most romantic forms, with its most magnificent, filled my mind with admiration both of the work and its Author.

On the morning of the 16th, I arose before day, called my Indians, and as soon as any light appeared, we again launched out into the broad river, in our frail canoe. For about ten miles, the surrounding country was mountainous, forming bold shores; after which the mountains recede, and the river spreads out in some places from one to three miles wide, and an extensive region around presents the appearance of a rich soil well adapted to agriculture. There are some fine prairies, but the greatest part is thickly wooded. In this part of the river are many fertile islands, some of which are large; the current moves on gently, and the whole scenery around is fascinating. As I descended towards the Pacific ocean, water fowl, such as geese, swans, and a very great variety of ducks, began to multiply; also every now and then seals made their appearance, so that I became cheered with the increasing exhibitions of animated nature, greater than I had witnessed since leaving the buffalo country. Unexpectedly, about the middle of the day, on the north shore in a thick grove of large firs, I saw two white men, with a yoke of oxen drawing logs for sawing. I hailed them, and enquired of them the distance to Fort Vancouver. They replied, "only seven miles around yonder point, down that prairie." Soon we came to a very large saw-mill, around which were large piles of lumber and several cottages. This looked like business upon a much greater scale than I had expected. I called a short time at this establishment, where I found several Scotch laborers belonging to the Hudson Bay Company, with their Indian families. Although it was then about noon, they offered me a breakfast of peas and fish,

taking it for granted that men who travel these western regions, eat only when they can get an opportunity. At two
in the afternoon, we arrived at Fort Vancouver, and never
did I feel more joyful to set my feet on shore, where I expected to find a hospitable people and the comforts of life.
Doct. J. McLaughlin, a chief factor and the superintendent
of this fort and of the business of the Company west of the
Rocky Mountains, received me with many expressions of
kindness, and invited me to make his residence my home
for the winter, and as long as it would suit my convenience.
Never could such an invitation be more thankfully received.

It was now seven months and two days since I left my
home, and during that time, excepting a few delays, I had
been constantly journeying, and the fifty-six last days, with
Indians only. I felt that I had great reason for gratitude to
God for his merciful providences toward me, in defending
and so providing for me, that I had not actually *suffered* a
single day for the want of food. For months I had no
bread nor scarcely any vegetables, and I often felt that a
change and a variety would have been agreeable, but in no
instance did I *suffer*, nor in any case was I brought to the
necessity of eating *dogs* or *horse flesh*. In every exigency
something wholesome and palatable was provided.

CHAPTER IX.

Description of Fort Vancouver—departure for Fort George and mouth of the Columbia—mouths of the Multnomah—Wappatoo island—May Dacre—Coffin Rock—Cowalitz river—Indian friendship—Pacific ocean—Gray's bay—Astoria.

FORT Vancouver is situated on the north side of the Columbia river, about sixty rods from the shore, upon a prairie of some few hundred acres, surrounded with dense woods. The country around, for a great distance, is generally level and of good soil, covered with heavy forests, excepting some prairies interspersed, and has a pleasing aspect. It is in north latitude 45° 37', and longitude 122° 50', west from Greenwich—one hundred miles from the Pacific ocean. The enclosure is strongly stoccaded, thirty-seven rods long, and eighteen rods wide, facing the south. There are about one hundred white persons belonging to this establishment, and an Indian population of three hundred in a small compass contiguous. There are eight substantial buildings within the enclosure, and a great number of small ones without.

October 17th. After a night's rest in this fort, I left for Fort George, situated ninety-one miles below, near the confluence of the Columbia with the Pacific, known in the United States by the name of Astoria. I took this early departure that I might visit the lower part of the river and the sea coast, and return before the rainy season should commence ; and also to avail myself of a passage in the May Dacre, from Boston, Capt. Lambert, a brig belonging

to Captain Wyeth and Company, which was lying twenty-
three miles below, at the lowest mouth of the Multnomah.
Mr. J. K. Townsend, an ornithologist from Philadelphia,
accompanied me to the brig.   Our canoe was large and propelled by Sandwich Islanders, of whom there are many
in this country, who have come here as sailors and laborers.
Five miles below the fort, we passed the main branch of the
Multnomah.   It is a large river, coming from the south, and
is divided by islands into four branches at its confluence
with the Columbia.   Here commences the Wâppatoo island,
so called from a nutritive root found in the small lakes
in the interior, which is much sought for by Indians as
an article of food.   This island is about eighteen miles
long, and five miles wide, formed by a part of the Multnomah, branching off about six miles up the main river, running in a westerly and north-westerly direction, and again
uniting with the Columbia eighteen miles below the main
branch.   The branch which flows around and forms the
island, is about fifteen rods wide, and of sufficient depth for
small shipping most of the year.   It was upon this island
the Multnomah Indians formerly resided, but they have become as a tribe, extinct.   The land is very fertile, and most
of it sufficiently high to be free from injury by the June
freshet.   Some parts of it are prairie, but the greatest part
is well wooded with oak, ash, balsam fir, and the species of
poplar often called balm of Gilead, and by most travelers, cotton-wood.   At the south-west of this island, there is
a range of mountains which render a space of the country
broken, but beyond these, it is said by hunters, that there is
an extensive valley well adapted to agriculture.

We arrived at the landing place of the May Dacre, at
five o'clock in the afternoon, and were politely received on

board by Capt. Lambert.   The brig was moored alongside
a natural wharf of basalt.

Sabbath, October 18th.   Part of the day I retired to a
small prairie back from the river, to be free from the noise
of labor in which the men were engaged in preparing for
their voyage; and part of it I passed in the state room
which was assigned me.   There is much reason to lament
the entire disregard manifested by many towards God's
holy Sabbath.   His justice will not always be deferred.
Those who will not submit to divine authority, must reap
the fruit of their disobedience.   None can slight and abuse
the mercy of God with impunity.

Monday, 19th.   The brig fell down the river with the
tide, about three miles, but for the want of wind anchored.
In the afternoon, I went on shore for exercise, taking with
me a *kanaka*, that is, a Sandwich islander, for assistance in
any danger.   I made a long excursion through woods and
over prairies, and found the country pleasant and fertile.
The grass on the prairies was green, and might furnish
subsistence for herds of cattle.   When will this immensely
extended and fertile country be brought under cultivation,
and be filled with an industrious population ?   From time
immemorial, the natives have not stretched forth a hand to
till the ground, nor made an effort for the earth to yield a
single article of produce, more than what springs up spontaneously ; nor will they, until their minds are enlightened
by divine truth.   No philanthropist, who is not under the
influence of Christian principles, will ever engage in the
self-denying work of enlightening their minds, and arousing
them from their indolence.   As on our frontiers, so on these
western shores, the work of destruction, introduced by those
who would be called the friends of man, is going forward.

The Indians in this lower country, that is, below the Cascades, are only the *remnants* of once numerous and powerful nations.

The evening was clear and pleasant, which gave us an opportunity to see the comet which was observed by Halley in the year 1682, and which was seen again in 1759, and now in 1835, proving its time of revolution to be about seventy-six and a half years. Its train of light was very perceptible and about twelve degrees in length.

We had a favourable wind on the 20th, which, with the current of the river, enabled us to make good progress on our way. Among the many islands, with which the lower part of this river abounds, Deer island, thirty-three miles below Fort Vancouver, is worthy of notice. It is large, and while it is sufficiently wooded along the shores, the interior is chiefly a prairie covered with an exuberant growth of grass and vines of different kinds, excepting the grape, of which there is none west of the Rocky Mountains of natural growth. In the interior of this island there are several small lakes, the resort of swans, geese and ducks. This island was formerly the residence of many Indians, but they are gone, and nothing is left except the remains of a large village.

Among some interesting islands of basalt, there is one called Coffin Rock, twenty-three miles below Deer island, situated in the middle of the river, rising ten or fifteen feet above high freshet water. It is almost entirely covered with canoes, in which the dead are deposited, which circumstance gives it its name. In the section of country from Wâppatoo island to the Pacific ocean, the Indians, instead of committing their dead to the earth, deposit them in canoes, and these are placed in such situations as are most secure from beasts of prey ; upon such precipices as this island, upon branches of trees, or upon scaffolds made for the purpose. The bodies of the dead are covered with mats, and split planks are placed over them. The head of the canoe is a little raised, and at the foot there is a hole made for water to escape.

A few miles below Coffin island, the Cowalitz, a river coming from the north-east, flows into the Columbia, which is about thirty rods wide, deep, and navigable for boats a very considerable distance. The country up this river is said to equal, in richness of soil, any part of the Oregon Territory, and to be so diversified with woods and prairies, that the farmer could at once reap the fruits of his labor.

We anchored for the night, on account of numerous sand-bars and windings of the navigable channel. The evening was cloudy, and there was the appearance of a gathering storm ; but we were so surrounded with high hills, that the situation was considered safe.

The wind, on the 21st, was light, which rendered our progress slow. This section of the country is mountainous, the ranges running from the south-east to the north-west, and covered with a very dense and heavy growth of wood, mostly fir and oak. A chief of the Skilloots with a few of his people came on board. He was very talkative and sportive. When he was about to leave, he told Capt. L. that as they had been good friends, and were now about to separate, he wished a present. Capt. L. told his steward to give him a shirt. The chief took it and put it on, and then said " how much better would a new pair of pantaloons look with this shirt." The captain ordered him the article asked for. Now, said the chief, " a vest would become me, and increase my influence with my people." This was also given.

Then he added, "well, *Tie**, I suppose we shall not see each other again, can you see me go away without a clean blanket, which would make me a full dress." The captain answered, "go about your business ; for there is no end to your asking so long as I continue to give." Then the chief brought forward a little son, and said, "he is a good boy ; will you not make him a present ?" Capt. L. gave him a few small articles, and they went away rejoicing over the presents which they had received, instead of regretting the departure of the May Dacre. We passed to-day Pillar rock, which stands isolated more than a half mile from the north shore, composed of basalt, and is about forty feet high and fifteen in diameter. We anchored a few miles below.

On the morning of the 22d, we waited for a favorable tide until nine o'clock, when we got under way with a brisk wind from the east. Here the river begins to spread out into a bay, but owing to many shoals, the navigation is difficult. We ran aground, but the increase of the tide set us afloat again, and soon the great Pacific ocean opened to our view. This boundary of the "far west" was to me an object of great interest; and when I looked upon the dark rolling waves, and reflected upon the vast expanse of five thousand miles, without an intervening island until you arrive at the Japan coast, a stretch of thought was required, like contemplating infinity, which can measure only by succession its expansion and sublimity. Like the vanishing lines of perspective, so is contemplation lost in this extent of ocean.

As we proceeded on our way, we left Gray's bay at the right, extending inland to the north some few miles, in which

---

* Chief, or gentleman.

on a voyage of discovery, the ship Columbia anchored, and from whose commander the bay took its name. Nearly opposite we passed Tongue Point, which extends about two miles into the bay or river, from the south. It is considerably elevated, rocky, and covered with woods. Soon after this, Astoria was announced. My curiosity was excited. I looked, but could not discover what to all on board was so plainly seen—I blamed my powers of vision—and reluctantly asked the captain, where is Astoria ? "Why," he replied, "right down there—that is Astoria." I saw two log cabins, and said within myself, is that the far-famed "New York of the west ?"

CHAPTER X.

Description of Fort George—mouth of the Columbia—dangerous bar
—mountainous coast—varieties of timber— good location for a missionary station—continued rains—dense forests—excursion in a
canoe down the bay—view of the coast—disasters at the entrance
of the Columbia—ship William and Anne—ship Isabella—Tonquin
—Japanese junk—reflections—water fowl—return to Fort Vancouver—the regard Indians show the dead—Indian kindness.

WHEN we arrived in the small bay, upon which Fort
George (Astoria) is situated, Captain L. manned a boat to
take me on shore, in which he also embarked to pay his
respects to the governor, who had the politeness to meet us
at the landing, and invited us, with hearty welcome, to his
dwelling. After having interchanged the customary salutations and made a short stay, the captain re-embarked and
made his way for Cape Disappointment ; and the wind and
tide being favorable, he passed the dangerous bar without
any delay, and shaped his course for Boston. Fort George
is situated on the south side of the bay, ten miles from Cape
Disappointment, is without any fortifications, has only two
small buildings made of hewed logs ; about two acres
cleared, a part of which is cultivated with potatoes and
garden vegetables. It is occupied by two white men of the
Hudson Bay Company, for the purpose of trade with the
few remaining Indians, who reside about these shores.
Though this is the present condition of Astoria, yet the time
must come, when at the mouth of this noble river there will
be a place of business, and especially may this be expected,

as this bay affords the only good harbor for a long distance on this coast. I should think the north side of the bay, a little above the cape, adjoining what is called Baker's bay, would be the most desirable location for a town, as that is the safest place for ships to ride at anchor. On that side of the Columbia bay, the country is more open and pleasant for a commercial town. On the south side, where Astoria was located, the mountains or high hills come down very near the shore, are rocky and precipitous, preventing a southern prospect, and in the short winter days of a north latitude of 46° 17′ they almost exclude the sun.

A difficulty, of a nature that is not easily overcome, exists in regard to the navigation of this river, which is the sand-bar at its entrance. It is about five miles across the bar from Ca̤ ᷄ Disappointment out to sea. In no part of that distance is the water upon the bar over eight fathoms deep, and in one place only five, and the channel is only about half a mile wide. And so wide and open is the ocean, that there is always a heavy swell, and when the wind is above a gentle breeze, there are breakers quite across the bar, and there is no passing it except when the wind and tide are both very favorable. Without the bar there is no anchorage, and there have been instances, in the winter season, of ships laying off and on, thirty days, waiting for an opportunity to pass; and a good pilot is always needed. Perhaps there have been more lives lost here, in proportion to the number of those who have entered this river, than in entering almost any other harbor in the world. But the calamities have been less frequent for some years past, than formerly ; and should a steam-boat be stationed at the cape, to tow vessels over, when business shall be sufficiently multiplied to warrant the expense, the delays and dangers would be greatly diminished.

The main bay is four miles wide at the mouth of the river, between Cape Disappointment and Point Adams; extends sixteen miles up the river; is nine miles wide between Chenook bay on the north and Youngs' bay on the south; and seven wide between Fort George and Chenook point. It is filled with many sand-bars, and one, which is called Sand island, a little within the capes, seen only when the tide is down, is dangerous to ships when not in the charge of skilful pilots.

The section of country about the sea coast is rough and mountainous, and covered with the most heavy and dense forest of any part of America of which I have any knowledge. The trees are almost all of the genus *pinus*, but I saw none of the species commonly called pine, any where below the Cascades. The balsam fir, of which there are three species, constitute the greatest part of the forest trees. White cedar, spruce, hemloc, and yew, are interspersed. Three species of oak, of which the white is most common, prevail in small sections; and in some low bottom-lands, the species of poplar, called the balm of Gilead, or bitter cotton wood, predominates. The balsam fir grows very large; not unfrequently four and six feet in diameter, and two hundred feet high. I measured one which was eight feet in diameter, and about two hundred and fifty feet high. As I do not here intend to enter upon the dendrology of this country, I pass farther remarks upon this subject for the present.

The quality of the land is good; and some tracts of this mountainous iron bound coast might easily be brought under cultivation. One section about Youngs' bay, extending to and about Point Adams. This would be a favorable location for a missionary station, where access could be had to the Clatsop and Killamook Indians, who are said to be numerous.

At this season of the year, there are but few Indians who reside about this trading post, finding it more for their comfort to retire into the forests during the rainy season of the winter, locating themselves upon small prairies along rivers and streams, where fuel is easily obtained, and where some game is found to add to their winter's stock of provisions.

During my continuance in this place it was my intention to cross the bay over to Chenook point, and from thence down to Cape Disappointment, which it is said affords a very extensive and interesting prospect. But from day to day it rained, and the high winds created such a sea in the whole bay, that it was not safe to attempt the passage.

On the 24th, the wind was high, and the weather very uncomfortable, and in the afternoon the storm increased, accompanied with snow, which, however, melted as fast as it fell. The sea fowl appeared to be alarmed by the severity of so early and unexpected a storm of snow, and came in from the ocean in great numbers, flying and screaming, as if in search of a safe retreat.

The storm being somewhat abated, on the 26th, Mr. Dunn, the superintendent of the fort, and myself, took our rifles to go back into the woods to hunt deer for exercise. But so dense was the forest, so filled and interwoven with various vines and shrubbery, that it was next to impossible to make any progress, and we did not penetrate the woods more than a mile, before we gave up the object, and turned our course back, but our return, with diligent efforts, occupied some hours. If a luxuriant growth of trees and shrubbery is indicative of a rich soil, no part of the world can surpass the country about these shores.

The morning of the 27th was pleasant and inviting for a water excursion ; but on account of sudden changes of weather, which are common at this season of the year, I did not think best to cross the wide bay, but took four Chenook Indians, and a half breed named Thos. Pish Kiplin, who could speak English, and went in a large canoe down to Clatsop and Point Adams, nine miles from the fort. There was a gentle wind from the east, which favored hoisting a small sail. This gave us a pleasant sail until it increased to the rate of eight miles an hour ; and by this time the waves had become so high, and the white caps were so numerous, that to one not acquainted with nautical adventures, the danger in a canoe appeared great. We could only run before the wind, and when we were upon the top of one wave, it seemed the next plunge would be fatal. Fears were of no avail in this situation, and I therefore kept up such conversation as was calculated to suppress any which might arise in the minds of the men. It was interesting to see how the Indians would take the waves with their paddles so as to favor the safety of the canoe. But our rapid progress soon brought us to the shore near Point Adams. Here a new and unexpected difficulty presented itself, and this was the almost utter impracticability of effecting a landing in the high surf; but my skilful mariners watched an opportnnity to shoot the canoe forward as far as possible on a flowing wave, and as soon as it broke, they leaped into the water and seized the canoe and lightened it over the returning surge, and drew it up beyond the reach of the waves. This management was an ocular demonstration of the skill of Indians on dangerous seas. I took Kiplin with me and walked several miles on the hard and smooth sandy beach, so far around to the south, that I had a view of the coast north and south, as far as the eye could reach. High basaltic rocks, in most parts perpendicular, lined the shores. Who but that Being, who sets bounds to the sea, and has said to the proud waves, hitherto shalt thou come and no farther, reared these volcanic walls ? This vast expanse of ocean and these stupendous works of God naturally fill the mind with awe.

In returning, I walked several miles beyond the place where we landed, along the shore towards Youngs' bay, and went on board the brig Lama, Captain McNiel, which was on its way up to the fort. In my excursion about Clatsop and Point Adams, I saw several canoes containing the dead, deposited as I have already described.

I have mentioned the bar at the mouth of the Columbia, and Sand island, as dangerous to those who were not well acquainted with the entrance into this river. In the year 1828, the ship William and Anne was cast away a little within the bar. All on board, twenty-six in number, were lost, and it could not be ascertained what were the circumstances of the lamentable catastrophe, as no one was left to tell the story. There were conjectures that after the ship had run aground, the Indians, for the sake of plunder, killed the crew. This is *only* conjecture ; but it is very strange, as they were not far from the shore, and the beach was sandy, that none escaped. The Indians carried off and secreted whatever of the goods they could find. The men of the Hudson Bay Company sent to the chiefs to deliver up what they had taken away. They sent Dr. McLaughlin at Fort Vancouver two small articles of no value. Dr. M. with an armed force went down to the Chenooks and demanded a surrender of the goods. The chief, with his warriors, put himself in the attitude of resistance, and fired upon the men of the Hudson Bay Company. They returned the fire with a swivel, not to injure them, but to let them know with what force they had to contend, if they persisted in their resistance. On this the Indians all fled into the woods. Dr. McLaughlin with his men landed and searched for the goods, many of which they found. Whilst they were searching, the chief was seen skulking and drawing near—and cocked his gun, but before he had time to fire, one of the white men shot him down. None besides were hurt. This was done, as the Hudson Bay Company say, not so much for saving the value of the property, as to teach the Indians not to expect profit from such disasters, and to take away temptation to murder white men for the sake of plunder.

On the 23d of May, 1830, the ship Isabella was cast away upon a sand-bar projecting from Sand island, which is a little within the capes. As soon as she struck, the men all deserted her, and without stopping at Fort George, made their way to Fort Vancouver. It is thought, that if they had remained on board and waited the tide, she might have been saved. The cargo was mostly saved.

In 1811, the Tonquin, sent out from New York by Mr. Astor, to form a fur trading establishment at or near the mouth of this river, lost eight men in crossing the bar. The calamity resulted from the ignorance of Captain Thorn of the dangers, and his great want of prudence.

About thirty miles south of this river, are the remains of a ship sunk not far from the shore. It is not known by whom she was owned, nor from what part of the world she came, nor when cast away. The Indians frequently get beeswax from her. It is highly probable that she was from some part of Asia.

A Japanese junk was cast away, fifteen miles south of Cape Flattery in March, 1833. Out of seventeen men only three were saved. In the following May, Captain McNeil, of the Lama, brought the three survivors to Fort Vancouver, where they were kindly treated by the gentlemen of the Hudson Bay Company, and in the following October, were sent to England, to be forwarded to their own country and home.* This junk was loaded with rich China ware, cotton cloths, and rice. In the same year eleven Japanese, in distress, were drifted in a junk to Oahu, Sandwich islands. It is not very uncommon that junks and other craft have been found by whale ships in the great Pacific ocean, in a state of starvation, without the nautical instruments and skill of mariners necessary to enable them to find their way to any port of safety. Undoubtedly many are entirely lost, while others drift to unknown shores.

May not such facts throw light upon the original peopling of America, which has engaged the attention of men for a long period. While one man demonstrates to his own satisfaction, that the first inhabitants of this continent must' have crossed from the north-east part of Asia, because of the resemblance of the people to each other, and the ease with

---

* From documents which have come to hand, since the publication of the first edition of this work, I have been led to admire the wisdom of Providence, as developed in the case of these three Japanese. On their way to their country, they were brought to Macao. It is a well known fact that the missionaries have been endeavoring to gain access to the island of Japan, and to obtain the means of acquiring the language of the inhabitants. These three Japanese, having been so long in foreign countries, were afraid to go to their own country, without permission from their government, and therefore Mr. Gutzlaff was enabled to obtain them as teachers, and to assist him in translating the Scriptures, and other tracts, for distribution among the otherwise inaccessible population of Japan, and thus to impart to them the riches of the Gospel of Jesus Christ.

which the strait is passed in canoes ; another, with no less certainty, proves from the diversity of languages, from the impossibility of tracing their origin, and from other reasons, that an equatorial union of Africa and America must have existed in some age of the world since the universal deluge, and that some violent convulsion of nature has since dissevered them. Others would confine the aborigines of this continent to the descendants of the Jews, and industriously trace in their customs, the ancient worship and rites of God's peculiar people. Some see in them the confirmation of their favorite theory, that human institutions and states, like human and vegetable nature, have their birth, growth, maturity, and decay ; and believe that, as it respects these tribes, these tendencies have already, for centuries, been in operation to produce their extinction. But from whatever single or numerical causes they have had their origin, their own traditions, and the histories of more civilized nations seem unable to inform us. Physical causes alone, we think, are adequate to account for the many features of resemblance which they possess, though they might, at different and distant periods of time have been drifted, or in any other manner found their way, from remote countries.

About this time of the year, water fowl of various genera and species begin to visit the bays and lagoons, and as the season advances, they gradually proceed into the interior of the country, and the rivers and lakes abound with them. Geese, swans, ducks, and gulls, wing their way over us, and their screams, particularly those of the swans, are at times almost deafening. The swan is not of the species common in the United States. It is the Bewick's swan, but is characterized by the same unsullied plumage ; its attitudes and motions, while sailing over its liquid element, are equally graceful, and its voice is even louder and more sonorous. Of the geese there are four kinds ; the white, white fronted, the Canada, and Hutchins. Of the ducks, there are the black or surf duck, the canvass-back, the blue-bill, the long-tailed, the harlequin, the pin-tail, and the golden-eyed. The number of these water fowl is immense, and they may be seen on the wing, swimming upon the waters, or search-ing for food along the shores. They constitute a large item of Indian living and trade, and find a conspicuous place up-on the tables of the gentlemen engaged in the fur business.

Wednesday, October 28th. I took passage on board a canoe, going on an express from the Lama, recently arrived from a northern voyage to and about Queen Charlotte's island, to Fort Vancouver. The canoe was large, carrying about fifteen hundred weight including men and baggage, manned by three white men and three Indians. The day was more pleasant than for some time past, which was a favorable circumstance for passing through the bay, and around Tongue Point, where the current was so strong that it required the full exertion of the men to double it. Ten miles further we passed Pillar Rock, a few miles above which we encamped on the north side, where the mountains came down so close to the shore, that we hardly found room to pitch my tent above high tide water. The men made a large fire, which was cheering and comfortable, and the supper which they prepared was eaten with a keener appe-tite than many a one amidst all the appliances of wealth and luxury.

On the 29th, we arose before day, and were willing to take an early departure from a place where tide and moun-tains disputed the territory. By diligently pursuing our way until eight in the evening, we made forty-five miles, which was a great day's work in going up the river against the current, which is strong when the tide is setting out. I noticed on my return a singular rocky point on the north shore, a short distance below the Cowalitz, rising nearly perpendicular about one hundred feet, separated from the adjacent high hills, and very much in the form of Coffin Rock. It was covered with canoes containing the dead. These depositories are held in great veneration by the Indians. They are not chosen for convenience, but for security against ravenous beasts; and are often examined by the friends of the deceased, to see if the remains of the dead repose in undisturbed quiet. And such is their watchful care, that the anatomist could rarely make depredations without detection, or with impunity. And if they have such regard for the dead, are they without affection for their living relatives and friends? Are they "callous to all the passions but *rage?*" Are they "steeled against sympathy and feeling?" And have they no happiness except what "exists in the visionary dreaming of those, who never contemplated their actual condition?" Have those, who charge upon the Indian character " sullen gloom, want of curiosity and surprise at what is new or striking," had extensive personal acquaintance with many different Indian nations and tribes? and have they gained their familiar friendship and *confidence?* I am firm in the belief, that the character of unabused and uncontaminated Indians will not lose in comparison with any other nation that can be named; and the only material difference between man and man, is produced by the imbibed principles of the Christian religion.

Wishing to avail ourselves of calm weather and a favorable moon, we kept on our way in the evening until thickening clouds and descending rain admonished us of the necessity of finding an encamping place; and while doing this, we ran upon a log, which came very near upsetting us in deep water. But by two men getting out upon the log and lifting the canoe, with much exertion we got off safely. After passing round a point we saw a light on the north shore, to which we directed our course and landed, where we found a small company of Indians encamped under a large projecting rock, giving shelter from the storm. They kindly shared their accommodations with us, and my tent was pitched under the concavity of the rocks; and mats, skins, and blankets upon small stones, made me a comfortable bed. A good fire and refreshing supper obliviscited the labors of the day and dangers of the evening.

Arose on the 30th before day, and although the morning was rainy, yet it was sufficiently calm for the express to prosecute their voyage. I arranged my mats and skins so as to shield myself and baggage from the rain; but the men whose business it was to propel the canoe, were exposed to the storm. After a few hours' labor and exposure, we arrived at the place where the May Dacre had made her harbor, near where the southern section of the Willamette discharges its waters into the Columbia. We brought our canoe into a small bay indented in the basaltic rocks, and drew it so far upon the shore, that it was thought safe without any other security; and all hastened to kindle a fire in a thatched building, which was constructed by some *Kanakas* for the accommodation of the May Dacre. This shelter was very desirable to protect us from the storm, and to give the men an opportunity to dry their clothes. Whilst we were preparing and eating our breakfast, the flowing tide, which swells the river and slackens the current, but does not stop it, took our canoe from its moorings, and drifted it a considerable distance down the river. Some Indians whose residence was far up the Cowalitz, and who were descending the river in their canoes, saw it and returned with it before we knew it was gone. This act proved them to be susceptible of kindness, and increased my confidence in their integrity. The canoe contained valuable baggage, and we should have been left without any means of going on our way. We could not have crossed the Willamette nor Columbia river, and if this had been accomplished, still to have attempted a return by land would have been an almost hopeless undertaking, as the forest had an undergrowth which rendered it quite impassable. The Indians are accustomed so much to travel in canoes, that even the poor accomodation of a trail was not to be found here, and we should have been compelled to dispute every inch of the way with our hatchets. Before the middle of the day, the storm abated, and the remainder of our way to Fort Vancouver was pleasant, at which place we arrived before evening. We were less than three days in accomplishing the passage from one fort to the other, and these were the only three calm days for a long time before and after.

CHAPTER XI.

HERE, by the kind invitation of Dr. McLaughlin, and welcomed by the other gentlemen of the Hudson Bay Company, I took up my residence for the winter; intending to make such excursions as the season will admit and the object of my tour demand. As this is the principal trading post of the company, west of the Rocky Mountains, it may be expected, that many Indians from different parts of the country for considerable distance around, will be seen here during winter, and more information may be obtained of their character and condition than in any other course I could pursue. Here also traders from different stations west of the mountains will come in for new supplies, of whose personal acquaintance with Indians I may avail myself.

Sabbath, November 1st. By invitation, I preached to a congregation of those belonging to this establishment who understand English. Many of the laborers are French Canadians, who are Roman Catholics, and understand only the French language.

This trading post presents an important field of labor, and if a Christian influence can be exerted here, it may be of incalculable benefit to the surrounding Indian population. Let a branch of Christ's kingdom be established here, with its concomitant expansive benevolence exerted and diffused, and this place would be a centre, from which divine light would shine out, and illumine this region of darkness. This is an object of so much importance, that all my powers, and energies, and time, must be employed for its accomplishment ; so that I do not feel that I have a winter of idle confinement before me.

Monday, 2d. In taking a review of my journeyings since I left my home, I can say, though long in time and distance, yet they have been pleasant and full of interest. So diversified has been the country through which I have passed, and so varied the incidents, and so few real hardships, that the time and distance have both appeared short. Although this mission was thought to be one which would probably be attended with as great, if not greater dangers and deprivations than any which had been sent into any part of the world, yet my sufferings have been so small, and my mercies so great, that I can say, if this is taking up the cross, let none be dismayed ; for surely Christ's yoke is easy and his burden light. I had thought much on the prospect of having an opportunity to see whether I could "rejoice in sufferings" for the heathen, "and fill up that which is behind of the afflictions of Christ in my flesh for his body's sake, which is the church," but the protecting providence of God was so conspicuous and his mercies so constant, that the opportunity did not appear to be presented. As to want, I experienced only enough to teach me more *sensibly* the meaning of the petition, "give us this day our daily bread ;" and the truth was comforting, that "the Lord giveth to all their meat in due season." I can truly say, "hitherto the Lord hath helped me."

I am very agreeably situated in this place. Rooms in a new house are assigned me, well furnished, and all the attendance which I could wish, with access to as many valuable books as I have time to read ; and opportunities to ride out for exercise, and to see the adjoining country ; and in addition to all these, the society of gentlemen, enlightened, polished, and sociable. These comforts and privileges were not anticipated, and are therefore the more grateful.

There is a school connected with this establishment for the benefit of the children of the traders and common laborers, some of whom are orphans whose parents were attached to the Company ; and also some Indian children, who are provided for by the generosity of the resident gentlemen. They are instructed in the common branches of the English language, such as reading, writing, arithmetic, grammar and geography ; and together with these, in religion and morality. The exercises of the school are closed with singing a hymn ; after which, they are taken by their teacher to a garden assigned them, in which they labor. Finding them deficient in sacred music, I instructed them in singing, in which they made good proficiency, and developed excellent voices. Among them was an Indian boy, who had the most flexible and melodious voice I ever heard.

It is worthy of notice, how little of the Indian complexion is seen in the half-breed children. Generally they have fair skin, often flaxen hair and blue eyes. The children of the school were punctual in their attendance on the three services of the Sabbath, and were our choir.

Monday, Nov. 23d. The weather being pleasant, though generally very rainy at this season of the year, as I wished to explore the country up the Willamette river, I embraced an opportunity of going with Mr. Lucier and family, who were returning in a canoe to their residence about fifty miles up that river. Doctor McLaughlin furnished and sent on board a stock of provisions, three or four times more than I should need, if nothing should occur to delay us, but such a precaution, in this country, is always wise. We left Fort Vancouver about one o'clock in the afternoon, and proceeded five miles down the Columbia to the entrance of the Multnomah, and about fifteen up the Willamette before we encamped. The name Multnomah, is given to a small section of this river, from the name of a tribe of Indians who once resided about six miles on both sides from its confluence with the Columbia, to the branch which flows down the southern side of the Wâppatoo island. Above this it is called the Willamette. The tide sets up this river about thirty miles, to within a few miles of the falls, and through this distance the river is wide and deep, affording good navigation for shipping.

The country about the Multnomah, and also some miles up the Willamette, is low, and much of it is overflowed in the June freshet ; but as we ascend, the banks become higher, and are more generally covered with woods. The country around contains fine tracts of rich prairie, sufficiently interspersed with woods for all the purposes of fuel, fencing and lumber.

A chain of mountains running from the south-east to the north-west, and through which the Columbia river passes below Deer island, extends along the west shore of this river for some distance, near and below the falls.

There are probably as many Indians who navigate this river with their canoes, as any of the rivers in the lower country ; many of whom I had an opportunity of observing to-day in their busy pursuits, the strokes of whose paddles broke in upon the general silence.   One company overtook us towards evening, and encamped with us upon the elevated shore on the east side of the river.   Owing to the dampness of the day, and previous rains, we had some difficulty in making a fire, but at length it was accomplished, and the wood was unsparingly applied.   With my tent pitched before a large fire, under the canopy of wide branching trees, I partook of the stores of my large wicker basket with as much satisfaction as could be felt in any splendid mansion. The blaze of dry crackling fir threw brilliancy around, softened by the dark forest, like the light of the astral lamp ; and the burning balsam perfumed the air.   The latter part of the night, I suffered more with the cold than at any time in all my journeying, not having taken with me as many blankets as the season required.

The morning of the 24th was overcast with clouds, and rendered chilly by a mist settled near the surface of the river, which collecting in a beautiful frosting upon the surrounding trees, exhibited one of those picturesque fancies, which works of art may intimate, but which only nature can perfect.   Soon after resuming the labor of the day, we passed several basaltic islands, some of them of sufficient magnitude to enclose a few acres, others only rocky points, between which the current was strong, requiring much effort for us to make headway.   Part of the way from our last encampment to the falls, which was six miles, I walked along upon the pebbled shore, where I found calcedony, agate, jasper, and cornelian of good quality.   Two miles below the falls, a large stream comes in from the south-east, called Pudding river.   Its entrance maks a strong current,

which we found difficult to stem, so that we were drifted
back in spite of all our efforts; but in the second attempt
we succeeded. We arrived at the falls of the Willamette
at two o'clock in the afternoon and hired eight Clough-e-wall-
hah Indians to carry the canoe by the falls, the distance of
half a mile, and proceeded about five miles farther before
evening. These falls with the scenery around have much
to charm and interest. The river above spreads out into a
wide, deep basin, and runs slowly and smoothly until within
a half mile of the falls, when its velocity increases, its
width diminishes, eddies are formed in which the water turns
back as if loth to make the plunge, but is forced forward by
the water in the rear, and when still nearer it breaks upon
the volcanic rocks scattered across the channel; then, as if
resigned to its fate, smooths its agitated surges, and precip-
itates down an almost perpendicular of twenty-five feet, presenting a somewhat whitened column. It was a pleasant
day, and the rising mist formed in the rays of the sun a
beautiful bow; and the grass about the falls, irrigated by
the descending mist, was in fresh green. The rocks over
which the water falls, and along the adjacent shores, are
amygdaloid and basalt. The opportunities here for water
power are equal to any that can be found. There cannot
be a better situation for a factory village than on the east
side of the river, where a dry wide-spread level extends
some distance, and the basaltic shores form natural wharves
for shipping. The whole country around, particularly the
east side, is pleasant and fertile. And can the period be far
distant, when there will be here a busy population? I could
hardly persuade myself that this river had for many thousand years, poured its waters constantly down these falls
without having facilitated the labor of man. Absorbed in

these contemplations, I took out my watch to see if it was not the hour for the ringing of the bells. It was two o'clock, and all was still, except the roar of the falling water. I called to recollection, that in the year 1809 I stood by the falls of Genesee river, and all was silence except the roar of the cataract. But it is not so now; for Rochester stands where I then stood.

Wednesday, 25th. As soon as the day dawned, we went on board the canoe and pursued our way up the river, which for thirty miles runs from a westerly direction, and at half past one, we arrived at McKey's settlement. This and Jarvis' settlement, twelve miles above, contain about twenty families. The settlers are mostly Canadian Frenchmen with Indian wives. There are a very few Americans. The Frenchmen were laborers belonging to the Hudson Bay Company, but have left that service, and having families they have commenced farming in this fertile section of country, which is the best of the Oregon Teritory that I have as yet seen. It is well diversified with woods and prairies, the soil is rich and sufficiently dry for cultivation, and at the same time well watered with small streams and springs. These hunters, recently turned to farmers, cultivate the most common useful productions—wheat of the first quality to as great an extent as their wants require. A small grist mill is just finished, which adds to their comforts. They have a common school in each settlement instructed by American young men who are competent to the business.

An opinion extensively prevails, that an American colony is located somewhere in this Territory, but these two settlements are the only farming establishments which exist here, if we except those connected with the trading posts of the Hudson Bay Company. The attempt which was made some few years since by a company of men from the United States, was an entire failure, and only a few individuals of whom I obtained any knowledge, have found their way back to the States.

The forest trees are mostly oak and fir, the latter growing remarkably tall. The misletoe, attached to the body and large branches of the oak, is very common. Beautiful dark green bunches of this plant, seen upon the leafless trees of winter, excite admiration that its verdure should continue, when the trees, from which it derives its life and support, are not able to sustain their own foliage.

I rode, on Thursday the 26th, twelve miles to Jarvis' settlement, and was delighted with the country. For richness of soil and other local advantages, I should not know where to find a spot in the valley of the Mississippi superior to this. I saw on the way a large number of horses, lately brought from California, fattening upon the fresh, luxuriant grass of the prairies.

Near this upper settlement, a short distance up the river, the Methodist church of the United States have established a mission among the Calapooah Indians, of whom there are but few remaining. Rev. Messrs. Jason Lee and Daniel Lee are the ordained missionaries, and Mr. Shepard teacher.

Their principal mode of instruction, for the present, is by means of schools. They have at this time fourteen Indian children in their school, supported in their family, and the prospect of obtaining others as fast as they can accommodate them. Their facilities for providing for their school are good, having an opportunity to cultivate as much excellent land as they wish, and to raise the necessaries of life in great abundance, with little more labor than what the scholars can perform, for their support. The missionaries have an additional opportunity of usefulness, which is to establish a Christian influence among the people of these infant settlements. Mr. J. Lee preaches to them on the Sabbath, and they have a very interesting Sabbath school among the half-breed children. These children generally have fair complexions, active minds, and make a fine appearance. The prospect is, that this mission may lay a foundation for extensive usefulness. There is as yet one important desideratum—these missionaries have no wives. Christian white women are very much needed to exert an influence over Indian females. The female character must be elevated, and until this is done but little is accomplished; and females can have access to, and influence over females in many departments of instruction, to much better advantage than men. And the model, which is furnished by an intelligent and pious family circle, is that kind of practical instruction, whether at home or abroad, which never fails to recommend the gospel.

At the time of my continuance in this place, a singular epidemic prevailed among the Indians, of which several persons died. The subjects of the complaint were attacked with a severe pain in the ear almost instantaneously, which soon spread through the whole head, with great heat in the part affected; at the same time the pulse became very feeble and not very frequent—soon the extremities became cold, and a general torpor spread through the whole system, except the head—soon they were senseless, and in a short period died. In some cases the attack was less severe, and the patient lingered, and after some days convalesced, or continued to sink until death closed his earthly existence.

Friday, Nov. 27th. I rode with Mr. J. Lee several miles south to see more of the country. The same rich, black soil continued, furnishing nutritive grass in abundance ; and also the same diversity of wood and prairie. This valley is generally about fifty miles wide east and west, and far more extended north and south.

Towards evening, we attended the funeral of an Indian boy, who belonged to the school, and who died last night with the epidemic. Most of the children of the school and the Sabbath school attended, and conducted with propriety.

On Saturday I returned to McKey's settlement, to fulfil an appointment to preach to the inhabitants on the Sabbath. I stopped with Mr. Edwards, who is temporarily attached to the mission, but now teaching school in this settlement.

Almost the whole of the inhabitants of this settlement assembled on the Sabbath, and made a very decent congregation, but not more than half of them could understand English.

After service I was called to visit a Mr. Carthre, who was taken severely with the epidemic. I bled him, which gave him immediate relief, and applied a blister, and, as I afterward learned, he recovered.

Early on Monday morning, the 30th, McKey furnished me with two young Indians to take me in a canoe to the falls, where we arrived safely at three o'clock in the afternoon. Here I engaged two Indians belonging to a small village of the Clough-e-wall-hah tribe, who have a permanent residence a little below the falls, to carry me in a canoe to Fort Vancouver. Wanaxka, the chief, came up to the falls, where I was about to encamp alone for the night, and invited me to share the hospitality of his house. I hesitated, not that I would undervalue his kindness, but feared such annoyances as might prevent my rest. On the other hand, there was every appearance of a cold, heavy storm,

and very little wood near, which I could procure for a fire
only with my hatchet, and I should be alone, exposed to
ravenous wild beasts—the latter consideration, however, I
scarcely regarded. But believing it would gratify the
chief, should I accept his invitation, I went with him to his
dwelling, which was a long permanent building on the west
side of the river, upon an elevation of one hundred feet,
and near which were several other buildings of nearly the
same dimensions. Besides the family of the chief, there
were two other families in the same building, in sections of
about twenty feet, separated from each other by mats hung
up for partitions. Their houses are built of logs split into
thick plank. These Indians do not sink any part of their
buildings below the surface of the earth, as some of the Indians do about and below the Cascades. The walls of the
chief's house were about seven feet high, with the roofs
more steeply elevated than what is common in the United
States, made of the same materials with the walls, except
that the planks were of less thickness. They have only
one door to the house, and this is in the centre of the front
side. They have no chimneys to carry off the smoke, but
a hole is left open above the fire-place, which is in the centre of each family's apartment. This answers very well
in calm weather, but when there is much wind, the whole
building becomes a smoke house. The fire-place of the
chief's apartment was sunk a foot below the surface of the
earth, eight feet square, secured by a frame around, and
mats were spread upon the floor for the family to sit upon.
Their dormitories are on the sides of the apartment, raised
four feet above the floor, with moveable ladders for ascent;
and under them they stow away their dried fish, roots, berries, and other effects. There was not an excess of neat-

ness within, and still less without. The Indians in the lower country who follow fishing and fowling for a livelihood are far from being as neat as those in the upper country, who depend more upon the chase. The latter live in moveable lodges and frequently change their habitations. But these Indians were also kind. They gave me most of one side of the fire-place, spread down clean new mats, replenished their fire, and were ready to perform any service I should wish. They filled my tea-kettle, after which I spread out the stores so bountifully provided by Doct. McLaughlin, and performed my own cooking. During the evening, the chief manifested a disposition to be sociable, but we had very little language common to us both, besides the language of signs. The next thing, when the hour of rest arrived, was to fortify myself against a numerous and insidious enemy. I first spread down the cloth of my tent, then my blankets, and wrapped myself up as securely as I could, and should have slept comfortably, had I not too fully realized my apprehensions.

As soon as daylight appeared, on December 1st, I left the hospitable habitation of Wanaxka, and with my two Indians proceeded down the Willamette about sixteen miles before we landed for breakfast. I find a great difference in going with or against the current of these rivers. Since going up this river, the number of swans and geese had greatly multiplied upon the waters and along the shores. Their noise, and especially that of the swans, echoed through the woods and prairies. The swan is a beautiful and majestic bird; its large body, long neck, clear white color, and graceful movements place it among the very first of the winged tribe. The common seal are numerous in this river. It is very difficult to shoot them, even with the

best rifles, on account of their diving with extreme sudden-
ness at the flash. I had a fair opportunity to shoot one to-
day, but with one splash he was out of sight and did not
again appear. When I came to the north-western branch
of the Multnomah, I proceeded down four miles to Fort
William, on the Wâppatoo island, an establishment which
belongs to Captain Wyeth and Company. The location is
pleasant, and the land around is of the first quality.

Some months ago, a tragical occurrence took place here
between two men from the United States. The subject of
their dispute was an Indian woman. Thornburgh was determined to take her from Hubbard, even at the risk of his
own life. He entered Hubbard's cabin in the night, armed
with a loaded rifle, but H. saw him and shot him through
the breast, and violently thrust him through the door. Poor
T. fell and expired. In the absence of any judicial tribu-
nal, a self-created jury of inquest, on examination into the
circumstances of the case, brought in a verdict of "justifia-
ble homicide."

In Thornburgh, was an instance of a most insatiable appetite for ardent spirits. Mr. Townsend, the ornithologist,
whom I have before mentioned, told me he was encamped
out for several days, some miles from Fort William, at-
tending to the business of his profession ; and that in addition to collecting birds, he had collected rare specimens
of reptiles, which he preserved in a keg of spirits. Several days after he was in this encampment, he went to his
keg to deposite another reptile, and found the spirits gone.
Mr. Townsend, knowing that Thornburgh had been several
times loitering about, charged him with having drank off
the spirits. He confessed it, and pleaded his thirst as an
apology.

On Wednesday, the 2d, I returned to Fort Vancouver, well pleased with my excursion. The weather was generally pleasant, free from winds and heavy storms. The whole country is adapted by nature to yield to the hand of cultivation, and ere long, I may say, without claiming to be prophetic, will be filled, through the whole extent of the valley of the Willamette, with farms spread out in rich luxuriance, and inhabitants, whose character will depend upon the religious advantages or disadvantages which benevolent and philanthropic individuals give or withhold. I found the people of the fort in their usual active business pursuits, and received a renewed and cordial welcome.

CHAPTER XII.

SABBATH, 6th. I have attended three services, morning,
afternoon, and evening, and expect to continue them during
my residence in this place. Through the week there will
be but few opportunities to do much for the spiritual benefit
of the common laborers; for in this high northern latitude,
the days in the winter are so short that the men are called
out to their work before daylight, and continue their labor
until near dark; and as their families do not understand
English, I have no direct means of benefiting them.

There is another circumstance which operates against
the prospects of benefiting many of the population here—
the common practice of living in families without being
married. They do not call the women with whom they live,
their wives, but their *women*. They know they are living
in the constant violation of divine prohibition, and acknowledge it, by asking how they can, with any consistency, attend to their salvation, while they are living in sin. I urged
the duty of entering into the marriage relation. They have
two reasons for not doing so. One is, that if they may
wish to return to their former homes and friends, they cannot take their families with them. The other is, that these

Indian women do not understand the obligations of the marriage covenant, and if they, as husbands, should wish to fulfil their duties, yet their wives might, through caprice, leave them, and they should be bound by obligations, which their wives would disregard.

There is no doubt, but that this subject is attended with real difficulties, but are they insurmountable ? Has God given a law, which if obeyed would not secure our greatest and best good ? Can a rational mind balance for a moment the pleasure of a sinful life against interests which stand connected inseparably with permanent happiness, and with a duration, compared to which, the whole of this mortal life is but a speck, a nothing. My heart is pained when I witness the things which are seen and temporal preferred to those that are unseen and pure, and which are commensurate with existence itself. I cannot believe, that if these men should marry the women with whom they live, and do all they could to instruct them, and treat them with tenderness and respect, that there would be many cases of their leaving their husbands. And whatever might be the results, it is always better to *suffer* wrong, than *do* wrong. But their social comforts are so strongly bound with the cords of sin, that they feel, as they express their own case, that it is useless to make any efforts to obtain spiritual freedom, until they shall be placed in different circumstances.

As much of my time, through the week, was occupied in study, and in digesting facts connected with the natural history of the country west of the Rocky Mountains, and the character and condition of the Indians, which came under my observation at different times and places ; and also that which I obtained from persons whose testimony could be relied upon, and which came

under their personal observation, I shall give them without particular dates.

I have already mentioned my agreeable disappointment,
in finding so many of the comforts of life, at different trading posts of the Hudson Bay Company; I have also given
a brief description of the local situation of Fort Vancouver.
This was taken from such observations as I could make in
a hasty view, as I was prosecuting my journey to the shores
of the Pacific ocean.   This establishment was commenced
in the year 1824.   It being necessary that the gentlemen,
who are engaged in transacting the business of the Company west of the mountains, and their laborers, should be
better and less precariously supplied with the necessaries of
life, than what game furnishes; and the expense of transporting suitable supplies from England being too great, it
was thought important to connect the business of farming
with that of fur, to an extent equal to their necessary demands, and as this fort is the central place of business to
which shipping come, and from which they depart for different parts of the north-west coast, and to which, and from
which, brigades of hunting parties come and go; the principal farming business was established here, and has been
progressing until provisions are furnished in great abundance.   There are large fertile prairies, which they occupy
for tillage and pasture, and forests for fencing materials and
other purposes.   In the year 1835, at this post, there were
four hundred and fifty neat cattle, one hundred horses, two
hundred sheep, forty goats, and three hundred hogs.   They
had raised the same year five thousand bushels of wheat, of
the best quality I ever saw; one thousand three hundred
bushels of potatoes ; one thousand of barley, one thousand
of oats, two thousand of peas, and a large variety of garden

vegetables. This estimate does not include the horses, horned cattle, &c. and produce raised at other stations. But little, however, is done at any of the others, excepting Colvile, the uppermost post on the northern branch of the Columbia. The garden of this station, enclosing about five acres, is laid out with regularity and good taste. While a large part is appropriated to the common esculent vegetables, ornamental plants and flowers are not neglected. Fruit of various kinds, such as apples, peaches, grapes, and strawberries, for the time they have been introduced, flourish and prove that the climate and soil are well adapted to the purposes of horticulture. Various tropical fruits, such as figs, oranges, and lemons, have also been introduced, and grow with about the same care that they would require in the latitude of Philadelphia.

In connection with this business and farming establishment, the Company have a flour-mill worked by ox power, which is kept in constant operation and produces flour of excellent quality. Six miles up the Columbia, at the confluence of a stream coming from the north-east, they have a saw-mill with several saws, which is kept in operation most of the year. This mill though large, does not furnish more lumber than a common mill would, with one saw, in the United States. There being no pine below the Cascades, and but very little within five hundred miles of the mouth of the Columbia river, the only timber sawed in this mill is fir and oak. Besides what lumber is used in the common business about this station, one, and sometimes two ship loads are sent annually to Oahu, Sandwich islands, and it is there called pine of the north-west coast, and sells for about fifty dollars the thousand feet. Spars and timber for shipping are also sent to that market. Boards of fir are not so durable, when exposed to the weather, as those of pine, nor so easily worked. One half of the grain of each annual growth is very hard, and the other half soft and spungy, which easily absorbs moisture and causes speedy decay. There is a bakery here, in which two or three men are in constant employment, which furnishes bread for daily use in the fort, and a large supply of sea biscuit for the shipping and trading stations along the north-west coast. There are also shops for blacksmiths, joiners, carpenters, and a tinner.

Here is a well-regulated medical department, and a hospital for the accommodation of the sick laborers, in which Indians who are laboring under any difficult and dangerous diseases are received, and in most cases have gratuitous attendance.

Among the large buildings, there are four for the trading department. One for the Indian trade, in which are deposited their peltries ; one for provisions ; one for goods opened for the current year's business ; and another for storing goods in a year's advance. Not less than a ship load of goods is brought from England annually, and always at least one in advance of their present use, so that if any disaster should befall their ship on her passage, the business of the Company would not have to be suspended. By this mode of management, there is rarely less than two ship loads of goods on hand. The annual ship arrives in the spring, takes a trip to Oahu during the summer, freighted with lumber to the island, and bringing back to Vancouver salt and other commodities, but generally not enough for ballast ; and in the last of September, or in October, she sails for England with the peltries obtained during the preceding year.

The fur business about and west of the Rocky Mountains, is becoming far less lucrative than in years past; for so extensively and constantly have every nook and corner been searched out, that beaver and other valuable fur animals are becoming scarce. It is rational to conclude that it will not be many years before this business will not be worth pursuing in the prairie country, south of the 50° of north latitude ; north of this, in the colder and more densely wooded regions, the business will not probably vary in any important degree.

But very few Americans who have engaged in the fur business beyond the Rocky Mountains, have ever succeeded in making it profitable. Several companies have sustained great loss, or entire failure, owing generally to their ignorance of the country, and the best mode of procedure. The conductors of these enterprises, mainly, were inexperienced in Indian trade, and, like Americans generally, they perhaps expected the golden fruits of their labor and industry, without the patience requisite to ensure it. Hence the results have frequently been disappointment. The Hudson Bay Company have reduced their business to such a system, that no one can have the charge of any important transactions without having passed through the inferior grades, which constitutes several years' apprenticeship. Their lowest order are what they call servants, (common laborers.) All above these are called gentlemen, but of different orders. The lowest class are clerks, then chief-clerks ; next traders, and chief-traders ; factors, and chief-factors ; and the highest, governors. Of the last office there are only two ; one resides in London, who is at the head of the whole business of the Company, and the other resides in Montreal, Lower Canada. There are only two chief-factors west of the Mountains, John McLaughlin, Esq. and Duncan Finlayson, Esq. and with them are associated in business several chief-traders and traders, and chief-clerks and clerks. The salaries of the gentlemen are pro-portioned to the stations they occupy. This being their system of business, no important enterprise is ever intrusted to any inexperienced person.

It is worthy of remark, that comparatively few of all those who engage in the fur business about, and west of the Rocky Mountains, ever return to their native land, and to their homes and friends. Mr. P. of Fort Walla Walla, told me, that to keep up their number of trappers and hunt-ers near, but west of the mountains, they were under the necessity of sending out recruits annually, about one third of the whole number. Captain W. has said, that of more than two hundred who had been in his employment in the course of three years, only between thirty and forty were known to be alive. From this data it may be seen that the life of hunters in these far western regions averages about three years. And with these known facts, still hundreds and hundreds are willing to engage in the hunter's life, and expose themselves to hardships, famine, dangers, and death. The estimate has been made from sources of correct infor-mation, that there are nine thousand white men in the north and in the great west, engaged in the various departments of trading, trapping and hunting, including Americans, Britons, Frenchmen, and Russians. It is more than one hundred and fifty years since white men penetrated far into the forests, in their canoes freighted with goods, coasting the shores of the remote lakes, and following up the still more remote rivers, to traffick with the Indians for their furs, not regarding hunger, toils, and dangers. These enterprises have been extended and pursued with avidity, until every Indian nation and tribe has been visited by the trader.

What is the power of that principle which draws these thousands from their country, and their homes, and all the ties of kindred ? Is the love of gain and hope of wealth the motive by which courage and daring are roused, and dangers defied ? And shall Christianity be a less powerful principle ? Has it only furnished twenty or thirty missionaries, whose sole motive is to carry the gospel to the many ten thousand Indians in the widely extended country, over which are ranging nine thousand traders, trappers and hunters ? Are these the only evidences the church of God can give of sincerity in her professions of attachment to Christ, and to the interests of the immortal soul ? If so, then Christians surely must suffer in comparison with worldly men, and our heaven-descended religion, if judged of by its restricted fruits, must be deemed unworthy of its name and origin. But this want of Christian enterprise, characterized by the late period in which it is begun, and carried forward with such slow and faltering steps, is not only to be lamented as a blot upon the Christian name, but incomparably more is it to be lamented that in consequence, generation after generation of the heathen, to say nothing of the thousands who are trafficking among them, are left in their ignorance of the Savior to perish eternally. How long shall it be, that when an adventurous man forms a plan for traffick in far distant wilds, in a short time a company is formed with a capital of fifty thousand dollars, and a hundred men are found to face hardships and dangers, and they are away ? But when a Christian heart is stirred up to go and carry the gospel to some far distant Indian nation, he may plead and plead for four men and two thousand dollars, and perhaps in vain.   But it is said, a great deal is now doing for the heathen world.   How much? *As much as to give five ministers to the United States.*   All that is doing for the conversion of the heathen is not more than it would cost to build, and man, and defray the expenses of one ship of war.

CHAPTER XIII.

Indian population—diseases—mortality—attributed to cultivation of the soil—destitute of medical science—holidays—customs at home—customs of the Indians—resemblance to Jewish customs in punishment—marriage contracts—condition of the females—slavery—division into tribes—two points of dissimilarity—sacrifices—language.

I HAVE found the Indian population in the lower country, that is, below the falls of the Columbia, far less than I had expected, or what it was when Lewis and Clarke made their tour. Since the year 1829, probably seven-eighths, if not as Dr. McLaughlin believes, nine-tenths, have been swept away by disease, principally by fever and ague. The malignancy of this disease may have been increased by predisposing causes, such as intemperance, and the influence of intercourse with sailors. But a more direct cause of the great mortality, was their mode of treatment. In the burning stage of the fever they plunged themselves into the river, and continued in the water until the heat was allayed, and rarely survived the cold stage which followed. So many and so sudden were the deaths which occurred, that the shores were strewed with the unburied dead. Whole and large villages were depopulated; and some entire tribes have disappeared, the few remaining persons, if there were any, uniting themselves with other tribes. This great mortality extended not only from the vicinity of the Cascades to the shores of the Pacific, but far north and south; it is said as

far south as California.   The fever and ague was never
known before the year 1829, and Dr. McLaughlin mentioned it as a singular circumstance, that this was the year in
which fields were ploughed for the first time.   He thought
there must have been some connexion between breaking up
the soil and the fever.   I informed him that the same fever
prevailed in the United States, about the same time, and in
places which had not before been subject to the complaint.
The mortality, after one or two seasons, abated, partly from
the want of subjects, and partly from medical assistance obtained from the hospital at Fort Vancouver.   The mortality
of Indians and their sufferings under diseases are far greater
than they would be, if they were furnished with a knowledge of medicine.   Indian doctors are only Indian conju-
rers.   But I shall have occasion to say more upon this subject when I describe Indian customs.

December 25th.   The holidays are not forgotten in these
far distant regions.   From Christmas until after the New
Year, all labor is suspended, and a general time of indulgence
and festivity commences.   Only this once in the whole year
are ardent spirits given to the laborers, when they have a free
allowance, furnishing them the opportunity to exhibit fully
what they would do, if spirits were easily and always acces-
sible.   On Christmas morning they dress themselves in their
best attire, accelerated movements are seen in every direction,
and preparation is made for dinners, which are sure to be furnished in their first style, and greatest profusion; and the
day passes in mirth and hilarity.   But it does not end with
the day; for the passions and appetites pampered through
the day, prepare the way for the night to be spent in dancing, and loud and boisterous laughter, shouts, and revelry,
consume the hours designed for rest.   They continue these

high-strung convivialities until they pass the portals of the new year, when labor and toil resume their place.

Such are often the customs of those who profess to be wiser and better. The expiring year vanishes, amidst the noise and revels of many, who pretend by such methods to honor the birth of our Savior, and the introduction of that only religion, which requires perfect purity and perfect order. And too many give as they profess, but a decent honor and respect to those festival days, when from house to house of their best or indifferent friends, the wine is circulated until they become genteelly inebriated. And is it so, that these days are baptized with the name of *holy days?* The piety of primitive Christians undoubtedly led them to observe the supposed anniversary of our Savior's birth, but whenever such uncommanded observances are greatly abused, the same piety will exert itself to bring about a reformation ; and if this cannot be done, then to abolish the custom altogether. Hezekiah, king of Judah, in the case of the brazen serpent, which was preserved as a memorial of the salvation wrought instrumentally by it for those who were bitten by the fiery serpents, destroyed it when the people idolized and burned incense to it.

The question whether there is any evidence that the Indians are descended from the ten lost tribes of Israel, though frequently and largely discussed, has not been satisfactorily answered. From all the personal observations I could make, and efforts at examination, I could not obtain any thing conclusive upon the subject, but am induced to believe that their origin will remain as problematical in future, as it has been in time past. There are some things in their belief and customs which favor the idea that they are of Israelitish descent. Their entire freedom from idolatry is a peculiar characteristic, by which they are distinguished from all other heathen. It will be remembered that this propensity of the Jews to idolatry was entirely subdued from the time of their captivity in Babylon. It was predicted by the prophet Hosea of the children of Israel, that "they should abide many days without a king, and without a prince and without a sacrifice." Among the Indians beyond the mountains, I found no idols, nor any appearance of idolatry. They believe in only one God, and all their worship, so far as they have any, is offered to Him, or as they would say, to the Great Spirit. They believe in the immortality of the soul, and future rewards and punishments. They have no sacrifices, no kings, and no prince. Their government is invested entirely in their chiefs, no one of whom has any special control over the others, or over the people, but they always act in united councils. Their minds are perfectly open to receive any truth in regard to the character and worship of God. They have many traditions and superstitions; and some persons can hardly see the distinction between a reverence for these, and idol worship—for instance, though they may believe that the Great Wolf and the Grey Bear scrambled together the mountains in a fight, yet they do not worship either.

Their custom of punishing the crime of murder, if it does not differ from that of all other heathen nations, yet coincides with what was the custom of the Jews. The nearest relatives of the murdered person are the "avengers of blood," the executioners, or "pursuers of blood." They kill the murderer if they can find him; and in their own tribe or nation, they do not extend the punishment to any other person, so that "the fathers are not put to death for the children, neither are the children put to death for the fathers;

every man is put to death for his own sin." As the Jews
did not regard other nations with the same benevolence as
their own, so the Indians make a distinction between their
own tribe or nation, and others.   If one is killed by a person belonging to another nation, if they cannot obtain and
put the murderer to death, they will take the life of some of
the relatives of the murderer ; or, if they fail of this, some
one of the nation must atone for the crime.   And if this
cannot be done immediately, the debt of blood will still be demanded, though years may pass away before it is canceled.

There is also some resemblance in their marriage contracts.   The negotiation is commenced, if not completed,
with the parents of the intended bride, as in the case of
Isaac's marrying Rebekah.   Abraham directed his servant
to go to his kindred and take a wife for his son Isaac.   He
went, and when God had shown him that Rebekah was the
appointed person, he first consulted her father and brother,
and when their approbation was obtained, Rebekah's ap-
proval closed the contract, and presents were made to the
several members of the family.   The customs of the Indians are substantially the same.   The bridegroom negoti-
ates with the parents, and the approbation of the daughter
being obtained, the stipulated commodities are paid and the
man takes his wife.   But as much or more is given in
dowry to the daughter.   The presents and dowry are pro-
portioned to the rank and wealth of the contracting parties.
Wanaxka, the first chief of the Clough-e-wall-hah Indians,
has refused more than one hundred dollars for a beautiful
daughter, whom I saw when I shared the hospitality of his
house.   A chief at the La Dalles has refused two horses
and six blankets, together with several other articles of
smaller value.   It is not, however, to be understood, that

marriage is a mere mercenary transaction; for fancy and choice have their influence with them, as well as among more refined people.

Another resemblance between the Indians and the Jews may be traced in the estimation in which the females are held. No doubt the degradation of Indian women is to be attributed in a large degree to heathenism, and that uncivilized and savage state in which we find them; yet in their respective occupations we find some features which are not dissimilar. Among those nations and tribes who do not possess slaves, the women cut and prepare wood for fire, as well as food for their families, they pack and unpack the horses, set up and take down lodges, gather roots and berries for food, dress the skins for clothing, and make them into garments. So the Jewish women drew water for flocks and camels, and watched over them; they gleaned the fields in harvest; they also performed the work of grinding in the mill. Our Savior refers to this, when he foretold the destruction of Jerusalem. "Two women shall be grinding at the mill, one shall be taken and the other left."

Slavery was suffered among the Jews, and undoubtedly for the same reasons that polygamy was, and the putting away their wives by writing a bill of divorcement. While the great law-giver did not at once abolish the practice, he brought it under modified restrictions. The stealing and selling a man was punishable with death. If a man bought a Hebrew servant, the time of his service was not to exceed six years. Intermarriages took place between these servants and the families of their masters; and the betrothed maid was to be treated like a daughter. The same restrictions were not, however, enjoined in relation to those bondmen who were bought of the heathen, until the days of the prophets, when they were commanded to break every yoke and let the oppressed go free.   So also slavery exists in a modified form among the Indians west of the mountains, not generally, but only among the nations in the lower country. They are bought; taken prisoners in war; taken in payments of debts, if they are orphans of the debtor; and sell themselves in pledges.   They are put to the same service which women perform among those Indians who have no slaves.   They are generally treated with kindness; live in the same dwelling with their masters, and often intermarry with those who are free.   They are exempt from one cruel practice which their masters inflict upon their own children, the flattening of their heads.   The reason, which those who possess slaves assign for flattening their own heads, is, that they may be distinguished from their slaves who have round heads.

Polygamy is practiced among the Indians, and with nearly the same regulations with which it was practiced among the Jews.   Though they do not write bills of divorcement and put away their wives, yet they send them away on slight occasions.   But this brings no disgrace upon the woman's character, and generally she is soon married to another, and often as advantageously.

Another resemblance between the Jews and the Indians is the division of their nations into tribes.   The tribes of the children of Israel were the descendants of distinguished families, and their government was patriarchal.   The tribes among the Indians are constituted much in the same way. Some important personage gains an influence, numbers become attached to him; and though they do not separate from their nation, nor at once become a distinct tribe, yet they are denominated a band, and these bands in many cases grow up into tribes.

How much allusion there may be to the ancient Jewish custom of wearing " fringes to the borders of their garments," I am not able to determine by eliciting any facts from Indian tradition, but the practice is universal among the tribes west of the mountains, as far as my observation extended—and so fond are they of this ornament to their dress, that every seam in their garments is furnished with it.

There is one consideration which should not be passed over, and which may appear to be against the evidences that the Indians are of Israelitish origin.

Every different nation has an entirely distinct language. These languages are more distinct than the different languages of Europe ; for in all the different languages of Europe there are words derived from Latin, common to each, which prove a common relation.   Now, if the Indians are descended from the Jews, and of course once had a common language, the Hebrew, notwithstanding their departure by different dialects from their original, might it not be expected that there would still remain words and idioms indicative of their common origin.   But it is not so, as may be seen in a vocabulary of a few languages which I shall subjoin.   They have some words in common with Latin, Greek and Hebrew, but these are used in an entirely different sense from that in which they are used in those languages.   As far as it respects language, the proof of a Jewish, or even of a common origin, is not only doubtful but highly improbable.

CHAPTER XIV.

The various animals beyond the Mountains..

It is generally supposed that wild animals, in all Indian countries and especially in the far regions beyond the mountains, are very numerous; but, excepting buffalo within their range, which is becoming more and more circumscribed, game is scarce. In giving an account of animals beyond the mountains, I shall not go into a minute description of those which are familiar to all classes of persons.

Among the animals of the genus *cervus*, the elk is the largest and most majestic. It exists in considerable numbers east of the Rocky Mountains, but is less numerous on the west side. It combines beauty with magnitude and strength, and its large towering horns give it an imposing appearance. Its senses are so keen in apprehension, that it is difficult to be approached; and its speed in flight is so great that it mocks the chase. Its flesh resembles beef, though less highly flavored, and is much sought for by the Indians and hunters. Its skin is esteemed, and much used in articles of clothing and for moccasons.

I did not see the moose; they are said to be found farther north, in the colder and woody regions.

There are three species of deer; the red, the black-tailed, and the common American deer. Like those found in other countries, they are of a mild, innocent, timid aspect; elegant in form, with slender, nervous limbs. When any object or noise alarms them, they throw up their heads, erect

and move their ears in every direction to catch the sounds;
snuff up the wind, and bound off with great celerity. The
deer west of the mountains are more lean and the flesh is
less inviting than those found in the United States. This
may arise from the nature of the food to which they are
confined, having less opportunity for browsing, especially
upon such shrubbery as is congenial to their natures, there
being but very few of the sacchariferous kinds found in
their country.

The red deer are generally found about the Rocky Mountains and upon the head waters of the Columbia.

The black-tailed deer, while they are of a dusky sallow
color, like the common American deer, are somewhat darker,
and their tails are larger and nearly black, which gives them
their name. Their eyes are large and prominent, their ears
are also large and long, and judging from those I saw, they
are smaller than the common deer. When they move faster
than a walk, they bound.

The antelope, which I have already described, page 61st,
are numerous in the upper and prairie country.

It is hardly necessary to say that the beaver, so noted for
its valuable fur, for its activity, and perseverance,—its social habits, its sagacity and skill in constructing its village,
and preparing its neat and comfortable dwellings, is an in-
habitant of this country. It has been sought with avidity,
and has been a source of wealth to many, but to multitudes,
of poverty, misery and death. It would be difficult to sum
up the woes of the last class of adventurers. Its flesh is
very good for food, and the trapper and hunter depend almost entirely upon it for subsistence, while in its pursuit.
Although I ate several times the flesh of the beaver, yet I
discovered no evidence of the truth of the assertion often

made, that while the flesh of the fore parts is of the quality of land animals, its hind parts are in smell and taste like fish. I should think it would require much assistance from imagination to discover the fish taste.

Here also the land otter is found, and is somewhat numerous, and next to the beaver is sought with avidity by the hunter and trader. The shades of its color vary from a light, to a deep, beautiful brown. The fur is rich and in great demand, and there is none found in any country of better quality than the skins I saw at different trading posts of the Hudson Bay Company. Its formation is adapted to land and water, having short and muscular legs, so articulated that it can bring them horizontal with its body, and use them as fins in the water; and its toes are webbed like water fowl. It subsists principally upon fish, frogs and other aquatic animals. It has a peculiar habit, which seems to be its pastime, for we know of no motive it can have, unless it be the love of amusement, which is to ascend a high ridge of snow, and with its legs thrown back, slide down head foremost upon its breast. When there is no snow, it will in the same manner slide down steep, smooth, grassy banks.

The sea otter, so highly and justly valued for its rich fur, is found only along the American coast and adjacent islands, from Kamschatka to upper California. They vary in size, are generally about four feet long when full grown, and nine inches in diameter. Its legs are very short, and its feet are webbed. Its fur is of the first quality, long and glossy, extremely fine, intermixed with some hairs; the outside is black, sometimes, however, dusky, and the inside a cinerous brown. They are amphibious, sportive, and often bask upon the shore for repose, and when asleep the Indians approach and slay them. They have been so much hunted for their valuable fur, that they are diminishing in numbers.

The hair seal is very frequently seen in the waters of Columbia river. Its head is large and round, its eye full and mild. I often saw it swimming after our canoe, presenting to view its head, neck, and shoulders, appearing, in some degree, like the mastiff dog. Its hair is of various colors, generally a dappled gray. It rarely goes far from its most natural element, water ; but is sometimes seen basking upon rocks on the shore, and this is the most favorable opportunity for killing it; for its motions are so quick in the water, that it will submerge at the flash of the rifle, and if killed in the water it sinks, and is difficult to be obtained.

In enumerating the animals beyond the Rocky Mountains, I am not able, as might be expected, to describe the Rocky Mountain, or big-horn sheep. I am unwilling to state, as facts, the descriptions of others, especially as there are so many wrong statements made in natural history. I did not see any of these animals, which probably I should have done, if they were as numerous as travelers have said they are. I saw their horns, which are enormously large, if, as it is said, their bodies are not much larger than a common deer. A horn which I measured, was five inches in diameter at its juncture with the head, and eighteen long. Its flesh, of which I had an opportunity to eat, was far preferable to the best mutton. They inhabit the mountains, and are said to select the most rough and precipitous parts where grass is found. They are not covered with wool, but with hair so bordering upon wool as to render its coat warm in the winter.

The mountain goat, and sheep, did not come under my observation. I was anxious to obtain specimens of them for description, but succeeded in obtaining only small parts of their skins.

The racoon is somewhat numerous in parts of this country, more especially towards the ocean. I could not discover any difference in their appearance and habits from those in the United States.

The badger inhabits this country, and is found on the plains west of the great chain of mountains. Having given a short description of this animal, page 62, when passing through the parts where it was seen, it is not necessary in this place to make any further remarks.

The weasel, the polecat, the marmot, the mink and muskrat, are common, though not numerous, in this country, and not differing from those on the eastern part of this continent, they do not need description.

The wolverine is said to inhabit these western regions, and I saw one in the Salmon river mountains, which my Indians killed. The animal differed in several particulars from the description given by Richardson. It was one foot nine inches from its nose to its tail ; its body was not large in proportion to the length, short legs, small eyes and ears ; the neck short, and as large as the head, and its mouth shaped like that of the dog. Its color was uniformly a dark brown, nearly black ; and its fur was more than an inch long and coarse. I had no opportunity of observing its habits.

The hedgehog is common in all parts of the Oregon Territory, does not differ from those found in other parts of America, and for its quills, is held in high estimation by the Indians. It is interesting to see with how much ingenuity, and in how many various forms, the Indians manufacture these quills into ornamental work, such as moccasons, belts, and various other articles.

There are three kinds of squirrels—two of which I have already described. The third is the gray, which differs from those in the United States in being larger and its color more beautifully distinct. I saw many of their skins made into robes and worn by the Indians about the Cascades.

Of the feline, or cat kind, there are the panther, the long tailed tiger cat, the common wild cat, and the lynx. The panther is rarely seen, and the difference of climate and country produces no change in its ferociousness and other habits, from those found in other parts of America. The long tailed tiger cat is more common, very large, and of a dull reddish color. Also the common wild cat is often seen. It is much smaller, its tail is short and its color is like the above named. I can only name the lynx, as they did not come under my observation. It is in the lower, wooded country they are found, and the Indians say they are numerous.

There are five different species of wolves ; the common gray wolf, the black, blue, white, and the small prairie wolf. The common gray wolf is the same as those found in the United States, and has all their common habits. The black wolf, I did not see, but as described by Mr. Ermitinger, a gentleman belonging to the Hudson Bay Company, is larger than the gray and more noble in its appearance, and is the strongest of the wolf kind. Those which the same gentleman called the blue wolf, are rarely seen, as also the white, and so far as their habits are known, they do not materially differ from others. The small prairie wolf is the most common, and bears the greatest resemblance to the dog, and has been called the wild dog. It differs from the dog in all the peculiarities of the wolf kind as much as the others do. It is as uniform in its color, size, and habits.

They are of a dull reddish gray, never particolored; the hair is always long, blended with brown fur at its roots, and like other wolves they are always prowling and cowardly. They are more numerous than the other kinds, and in considerable numbers follow the caravans to feed upon the offals. Although we frequently heard them howl and bark around our encampments, yet they never disturbed our rest.

Much has been said about the immense number of wolves beyond the Rocky Mountains, but I did not find them so numerous as I expected. I do not make this assertion solely from the fact that I saw or heard only a few, but from the testimony of those whose long residence in this country entitles them to credit. It is the traveler who never saw the country he describes, or the lover of the marvelous, or he who does not expect soon to be followed in his route through dreary and uninhabited wilds, who sees, and minutely relates, adventures with the reptiles and monsters of the desert.

The fox, which is generally dispersed through the world, is found here in three different kinds; the red, gray, and silver. They do not differ from those found east of the mountains. The silver gray fox is scarce, and highly esteemed, and takes the highest rank among the furs of commerce. Its color is dark, sometimes nearly black, the ends of the hairs tipped with white, and in addition to the uncommon fine texture, the fur presents a beautiful glossy appearance.

Martins are not abundant; some are found about the head waters of the Columbia in woody mountains, but they are more numerous and of superior quality farther north.

The inoffensive, timorous hare, in three different species,

abounds in all parts of this country. Its natural instinct
for self-preservation, its remarkably prominent eye, its large
active ear, and its soft fur, are its characteristics in this, as
in other regions. The three species are, the large common
hare, which is generally known, the small chief hare with
large round ears, and a very small species, only five or six
inches long, with pointed ears. If the first named differs
in any particular from those in the United States, it is in
its manner of running, and its speed. Its bound is not regular, but its motions are an alternate running and leaping
at an almost incredible distance, and with such swiftness
that I frequently mistook it, at first view, for the prairie
hen, which I supposed was flying near the surface of the
ground. Its flesh, when used for food, is tender and of a
pleasant flavor.

The only dress which many of the Indians have to protect them from the cold, is made of the skins of these animals, patched together into a scanty robe.

There is a small species of the marmot, of which I have
seen no description in any work on natural history, which
is probably peculiar to this country. It is called by the
Nez Percés, *ēluet ;* is five inches long from the tip of its
nose, exclusive of its tail, which is two in length—its body
is one inch and a third in diameter, the color is brown,
beautifully intermixed with small white spots upon its back.
It has eight long hairs projecting from the nose, on each
side, and two over each eye. Its habits resemble those belonging to its genus. It is remarkably nimble in its movements. The Indians esteem its flesh a luxury.

There are four varieties of bears, though it is supposed
there are only two distinct species. These are the white,
grizzly, brown, and black. The white bear is ferocious and

powerful, but their numbers are so small in the region of the Oregon country, that they are not an object of dread. But the grizzly bear is far more numerous, more formidable, and larger, some of them weighing six or eight hundred pounds. Their teeth are formed for strength, and their claws are equally terrific, measuring four or five inches; and their feet, which are astonishingly large, exclusive of the claws, measuring not far from ten inches long, and five inches wide. There are some even larger. The shades of their color vary from very light gray to a dark brown, always retaining the grizzly characteristic. Among a multitude of their skins which I saw, there were some beautifully dappled, and as large as buffalo robes. These were held in high estimation. Their hair and fur is longer, finer, and more abundant than of any other species. They depend more upon their strength than speed for taking their prey, and therefore generally lurk in willows or other thickets, and suddenly seize upon any animal which may be passing near. The mountain men tell as many wonderful stories about their encounters with these prodigies of strength and ferocity, as some mountain travelers tell us about constant battles with the Blackfeet Indians, and starvation, and eating dogs. Now I may be considered deficient in a *flexible* and fruitful imagination, if I do not entertain my readers with *one* bear story, after having traveled thousands of miles over prairies, and mountains, through valleys, ravines, and amongst caves, chasms and deserts. But as I did not myself have any *wonderful* encounters, I must borrow from a gentleman of established good character, belonging to the Hudson Bay Company, who gave me an account of a case which he witnessed. He and a number of others were traveling in canoes up the Athabasca river, and one morning one of their hunters shot upon the shore a large cub of a grizzly bear, which they took on board a canoe, and of which they made their supper on encamping for the night. While seated around their fire in conversation, the supposed mother of the slain cub approached, sprang across the circle and over the fire, seized the hunter who had shot the cub, threw him across her shoulder, and made off with him. They all laid hold of their rifles and pursued, but feared to fire lest they should injure their companion. But he requested them to fire, which one of them did and wounded the bear. She then dropped the first offender, and laid hold of the last in like manner as the first, but more roughly, and accelerated her departure. There was no time to be lost, and several fired at the same time, and brought her to the ground. The last man was badly wounded but recoved. The "*great medicine,*" or mystery in this case, I shall not attempt to explain, but let every one account for it in his own way.

The brown bear is less ferocious, more solitary, and not highly esteemed either for food or for its skin. The black bear is somewhat similar in its habits to the brown, but lives more upon vegetable food, and is more in estimation for its pure black, well-coated skin.

I close with the buffalo, which is of the *bovine* genus, and is the largest and the most important for food and covering of any of the animals in our country. I need not in this place go into so long description, as otherwise would be important, having already spoken of them as I was passing through their range of country. After having seen thousands and ten thousands of them, and having had months of time to examine their forms and habits, I do not think they should be classed with the buffalo or bison of the eastern continent.

Not with the buffalo, if historians have given a correct description of those on that continent. The flesh of those is
said to be "black, hard, and very unpalatable; their hides
impenetrable, making soft and smooth leather—their race
is so fierce and formidable, that there is no method of
escaping their pursuit but by climbing up into some immense
tree; for a moderate tree would be broken down by them,
and many travelers have instantly been gored to death by
them and trampled to pieces under their feet." It is said
"their voice is a hideous loud bellow." But none of these
things are true of the buffalo of our country.

If a true account has been given of the bison of the eastern continent, our buffalo differ from them in several material traits of character and habits. Those of the eastern
continent, are said to have "small heads, with horns so wide
spread, that three men can sit between them,—that their
eyes are small, red and fiery,—that they have a hump upon
their backs like a camel, and which is preferred to be eat-
en for its delicacy—that they are fierce and vindictive, so
that men have to fly to trees for safety,—that the bulls and
cows live in separate bands." These things do not corres-
pond with the buffalo or bison of our western prairies.

The buffalo or bison of our country are generally about
as large as our domestic neat cattle, and the long, shaggy,
woolly hair which covers their head, neck, and shoulders,
gives them a formidable appearance, at a distance something like the lion. In many particulars they resemble
our horned cattle; are cloven footed, chew the cud, and
select the same kind of food. Their flesh is in appearance
and taste much like beef, but of superior flavor, and remarkably easy of digestion. Their heads are formed like the ox,
perhaps a little more round and broad, and when running,

they carry them rather low. Their horns, ears and eyes, as seen through their shaggy hair, appear small, and cleared from their covering, they are not large. Their legs and feet are small and trim, the fore legs covered with the long hair of the shoulders as low down as the knee. Though their figure is clumsy in appearance, yet they run swiftly and for a long time without much slackening their speed; and up steep hills or mountains they more than equal the best horses. They unite in herds, and when feeding, scatter over a large space, but when fleeing from danger, they collect into dense columns, and having once laid their course, they are not easily diverted from it, whatever may oppose. Their power of scent is great, and they perceive the hunter when he is on the windward side, at a great distance, and the alarm is taken, and when any of them manifest fear, they are thrown into confusion, until some of the cows, from the instinct of fear, take the lead to flee from the pursuer, and then all follow at the top of their speed. So far are they from being a fierce and revengeful animal, they are very shy and timid; and in no case did I see them offer to make an attack, but in self defense when wounded and closely pursued, and then they always sought the first opportunity to escape. When they run they lean alternately from one side to the other. The herds are composed promiscuously of bulls and cows, except some of the old bulls, which are often found by themselves in the rear or in advance of the main bands. Sometimes an old blind one is seen alone from all others; and it was amusing to see their consternation when they apprehend the approach of danger. The natural instincts of fear and prudence lead them to fly alternately in every possible direction for safety. I was pleased to find our most thoughtless young men respect their age and pity their calamity ; for in no instance did I see any abuse offered them.   They are fond of rolling upon the ground like horses, which is not practiced by our do-mestic cattle.   This is so much their diversion, that large places are found without grass and considerably excavated. The use of their skins for robes, and the woolly fur, with which they are covered, are so universally known, that a description is entirely unnecessary.   Another peculiarity which belongs to them is, that they never raise their voice above a low bellow ; in no instance were we disturbed by their lowing, even when surrounded by thousands, and in one of our encampments, it was supposed there were five thousand near.   It has been said they do not visit any of the districts formed of primitive rocks.   This is said with-out reason, for I saw them as frequently in those districts, in proportion to their extent, as where other formations ex-isted.   It is also said as they recede from the east they are extending west.   This is also incorrect ; for, as I have be-fore said, their limits are becoming more and more circum-scribed.   And if they should continue to diminish for twenty years to come, as they have during the last twenty, they will become almost extinct.

CHAPTER XV.

Fish—description of salmon—salmon fishery—ornithology—dendrology—shrubbery—nutritive roots—geography—mountains—valleys
—plains—forests—rivers—soil—seasons.

I PASS to a brief notice of the fish found in the waters of
the Columbia. Their number is great, but their variety is
small. The salmon, sturgeon, anchovy, rock cod, and trout
are all that I shall mention. The sturgeon of good quality
and in large numbers, commence ascending the rivers in the
fore part of April, and furnish food to the suffering Indians.
I say suffering, for before the opening of the spring, their
stock of provisions are consumed, and they are seen searching for roots and any thing which will sustain life; and
though I do not feel authorized to say what others have said,
that in the latter part of the winter and fore part of spring,
they die with starvation in great numbers, yet they are
brought to extreme want, and look forward to the time when
the sturgeon shall come into the river with great solicitude.
A small fish, like the anchovy, about six inches long, very
fat and well flavored, come into the river in great numbers
about the same time or a little before the sturgeon. The
Indians obtain large quantities of oil from them, by putting
them into a netting strainer and exposing them to gentle
heat.

The rock codfish were not known to inhabit the waters
about the mouth of the Columbia, until the present year.
They are very fine and easily caught.

The salmon is far the most numerous and valuable fish found in these waters, and is of excellent flavor. It is well ascertained that there are not less than six different species of the true salmon that ascend these waters, commencing about the twentieth of April. Their muscular power is exceedingly great, which is manifested in passing the falls and rapids, which would seem insuperable. They are never known to return, but are constantly pressing their way upwards, so that it is not uncommon to find them in the small branches of the rivers near the very sources. We found them in September near the Rocky Mountains, where they are said to be as late as November and December. I saw some with parts of their heads worn to the bone and the skin worn from various parts of their bodies, which appears to be the result of efforts to ascend until they perish. Late in the season, great numbers are found dead, furnishing food for crows, and even Indians; for I have seen them drive away the crows and appropriate the remnants to themselves. When the salmon become much emaciated, the flesh loses its rich redness, and it is seen in the skin, which gives the fish a beautiful appearance; but when in this state it is hardly edible. It is worthy of notice, that the salmon has its preferences of water, selecting some branches of the Columbia river and passing by others; and those taken in some of the tributary streams are far better than those taken in others. While those which ascend the rivers never return, the young are seen in September descending on their way to the ocean, in immense numbers. It is believed these return the fourth year after their descent; but this may be only conjecture. It is difficult to estimate how many salmon might be taken in these rivers, if proper measures were pursued; and also what would be the results upon the numbers which would continue to enter and ascend. I think without doubt a plan might be devised and adopted to carry on a salmon fishery in this river to good advantage and profit. The experiment was made by a company from the United States, which failed, for it contained the elements of its own overthrow. The company sent out large quantities of rum, probably calculating on the fact that the Indians are fond of ardent spirits, and if they should gratify this appetite, they should enlist them in their favor, and as Indians will do anything for rum, they would catch and sell the fish to them. Whatever the object of the company might have been in sending and dealing out so much rum, the Indians were highly pleased with receiving it in pay for their salmon. But when they had thus obtained it they would become intoxicated and disqualified for labor, and more time was wasted in drunkenness, than employed in fishing. Besides, the salmon were often suffered to lie in the hot sun until they were much injured, if not wholly spoiled. The result was, that the company, as I was informed, obtained only about four hundred barrels of salmon, and made a losing voyage; and the superintendent of Fort Vancouver told me, that when the company abandoned their business, they stored many barrels of rum at his fort. My information was not wholly derived from those who had been in the employment of that company, and gentlemen of the Hudson Bay Company, but in part from the Indians, who often spoke to me upon the subject by way of praise. They would say, "*close, hias lum*," signifying, good, plenty of rum.

The birds of Oregon are not as numerous as those which inhabit civilized countries, probably because they have not access to the grain and fruit of cultivated fields, and the woods and groves are more widely dispersed. But they are sufficiently numerous to employ an ornithologist profitably, for a great length of time in collecting and preserving specimens. This region is particularly interesting from the fact, that in this as in other departments of natural science, it has hitherto been an unexplored field—no competent scientific person having visited this country to classify the different genera and species. Mr. J. K. Townsend, of Philadelphia, an ornithologist, has spent two years in examining scientifically this field, and will probably give to the public the result of his labors. I am indebted to him for assistance in the following summary.

The largest part of the feathered race are migratory, and are seen only a part of the year ; there are many, however, that reside here during the whole year. Among these are the majestic white-headed eagle, and the golden eagle, and three or four species of hawks, two species of jay, the magpie, and thousands of ravens and crows ; several species of small sparrows, and two or three species of grouse, the common partridge of the United States, and the dusky grouse of the Rocky Mountains ; and also an interesting species of the dipper or water ousel. The habits of this bird are very curious and peculiar, particularly that of descending to the bottom of ponds and swiftly running streams, and there in search of small shell-fish, remaining under water, for at least two minutes, during which time it will course about upon the pebbly bottom, with as much apparent ease and satisfaction, as if upon dry land. The red-winged black-bird and the robin continue through the year. The notes of the latter are heard even in the chill of the winter, though in feeble strains.

As the autumn advances, the number of swans, geese, and ducks multiply. I have already mentioned these water fowl. The black cormorant is common upon the Columbia river, and there are other species of the same genus, seen about the shores of the Cape, which do not ascend the rivers. Among these is the violet green cormorant, the most splendid of all the known species of cormorants. The loon, or great northern diver, is very plentiful in this river. Gulls, terns, auks, and petrels, in great numbers, visit this river to seek shelter from the violent storms which agitate the ocean during the winter.

The spring, with rising vegetation and opening flowers, brings its hosts of lovely feathered tribes, which remain for different periods of time; many of them continue only a few weeks, and then retire to other parts for nidification. There are, however, great numbers that remain through the summer, and their delightful songs add to the charms of a fine morning of April and May. Among these are hundreds of warblers, wrens, titmice and nuthatches. Of the warblers there are eleven species, six of which are new; the other five are common to the States. Several of the species are but transient visitors, but most of them remain through the season. Of the wrens there are six species; three of the titmice, and two of the nuthatches. And in the train follow the thrushes, of which there are seven species, two of which are new; of these Wilson's thrush is pre-eminent in sweetness of song. The fly catchers number eight species, three of which are new; and there are thirteen species of the finches, three of which are new. These are a large and musical band, among which are several of the finest songsters known in the world. In no instance do we find more richness and delicacy of plumage, with the most sweet melody of voice, than in a new species of large bullfinch, which visits this section of country in the spring. If these were domesticated, they would form a most valuable addition to any aviary. There are eight species of woodpeckers, four of which are new ; and of the swallow tribe there are five species, one of which is new, and the most beautiful of the family, characterized by a splendid changeable green plumage on the head and back, while the other parts are purple and white. About the middle of March, the splendid little Nootka humming bird makes his appearance, coming so suddenly that you wonder from whence he came, as the fact of his performing a long migration of weeks, with his delicate little wings, over a cold and flowerless country, or across the sea, seems incredible. The neck of this beautiful bird presents fine variations of color; now it is ruby red, with a metallic lustre; turn it, and the tints vary from purple to violet and crimson, according as the light falls upon it.

I pass over the mention of many genera, and still more numerous species of the different birds of this region, as it is not my design to attempt a history of them, but only to give a succinct sketch, that some idea may be formed of the ornithological treasures of this interesting country.

Having frequently made mention of the trees and shrubbery west of the great mountains, I shall in this place only enumerate the principal, describing a few. I have said there are three species of fir, and that they constitute far the greatest part of the forest trees, and are very large. The three kinds are the red, yellow and white. They differ not only in the color of the wood, but also in their foliage. The foliage of the red is scattered on all sides of the branchlets in the same form as those found in the United States ; the yellow only on the upper side, or the upper half of the twigs ; the white is oppositely pinnated. The balsam is alike in the three different species, found in blisters upon the bark in the same form as in other countries.

White pine is not native in the lower country, nor far west of the main chain of the Rocky Mountains ; a few pitch are found in the same region with the white. Norway and yellow pine are native farther west, but not below the Cascades. The new species, which I have called the elastic pine, is far the most numerous, but I did not see any of these as far west as Walla Walla.

The cedar is the common species, grows *very* large and tall, and is the best of the forest trees for various mechanical uses. The yew is also found among the evergreens, though it is scarce. The tamarisk is found in small sections of the country. The white oak of good quality, and often large, is a common tree of the forest, and also the black, rough-barked oak grows in some of the mountainous parts. In an excursion down the rich plains below Fort Vancouver, where there are trees scattered about like shade trees upon a well cultivated farm, I measured a white oak, which was eight feet in diameter, continued large about thirty feet high, and then branched out immensely wide, under which Mr. T. and myself, with our horses, found an excellent shelter during a shower of rain. There are two kinds of ash, the common white ash and the broad leafed. The latter is very hard. There is also alder, which I have mentioned as growing very large, and on dry ground as well as on that which is low and swampy.

There are three species of poplar, the common aspen, the cotton and balm. The first is common in various parts of the United States, and is well known ; the second commonly called cotton-wood, skirting rivers and streams as in the western States ; the third is the *Populus balsamifera,* often

called the balm of Gilead. Its distinguishing properties
are ovate leaves, and a bitter balsam in a glutinous state
found in the small twigs, but mostly in the buds. This last
species in some places spreads over large sections of bottom-
land, where the soil is uncommonly good. White maple is
found, but only in small quantities. Willows of various
species are common in all parts of the country. There is
a tree in the lower country which grows much in the form
of the laurel or bay tree, but much larger,—the bark is
smooth and of a red bay color, its leaves are ovate. It has
been called the strawberry tree, but I do not know with what
propriety. There are no walnut or hickory trees west of
the great mountains, nor chestnut of any species, or hard
or sugar maple, or beach, linden or bass-wood, black cherry,
cucumber, white wood, elms, or any kind of birch, except
a species of black birch which grows small; nor are there
any of the species of locusts, hackberry, or buckeye. I
might lengthen out the catalogue of negatives, but the above
observations are sufficient to give a general view of the forests trees of the country.

The variety of shrubbery and plants is so numerous, that
their examination would employ the botanist many months.
I shall only sketch a few of those which are scattered over
the prairies and through the forests. Among these are several varieties of the thorn-bush, many of which are large and
fruitful. Those bearing the red apple, present, when they
are ripe, a very beautiful appearance. There is one species
peculiar to the country west of the mountains, the fruit of
which is black and of a delightfully sweet taste, but not generally dispersed through the country. It is principally native about the Blue Mountains, the Walla Walla and Um-
matilla rivers. The choke cherry is common to all parts of

the country, and its fruit is very grateful where animal food is principally depended upon for subsistence. The salalberry is a sweet and pleasant fruit, of a dark purple color, oblong, and about the bigness of a grape. The serviceberry is about the size of a small thorn apple, black when fully ripe, and pleasantly sweet like the whortleberry; and the pambina is a bush cranberry. The varieties of the gooseberry are many,—the common prickly, which grows very large on a thorny bush,—the small white, which is smooth and very sweet,—the large smooth purple, and the smooth yellow, which are also of a fine flavor. All of these attain to a good maturity, and those growing on the prairies are very superior. There are three varieties of the currant, the pale red, the yellow, which is well tasted, and the black. Though these are a pleasant acid, yet they are not so prolific and desirable as those which grow under the hand of cultivation. The beautiful shrub *Symphoria racemosa,* called the snowberry, which is found in some of our gardens, grows here wild and in great abundance.

Besides the common raspberries, there is a new species which grows in the forests, the berry of which is three times as large as the common, is a very delicate rich yellow, but the flavor is less agreeable. There is a new species of sweet elder which I have already described. The trailing honeysuckle is among the first ornaments of nature.

The sweet flowering pea grows spontaneously, and in some places embellishes large patches of ground. In some small sections red clover is found, differing, however, from the kind cultivated by our farmers, but not less sweet and beautiful; white clover is found in the upper and mountainous parts. Strawberries are indigenous, and their flavor more delicious than any I have tasted in other countries.

Wild flax I have mentioned and described on page 90.

Sun-flowers are common, but do not grow large; also a species of broom-corn, is found in many places of the bottom-lands of the Columbia and other streams. To these may be added a wild grain somewhat resembling barley, or rye.

Among the nutritive roots, I have mentioned the wâppatoo and the cammas. The wâppatoo, is the common *sagittaria*, or arrow head, and is found only in the valley of the Columbia below the Cascades. The root is bulbous, and becomes soft by roasting, forming a nourishing and agreeable food, is much used by the Indians, and is an article of trade. It grows in shallow lakes, and in marshes which are covered with water. The Indian women wade in search of this root, feel it out in the mud and disengage it with their feet, when it rises to the surface of the water and is secured. The cammas, a tunicated root, in the form of an onion, is of great importance to the Indians and grows in moist, rich ground. It is roasted, pounded, and made into loaves like bread, and has a taste resembling licorice. The cowish, or biscuit root, grows on dry land, somewhat larger than a walnut, tastes like the sweet potato, is prepared in the same manner for food as the cammas, and is a tolerable substitute for bread. To these may be added the *racine amére*, or bitter root, which grows on dry ground, is fusiform, and though not pleasant to the taste, is very conducive to health; also the common onion, and another characterized by its beautiful red flower, which often grows upon patches of volcanic scoria where no other vegetation is seen.

Although a description of the Oregon Territory has been necessarily interwoven in the narrative, yet a condensed account of its geography may with propriety be given here.

In comparing the country west with that east of the mountains, especially the great valley of the Mississippi, we are impressed very powerfully with the strong contrast which their distinguishing features present. The valley of the Mississippi may be called the garden of the world—every part abounding in rich soil inviting cultivation. We see no barren or rocky wastes, no extended swamps or marshes —no frozen mountains. Destitute of prominent land-marks to catch the eye of the traveler, he sees in the wide distance before him only the almost horizontal lines of level or rolling meadow. No one points him to the peaks of dim mountains and tells him that the range divides two sister states, or separates two noble rivers. He sees no clouds resting on the shoulders of lofty Butes and blending their neutral tint with the hazy blue of the landscape before him—nor Tetons rearing their heads into the region of perpetual snow—and day after day he pursues his journey without any thing to create in his bosom emotions of the grand, and sublime, unless it be the vastness of the expanse.

Beyond the Rocky Mountains, nature appears to have studied variety on the largest scale. Towering mountains and widely extended prairies, rich valleys and barren plains ; and large rivers with rapids, cataracts and falls, present a great diversity of prospect. The whole country is so mountainous, that there is not an elevation from which a person cannot see some of the immense ranges which intersect its different parts. On an elevation a short distance from Fort Vancouver, five isolated conical mountains, from ten to fifteen thousand feet high, whose tops are covered with perpetual snow, may be seen rising in the surrounding valley. There are three general ranges, west of the rocky chain of mountains, running in northern and

southern directions. The first above the Falls of the Columbia river ; the second at and below the Cascades ; the
third towards and along the shores of the Pacific. From
each of these, branches extend in different directions. Besides these there are others which are large and high,
such as the Blue Mountains south of Walla Walla—
the Salmon ·river mountains between Salmon and the
Cooscootske rivers ; and also in the regions of Okanagan and Colvile.

Between these mountains are wide-spread valleys and
plains. The largest and most fertile valley is included between Deer island on the west, to within twelve miles of
the Cascades, and is about fifty-five miles wide, and extending north and south to a greater extent than I had the means
of definitely ascertaining ; probably from Pugets sound on
the north, to the Umbiquâ river on the south. The Willamette river and a section of the Columbia are included in
this valley. The valley south of the Walla Walla, called
tho Grand Round, is said to excel in fertility. To these
may be added Pierre's Hole and adjacent country ; also
Racine Amére, east of the Salmon river mountains. On
Mill river, which unites with the Columbia at Colvile, from
the south, through a valley of more than fifty miles, there
are rich bottom lands. While these are open and ready
for cultivation, the hills on both sides of the valley are covered with woods. Other fertile sections of considerable
magnitude are dispersed over different parts of the country.
To these may be subjoined extensive plains, most of which
are prairies well covered with grass. The whole region
of country west of Salmon river mountains, the Spokein
woods, Okanagan, and quite to the range of mountains
which cross the Columbia at the Falls, is a vast prairie

covered with grass, and the soil is generally good. Another large plain, which is said to be very barren, lies off to the south-west of Lewis' or Snake river, including the Shoshones' country ; and travelers who have passed through have pronounced the interior of America a great barren desert ; but this is drawing a conclusion far too broad from premises so limited. So far as I have had opportunity for observation, I should feel warranted in saying, that while some parts of Oregon are barren, large portions are well adapted to grazing ; and others, though less extensive, to both tillage and grazing.

Upon the subject of forests, I would only observe, that a large proportion of the country west of the mountains is destitute, while some parts are well supplied. I have already mentioned the lower country, from below the Falls of the Columbia to the ocean, as being well wooded, and densely in many parts, especially near the ocean. The mountains north of the Salmon river, and the country about the Spokein river, and so on still farther north, are well furnished with forests, and in some other sections there are partial supplies.

The country in general is well watered, being intersected with lakes, and many large rivers and tributary streams. This might be inferred from the fact that there are so many mountains, upon the sides and at the bases of which are multitudes of the finest springs. No country furnishes water more pure and of such crystal clearness. As the spring and summer heat commences, the snows of the mountains melt, and begin to swell the rivers in the beginning of May, and the freshet continues to increase until June, when it is the greatest, and overflows large sections of the low lands of the valleys, which have the appearance of inland seas.

While the rivers of this country are numerous, and several
of them are large, yet inland navigation will be attended
with difficulties, not only from the many falls and rapids,
but from the labor and expense necessary to construct canals through the immensely hard basaltic rock formation.
The Columbia has three large falls in the distance of seven
hundred miles ; the Cascades, one hundred and thirty miles
from the ocean at the head of tide water ; the Falls of the
Columbia, forty miles above the Cascades ; and the Kettle
Falls, five hundred and thirty miles above the Falls of the
Columbia.   There are many rapids, but the Nine-mile Rapids, thirty miles above Walla Walla, are the most embarrassing.   The other rivers are still more obstructed with
falls and rapids, except the Willamette, which has only
one fall at the head of its tide water, thirty miles above
its junction with the Columbia.   The obstruction to a
canal around this, is far less than around the above
named falls ; and when constructed, the navigation may
be extended fifty miles farther into the country.   While
such is the condition of the country in respect to its internal navigation and commerce, the ingenuity of man in our
day, has provided something which can be most advantageously applied as a remedy. I mean rail-roads. In
making observations, with reference to this very subject,
I was interested to see the wisdom and benevolence of
the Creator, in providing passes through those stupendous ranges of mountains, running generally from north
to south, and I thought how easily the whole territory
might be traversed in this way ; and the large pentagonal basaltic columns are ready at hand to facilitate
the work.   No country in the world furnishes better
opportunities for water power to be applied to manufac-

turing purposes ; every river and stream having falls, cascades and rapids.

The seasons.   These are divided into two, the rainy in the winter, commencing in November and terminating in May ; the dry in the summer, which is entirely destitute of rain, and during which time the atmosphere is remarkably serene ; the daily prairie winds relieve the heat of the sun, and the season is most delightful.   The climate is far more temperate and warm west of the Rocky Mountains, than east in the same latitude, there being at least ten degrees difference of latitude, as may be seen by the subjoined meteorological table.   There were only three days in the whole winter of my residence in the country, that the thermometer sunk as low as 22° Fahrenheit, at Fort Vancouver ; and there were only two mornings in the whole month of March when white frost was seen.   Snow does not fall deep excepting upon the mountains ; in the valleys it rarely continues more than a few days, or at the farthest only a few weeks ; and by the latter part of February or the first of March, ploughing and sowing is commenced.   And not only is the climate uncommonly delightful, but it is also healthy, and there are scarcely any prevailing diseases, except the fever and ague in the lower country, which, as has been stated, commenced in 1829 ; and the ophthalmy, which is very general among the Indians of the plains. It is worthy of notice, that thunder and lightning are seldom witnessed west of the mountains, but in the valley of the Mississippi, they are very frequent and unusually heavy.

The entire destitution of rain, showers and dew, during summer, does not exclude fertility ; nor is it peculiar to this country, for the same is true of the whole Pacific coast west of the Andes, and also of the Sandwich and Society Islands—yet by various methods of irrigation the soil is rendered productive. In the country which I am describing, the winter being so mild, the grain sown in the fall and spring advances beyond injury before the drouth becomes severe, and the grass attains its growth and dries into hay upon the ground; and there being no moisture to decompose it, retains its nutritive properties.

CHAPTER XVI.

Character and condition of the Indians—Indians of the plains—their
persons—dress—wealth—habits—physical character.—manufactures
—their religion—wars—vices—moral disposition—superstitions—
medicine men.

As it was the principal object of my tour to ascertain the
character and condition of the Indians beyond the Rocky
Mountains, their numbers, and the prospects of establishing
the gospel among them, it will not only be proper but important to give a full and connected description of them in
these respects.   In doing this, while I have availed myself
of information collected from men of intelligence and integrity, I have confined my statements to those things which
have been corroborated by, or came under my own observations; feeling it a duty to avoid the many fabulous ac-
counts which have been given of Indian character and customs.   Romance may please and excite admiration, fiction
may charm, but only truth can instruct.

I will first describe the Indians of the plains.   These
live in the upper country from the Falls of the Columbia to
the Rocky Mountains, and are called the Indians of the
plains, because a large proportion of their country is prairie
land.   The principal tribes are the Nez Percés, Cayuses,
Walla Wallas, Bonax, Shoshones, Spokeins, Flatheads,
Cœur d'Aléne, Ponderas, Cootanies, Kettlefalls, Okanagans,
and Carriers.   These do not include probably more than
one half of those east of the Falls, but of others I have ob-

tained but little definite knowledge. They all resemble each other in general characteristics. In their persons the men are tall, the women are of common stature, and both are well formed. While there is a strong natural as well as moral resemblance among all Indians, the complexion of these is a little fairer than other Indians. Their hair and eyes are black, their cheek bones high, and very frequently they have aquiline noses. Their hands, feet, and ankles, are small and well formed; and their movements are easy, if not graceful. They wear their hair long, part it upon their forehead, and let it hang in tresses on each side, or down behind.

There is a great resemblance in the dress of different tribes, which generally consist of a shirt, worn over long, close leggins, with moccasons for the feet. These are of dressed leather made of the skins of deer, antelope, mountain goat and sheep; and over these they wear a blanket or buffalo robe. The borders of their garments are ornamented with long fringes. They are fond of ornaments, and their heads and garments are decorated with feathers, beads, buttons, and porcupine quills; these last are colored red, yellow, blue, and black, and worked with great skill and variety of design. They appear to have less of the propensity to adorn themselves with painting, than the Indians east of the mountains; but not unfrequently vermilion, mixed with red clay, is used not only upon their faces, but upon their hair. The dress of the women does not vary much from that of the men, excepting, that instead of the shirt, they have what we may call a frock coming down to the ankles. Many of them wear a large cape made of dressed skins, often highly ornamented with large oblong beads of blue, red, purple, and white, arranged in curved lines covering the whole. Some of the daughters of the chiefs, when clothed in their clean, white dresses of antelope skins, with their fully ornamented capes coming down to the waist, and mounted upon spirited steeds, going at full speed, their ornaments glittering in the sun-beams, make an appearance that would not lose in comparison with equestrian ladies of the east.

Their horses are not less finely caparisoned with blue and scarlet trimmings about their heads, breasts, and loins, hung with little brass bells.

While a want of cleanliness is a characteristic of all heathen, the Indians of the plains are less reprehensible than others, and far more neat than those of the lower country towards the Pacific. It is not to be understood that there are not those who are poor, suffering from the want of food and clothing.

Their wealth consists in their horses, and their consequence depends in a great degree upon the number they possess, some owning several hundreds ; and that family is poor whose numbers are not sufficient for every man, woman and child to be mounted, when they are traveling from place to place ; and also to carry all their effects. In these respects they are far better supplied than any tribes I saw east of the mountains. While their horses are their wealth, they derive but little from them for the support of themselves and families; for they do not employ them to cultivate the earth ; and the market for them is so low, that they command but a small price. A good horse will not sell for more than enough to purchase a blanket, or a few small articles of merchandize. For subsistence, they necessarily depend upon hunting and fishing, and gathering roots and berries. Their mode of cooking is plain and simple. Most of their food is roasted, and they excel in roasting fish. The process is to build a small fire in the centre of their lodge, to fix the fish upon a stick two or three feet long, and place one end in the ground so as to bring the fish partly over the fire, and then by a slow process it is most thoroughly roasted without scorching, or scarcely changing the color. The principal art consists in taking time, and our best cooks might improve by following their mode.

The habits of Indians are said to be indolent. As a general remark it may be true, but I saw but very little to confirm its truth among the Indians of the plains ; for I rarely saw any of these Indians not engaged in some object of pursuit; not the most productive perhaps, but such as enlisted their attention. While I believe that the resemblance, both physical and moral, of all the different nations and tribes of Indians, spread over large portions of the continent of America, is greater than is seen in any people of any other country of equal extent, yet if it is true, that as a general fact, "they are morose and gloomy in their countenances ; sullen, or bacchanalian in their dispositions ; that they are rarely so joyful as to laugh unless excited by ardent spirits ; that they are taciturn and never indulge in mirth ; that they are obtuse in sympathy, and destitute of social affections ; that in proud disdain they turn away from whatever would excite curiosity ; that no common motives or endearments excite them to action ;" if these things are true, then the Indians in Oregon are an exception to the general fact. In all the above named particulars, I saw no special difference between them and other nations. As a part of the human family, they have the same natural propensities and the same social affections. They are cheerful and often gay, sociable, kind and affectionate ; and anxious to receive instruction in whatever may conduce to their happiness here or hereafter. It is worse than idle to speak of " physical insensibility inwrought into the animal nature of the Indians, so that their bodies approximate to the insensibility of horses' hoofs." The influence of this kind of remark is to produce, in the bosoms of all who read them, the same insensibility that is charged upon the native character of the Indians. To represent their characters and their restoration to the common feelings of humanity so hopeless, is to steel the heart of even Christianity itself, if it were possible, against all sympathy, and to paralize all exertions and effort to save them from the twofold destruction to which they doom them, temporal and eternal. Is this the reason that Christians are sitting in such supineness over their condition, and that the heart-thrilling appeals for teachers to enlighten them are disregarded? Is this the reason, that while the philanthropy of the United States' citizens towards them is so widely blazoned, those who are sent to teach them the arts of civilized life, are sitting quiet on the borders in govermental pay, while the Indians are roaming still over the prairies in search of uncertain and precarious game? I forbear to tell the whole story.

They have but few manufactures, and those are the most plain and simple, not extending much beyond dressing the skins of animals, and making them into clothing ; making bows and arrows and some few articles of furniture. In dressing skins they never make any use of bark or tannin. Their process is to remove the hair and flesh from the skins by scraping them with a hard stone or wood, or when it can be obtained, a piece of iron hoop, and then besmearing them with the brains of some animal, they smoke them thoroughly and rub them until they are soft; and after this bleach them with pure white clay. Their mode of smoking them is to excavate a small place in the ground, about a foot deep, and over this to construct a fixture in the form of a lodge, a few feet wide at the base and brought to a point at the top. Then they build a small fire in the centre, and place the skins around upon the frame work, so as to make the enclosure almost smoke tight. The process occupies about one day. Their mode of dressing buffalo robes is different. They stretch the skin upon the ground, flesh side up, fastening it down with pins around the border, and then with an instrument formed somewhat like a cooper's adz, made of stone, or wood overlaid with a piece of iron, brought to a blunt edge like the currier's knife, they clear from it all remaining flesh, and let it thoroughly dry. After this, with the same instrument, they work upon it with a pounding, hewing stroke, until they have brought it to a suitable thickness and rendered it soft and white, as our buffalo robes are when brought into market It is a work of great labor, and is performed by the women. We little think how much toil it costs a woman to prepare one of these robes, and then how little is paid for it by the purchaser; a pound of tobacco or a bunch of beads, is as much as the Indian generally receives.

Their bows are made of the most elastic wood, strengthened with the tendons of animals glued upon the back side, and the string is made of the same substance. Their arrows are made of heavy wood, with one end tipped with a sharp stone or pointed iron, and the other pinnated with a feather. While the first is to pierce, the latter is to govern the direction. Their bows and arrows perform astonishing execution, and they manage them with great dexterity.

Most of the cooking utensils, which they now use, are obtained from traders, and do not often extend beyond a brass kettle, tin pail, and a very few knives. They have bowls which they manufacture very ingeniously from the horns of buffalo ; and sometimes, those that are larger and more solid, from the horns of the big horn mountain sheep. They have spoons of very good structure made of buffalo horns ; also various kinds of baskets of rude workmanship. Their saddles are rude, somewhat resembling the Spanish saddle, having a high knob forward, and rising high on the back part ; generally sitting uneasily upon the horse's back. Their bridles consist of a rope well made of the hair, or shag of the buffalo, eight or ten feet long, fastened in the centre to the under jaw of the horse, and the ends are brought over the neck for reins. The lasso, which is used for catching horses and some kinds of wild animals, is a long rope with a large noose at one end, and the other end is held firmly in the hand ; the whole is coiled, and when the distance permits it to be thrown, it is usually so dexterously done, as to bring the noose over the animal's head. When mounted, they often have a long leather thong, or a rope, fastened upon the horse's neck, which trails upon the ground, and is frequently suffered to remain when the horse is turned loose, for the convenience of more easily catching him again.

Their canoes, before they obtained iron hatchets of the traders, were, with great labor and patience, made with hatchets of stone ; and even now, cost them no small effort. A canoe of good construction is valued as high as one or two good horses. Their fishing nets are another article which is well constructed, formed of wild flax ; and in every particular like our scoop nets.

As regards the religion of the Indians, I have already stated that they believe in one God, in the immortality of the soul, and in future rewards and punishments. But while these are the prominent points of their belief, definite ideas of a religious nature appear to be extremely limited, both in number and in comprehensiveness. As much as this, however, appears to be true. They believe in one Great Spirit, who has created all things, governs all important events, who is the author of all good, and the only object of religious homage. They believe he may be displeased with them for their bad conduct, and in his displeasure bring calamities upon them. They also believe in an evil spirit, whom they call *cinim keneki meohōt cinmocimo ;* that is, the black chief below, who is the author of all the evils which befall them, undeserved as a punishment from the Great Spirit above. They believe that the soul enters the future world with a similar form, and in circumstances like those under which it existed in this life. They believe that in a future state, the happiness of the good consists in an abundance and enjoyment of those things which they value here, that their present sources of happiness will be carried to perfection ; and that the punishment of the bad will consist in entire exclusion from every source of happiness, and in finding all causes of misery here, greatly multiplied hereafter. Thus their ideas of future happiness and misery are found to vary according to their different situations and employments in life. It is difficult, if not impossible, to ascertain any thing of their religious belief beyond these general notions. The number of words and terms in their language expressive of abstract and spiritual ideas, is very small, so that those who wish to instruct them in these subjects, are compelled to do it by

means of illustrations and circumlocutions, and the introduction of words from foreign languages. Besides, conscious of their ignorance, they are, for the most part, unwilling to expose it, by revealing the little knowledge which
they possess. Indeed, wherever a feeling of ignorance upon
any subject prevails, we find that all endeavors to elicit the
true amount of knowledge, are repelled or evaded. Even
men of talents, with us, who converse fluently upon most
subjects, are often silent when religious topics are introduced.

I am far from believing the many long and strange traditions, with which we are often entertained. It is more
than probable, that they are in *most* instances the gratuitous offerings of designing and artful traders and hunters to
that curiosity, which is ever awake and attentive to subjects of this description. The Indians themselves would
often be as much surprised at the rehearsal of these traditions, as those are for whose amusement they are fabricated.
My own opinion is confirmed by that of several gentlemen
of integrity and veracity, who stand at the head of the Hudson Bay Company, who have long been resident in the Indian country, and have become extensively acquainted with
their languages.

The Indians west of the great chain of mountains, have
no wars among themselves, and appear to be averse to
them, and do not enter into battle except in self-defense,
and then only in the last extremity. Their only wars are
with the Blackfeet Indians, whose country is along the east
border of the Rocky Mountains, and who are constantly
roving about in war parties, on both sides, in quest of plunder. When the Indians on the west meet with any of these
parties, they avoid an encounter if possible, but if compelled

to fight, they show a firm, undaunted, unconquerable spirit,
and rush upon their enemies with the greatest impetuosity;
and it is said that one Nez Percé, or Flathead warrior, is a
match for three Blackfeet. The only advantage which the
latter have over the former consists in their numbers, there
being more than twenty thousand of the Blackfeet Indians.
When an enemy is discovered, every horse is driven into
camp, and the women take charge of them, while every
man seizes his weapons of war, whatever they may be,
mounts his horse, and waits firm and undismayed to see if
hostilities must ensue. If a battle cannot be avoided, they
rush forward to meet their foes, throwing themselves flat
upon their horses as they draw near, and fire, and wheel,
and reload, and again rush full speed to the second encounter. This is continued until victory is decided, which is as
often by the failure of ammunition, as by the loss of men.
Very frequently, when the Blackfeet see white men with
the Nez Percés or Flatheads, they decline a battle, though
far superior in numbers, knowing that the white men can
furnish a large supply of ammunition; and in such cases
they will raise a white flag, and come in to smoke the pipe
of peace. The Nez Percé or Flathead chief, on such an
occasion, will say " we accept your offer to smoke the pipe
of peace, but it is not in ignorance that your heart is war,
and your hand blood, but we love peace. You give us the
pipe, but blood always follows."

But these Indians are not without their vices. Gambling
is one of the most prominent, and is a ruling passion which
they will gratify to the last extremity. It is much practiced in running horses, and foot races, by men, women and
children, and they have games of chance played with sticks
or bones. When I told the Nez Percés that gambling is

wrong, and a violation of the tenth commandment; for it is coveting the property of another, and taking it without an equivalent, as much as stealing; they said they did not know it before, but now they know God forbids it they will do so no more.   Theft is generally supposed to be inbred in the Indians, but I was pleased to discover that the tribes of the plains held it in abhorrence, and would punish it severely should it occur.   The Shoshones are said to be addicted to this habit in some degree.   Drunkenness is a stranger vice among these nations, their remove from the sources of this evil being their security.   It is not to be supposed that their virtue, any more than that of other tribes, would be invulnerable if exposed to temptation, for this habit, like their proverbial love for finery and ornament, is acquired by the facilities for indulgence which are thrown in their way. The trader goes far into the interior with his packs of beads, buttons, paints, &c., to exchange for furs, and teaches this ignorant people to set the same value on his articles, that theirs are intrinsically worth—but who supposes that they would not know the comparative worth of more useful goods, if they were offered them ?*

The moral disposition of these Indians is very commendable, certainly as much as that of any people that can be named.   They are kind to strangers, and remarkably so to each other.   While among them I saw no contentions, and heard no angry words from one to another.   They manifest an uncommon desire to be instructed that they may obey and fulfil all moral obligations.   Harmony and peace prevail in all their domestic concerns.   But when they have

---

* An attempt was made not long since, by an United States citizen, to construct a distillery on the Willamette river, but for want of suitable materials he failed in his object.

any difficult subject, which they know not how to dispose of, they go to their chiefs, and if it involves any important principle, the chiefs bring the case to any white man, who may be among them, to obtain his opinion, which is generally followed. They are scrupulously honest in all their dealings, and lying is scarcely known. They say they fear to sin against the Great Spirit, and therefore, have but one heart, and their tongue is straight and not forked. And so correctly does the law written upon their hearts accord with the written law of God, that every infraction of the seventh command of the decalogue is punished with severity.

I have witnessed but few things among them indicative of superstition. The practice of the Shoshones of cutting themselves for the dead, I have already mentioned. The Carriers burn their dead. When a person dies, all the relations must be assembled, which often occupies many days ; and if a husband is deceased, the wife must lay her head upon the bosom of her husband every night, to show her affection for him ; and when the funeral pile is constructed, the corpse laid upon it, and the fire enkindled, during the burning of the body, she must frequently put her hands through the flame and lay them upon his bosom, to show her continued affection. Their first chief lost his wife. He was asked if he would show the affection for her, which was required of others. He thought on account of his chieftainship he might be excused. The people were urgent, and he consented, but so great was the pain which he endured, that he was willing the practice should be ameliorated, and it is hoped it will soon be abolished.

They have no unlucky days, but as a substitute for the white man's Friday, they have a portentous howling of a large wolf, which they call the medicine wolf. If they hear this when traveling, sadness is at once visible in their countenances, for it is considered as foreboding some calamity near.

Among their superstitions may be classed their mode of curing diseases. They have what are called medicine* men, who make no pretensions to any knowledge of diseases or skill in medicine ; but they have a bag in which is deposited various relics. The patient is stretched upon the ground ; a number of persons encircle him and sing the medicine song. The medicine man enters the circle and commences his magical incantations by holding the medicine bag over him, which is to operate as a charm; he uses many gestures, grimaces, and inarticulate sounds ; pats or kneads the patient with his hands, beginning very softly, and gradually increasing to a considerable degree of severity ; blows into his ears, and practices other like ceremonies. By this process the patient is often much fatigued, and thrown into a free perspiration, and his imagination is much excited. When the friction has been sufficiently employed, the imagination well wrought upon, and the medicine bag has invisibly imparted its virtues, the medicine man presents some trifling article, such as a small bone, a stick, or pebble, and says he has taken it from the body of the patient, and that it was the cause of the disease ; or he gives a heavy puff upward, and says the disease has come out of the patient and gone upward, and then asks him if he does not feel better. The patient says yes ; for he certainly feels better in being relieved from the process. And often the relief is permanent ; for the friction may have been beneficial, and the imagination often performs wonders. The medicine man stands respon-

---

* The word *medicine*, as used by Indians, signifies any thing mysterious.

sible for the life of his patient, and if the patient dies, not unfrequently his own life is taken by some of the relatives of the deceased. He makes a heavy charge for his services, often a horse, and why should he not ? for who in such cases would endanger his life without being well paid ? In some parts of the country, but more especially in the lower country, the lives of medicine men are short, and it would be supposed this would deter others from entering into the profession. But the love of fame and wealth is powerful among heathen as well as among civilized communities. Undoubtedly the medicine men, when they begin their profession, know that they are practicing deception, but by habitual deceit, by the confidence others place in their skill, and by the effects produced through the medium of the imagination, they finally believe in the efficacy of their own enchantments, and that they are consequential men.

I have seen no " root doctors " in any tribe east or west of the mountains. The Indians, so far as I have had an opportunity of ascertaining, have but few diseases, and for the cure of these, they use but little medicine ; nor do they profess to have any knowledge of remedies beyond a few specifics.

The warm bath is used both by sick and healthy persons in the following manner. They construct a steam bath in the form of an oblong oven, two or three feet high, about six feet long, made of willow branches, each end inserted into the ground, forming an arch, which is covered with grass and mud, or more generally with skins. In this they place a number of hot stones, upon which they pour water. The person who is to go through the process, enters and is enclosed nearly air tight, and remains until a very profuse perspiration is produced, and often until nearly suffocated.

He then comes out and plunges at once into cold water, and no regard is paid to the season of the year, whether summer or winter.

They are wholly destitute of the means of obtaining an education, and therefore are ignorant of all the sciences. In things with which they are conversant, such as appertain to hunting, war, and their limited domestic concerns, they manifest observation, skill, and intellect; but beyond these their knowledge is very limited. They necessarily compute by numbers, but their arithmetic is entirely mental. It is an interesting fact, that of four different languages, which I examined, the mode of counting is by tens.

The Klicatat nation count with different words up to ten, *Lah's*, one; *neep't*, two; and so to ten; then they add *wappena* to *lah's;* as *lah's wappena*, eleven; *neep't wappena*, twelve; *neep't tit*, twenty; and in like manner to one hundred, and so on to a thousand by hundreds. In the Nez Percé language, *nox* is one, *lapeet*, two, *metait*, three, &c. After ten they repeat the radical numbers with the addition, *tit*, as *noxtit*, eleven; *laaptit*, twenty; *metaptit*, thirty. This may be a sufficient specimen for the four languages, as the other two proceed in the same manner.

They count their years by snows; as, *maika elaix*, snows six, that is, six years; and months by moons, and days by sleeps; *pinemeek pe-e-lep*, sleeps four, (four days.) It is not common that they know their exact age; nor are they very accurate in chronology.

They are very fond of singing, and generally have flexible and sweet-toned voices. Most of their singing is without words, excepting upon some special occasions. They use *hi*, *ah*, in constant repetition, as we use fa, sol, la; and instead of several different parts harmonizing, they only take eighths, one above another, never exceeding three. They are conscious of the inferiority of their tunes to ours, and wished to be instructed in this department of knowledge. In this land of moral desolations, it was cheering to hear even the most simple strains of melody and harmony.

CHAPTER XVII.

The Indians of the lower country.

THE Indians of the lower country are those between the shores of the Pacific and the Falls of the Columbia river, and from Pugets Sound to upper California.   The principal nations are the Chenooks, the Klicatats, the Callapooahs, and the Umbaquâs.   These nations are divided into a great number of tribes, which have their respective chiefs, yet each nation has its principal chief, who is head over all the several tribes, and has a general superintending control. Their persons are rather below a middle stature, and not generally as well formed as the Indians of the plains or up- per country.   The women are uncouth, and from a com- bination of causes appear old at an early age.   Among these causes the habit of painting, in which they indulge, destroys the smooth and healthy appearance of the skin.

These Indians appear to have less sensibility, both phys- ical and moral, than those of the upper country.   Their dependence for subsistence being mostly confined to fishing and fowling, they are not so well supplied with clothing as the upper Indians, who hunt the buffalo, the elk, the ante- lope and other game.   The lower Indians obtain some game, and clothing from the posts of the Hudson Bay Com- pany.   I have often seen them going about, half naked, when the thermometer ranged between thirty and forty de- grees, and their children barefooted and barelegged in the snow ; and yet when exposed to fatigue, they cannot endure

the intensity of the season as well as civilized people.   I
have noticed this, when I have had them employed in con-
veying me any considerable distance in a canoe.   Their
taste and smelling are obtuse, rendered so by their filthy
habits and contaminated food.   But they are quick to catch
correctly a distant sound, and remarkably keen-sighted,
acquired by their habits of closely and carefully watching
for game.   These nations being, from their mode of subsistence, more stationary than those of the plains, have more
durable and comfortable habitations, which are built of split
plank, after the manner of Wanaxka's, near the falls of the
Willamette, which I have described.   Some of them indulge
the fancy of making their doors like the face of a man, the
mouth being the place of entrance.

The lower Indians do not dress as well, nor with as good
taste, as the upper.   Their robes are much shorter, and are
made of inferior materials ; such as deer skins with the hair
on, and skins of hares and of squirrels.   I saw many women
of the poorer class, dressed in a short petticoat or skirt,
made of cedar bark, or a species of strong grass twisted
into strands, one end of which is secured in a girdle or band
to the waist, while the other is suspended, knotted and
fringed.   These are a substitute for cloth, which they are
too poor to obtain.   The nations near the ocean, who have
intercourse with sailors, and access to ardent spirits, are as
degraded as those on our frontiers, and from the same causes.
By their communication with those who furnish them with
the means of intoxication, and who have introduced kindred
vices, they have become indolent and extremely filthy in their
habits, and more debased than the beasts of the earth.   How
perfectly neat are the deer and the antelope ; how industrious the beaver and the bee ; how cleanly is the plumage

of the bird ; how well adapted to repose are their habitations ; in a word, how different are all their habits, from
those of fallen, polluted man.   It is not the want of rational
powers, but their abuse by sin which has thus degraded
him, and nothing but Christianity can bring him back to
God, and the comforts and decencies of life.

The want of moral instruction, the influence of bad examples, and unrestrained licentiousness, have brought the
lower Indians into a state of wretchedness which will be en-
tailed upon future generations, and which nothing but the
healing power of the gospel can ever eradicate.   There
are some exceptions, but not enough to save these remnants
of once populous nations, if benevolence and humanity do
not soon break their slumbers.   It is to be hoped the missionaries, now in the field, by the blessing of God, will interpose a barrier to these sweeping desolations.

In their religious belief, they do not materially differ from
the upper Indians.   While they believe in one Great Spirit,
they in addition believe in subordinate spirits, or invisible
agencies, to whom they ascribe much the same power as
has been ascribed to witchcraft.   We had a specimen of
this, when the May Dacre was passing down the river in
October.   On the north side of the Columbia, near the confluence of the Cowalitz, there are some dark recesses in
the basaltic rocks.   An Indian chief on board warned Capt.
L. not to approach those dark places ; for they were the
residence of bad spirits who would destroy the ship and all
on board.   Capt. L. purposely passed near the place ; and
the Indian was astonished that we escaped unhurt, and concluded there must have been some great "medicine" in the
ship which defended us.   They believe in the immortality
of the soul, and that in the future state we shall have the

same wants as in this life.   Under the influence of this belief, the wife of Calpo, an influential chief of the Chenook
village near Cape Disappointment, on losing a daughter in
the year 1829, killed two female slaves to attend her to the
world of spirits, and for the particular purpose of rowing
her canoe to the far off happy regions of the south, where
they locate their imaginary elysium.   She deposited her
daughter, with the two slain females by her side in a canoe,
with articles of clothing and domestic implements.   She
was the daughter of Concomly, and a woman of distinguished
talents and respectability, a firm friend of white men, and
had more than once saved them from death.   How dark was
the mind of this talented woman, and how differently would
she have conducted under the influence of divine revelation !
These Indians never mention the name of their relatives
after they are dead.

It is only in the lower country of the Oregon Territory,
and along the coast that slavery exists.   It was formerly
practiced in the upper country, but was long since abolished.
The Walla Walla tribe are descended from slaves formerly
owned and liberated by the Nez Percé Indians.   They permitted, as I have stated above, their slaves to reside and to
intermarry in their families, and reasoning on the principles of natural justice, they concluded that it was not right
to hold in slavery their own descendants, and liberated them,
and they are now a respectable tribe.

Gambling is also practiced among the lower Indians, and
carried to perfection.   After they have lost every thing
they possess, they will put themselves at stake; first a hand,
and if unsuccessful, the other; after this an arm, and in the
same manner, piece by piece, until all is lost except the head,
and at last their head; and if they lose this, they go into

perpetual slavery. If civilized men *will* gamble, it is desirable they should carry gaming to the same perfection ; for then they would cease to be pests in society, and however different may be our sentiments upon the subject of slavery, in this we should generally be agreed, that such slaves would not deserve much commiseration. The Indians, however, do not set their souls at the hazard of the game, as civilized gamblers do, when they imprecate the eternal vengeance of God upon themselves if they are not successful. The Indian gambles away his inalienable rights for time only.

It is a universal practice to indulge in smoking, but they do it in a dignified manner. They use but little tobacco, and with it they mix freely a plant which renders the fume less offensive. It is a social luxury, and for its enjoyment they form a circle, using only one pipe. The principal chief begins by drawing three whiffs, the first of which he sends upward, and then passes the pipe to the next person in dignity, and in like manner it passes around until it comes to the first chief again. He then draws four whiffs, the last of which he blows through his nose in two columns, in circling ascent, like a double-flued chimney. While thus employed, some topic of business is discussed, or some exploit in the chase, or some story of the battle-field, is related ; and the whole is conducted with gravity. Their pipes are variously constructed, and of different materials. Some of them are wrought with much labor and ingenuity of an argillaceous stone, of very fine texture, of a blue black color, found at the north of Queen Charlotte's island. It is the same kind of stone except in color, as that found upon the head waters of the Missouri, which is brick red. These stones, when first taken out of the quarries, are soft and easily worked with a knife, but on being exposed to the air, become hard, and are susceptible of a very good polish.

The Indians in the lower country are more indolent than in the upper ; and the common motives for industry operate reversely from those in civilized communities.   The more they can get for their labor, the less they will do ; the more they can get for an article in sale, the less they will bring into market.   Their wants are but few, and when these are supplied, they will do no more.   They have no disposition to hoard up treasures, nor any enlarged plans to execute, requiring expense and labor.   If they have any particular present want to supply, they will do what is sufficient to satisfy it, and make no farther effort until urged by a returning necessity.   To make them industrious and provident, you must induce them to set a higher estimate upon the comforts of life, and show them that they are attainable, and that there is an increase of happiness growing out of industry ; and all this must be learned by experience, for abstract reasoning and theories are of no avail.   An Indian may be taken abroad and instructed, and convinced of the advantages of civilization, but if sent back to his country alone, he will become discouraged, and return to his former habits.   Missionaries, and practical farmers, and artisans, must go among them, and make it the business of their lives to do them good, and identify their own interests with theirs.   Charging them with indolence, and insensibility, and cruelty, will never make them wiser or better.   He is the true philanthropist, who, instead of passing by on the other side, goes to them, and does all in his power to raise them from their degradation, and bring them to God and to heaven.

The Indians of the lower country, although less anxious

to be instructed in the things of religion, than those of the upper country, express a readiness to receive instructors. I have not found among them, nor any Indians beyond the influence of frontier settlements, any thing like what has been stated to have taken place in other sections of our country : that they will listen to statements made by missionaries, and give their assent to what is said as very good; and then state their own theories of religion, expecting the same courteous assent in return. Neither have I seen any disposition manifested, to say that the Christian religion is good for white men, but as red men differ, they need a different religion and mode of life. They have not yet been instigated by infidels to say such things. They are conscious of their ignorance of God and salvation, and of the various arts and sciences. While an indifference and apathy characterize some, which is discouraging, yet I know of no insuperable obstacles to their improvement.

While gratitude is a general characteristic of Indians, they have in some cases their peculiar way of expressing it. An Indian had a son laboring for a long time under a lingering and dangerous complaint. Their medicine men had done all they could for him, but without success. The father brought his son to the hospital at Fort Vancouver, and earnestly desired to have him treated with care and with the best medical attendance. The sick son was received, and in about six months was restored to health. When his father came to take him home, he remarked to Dr. McL. " My son is a good boy, he has been with you a long time, and I think you must love him ; and now as he is about to leave you, will you not give him a blanket and shirt, and as many other small things as you think will be good? We shall always love you."

The lower Indians " make their medicine," in some particulars, differently from those farther east. Their professed objects are to obtain present relief, if not a radical cure; to make his exit more easy if the patient dies, and that his soul may be rendered capable of performing its journey to its far distant and happy country, and also to assuage the sorrow of surviving relatives. The process is simple, and occupies five or six hours. The patient is laid upon a bed of mats and blankets, sometimes a little elevated, and surrounded by a frame work. Two " medicine men" place themselves upon this frame, and commence a chant in low long-drawn tones, each holding a wand in his hand, three or four feet long, with which they beat upon the frame, keeping time with their tune. They gradually increase the loudness and the movement of their medicine song, with a correspondent use of their wand, until the noise becomes almost deafening, and undoubtedly often hurries the patient out of the world. During this time the near relations affect indifference to the condition of the sick person, lest their anxiety should counteract the influence of the charm, and they are generally employed about their common business, the women in making mats, baskets, and moccasons; and the men lolling about, smoking, or conversing upon common subjects. In some cases, especially if their confidence in the medicine man is small, they manifest much affliction and concern ; and in all cases after the person dies, they make great lamentation.

I have already mentioned the practice of the lower nations of flattening their heads and piercing their noses. But another reported custom, of having pieces of sea-horse's tusks, or oval pieces of wood an inch and a half long and an inch wide, inserted into a hole in their under lip, made for the purpose, is not correct in regard to any of the Indians in this section of country. Captain Beechy mentions it as a common practice from Norton's island and northward; which was noticed by Deshnow, as long ago as 1648, that this ornament was worn by men and women about Prince William's sound, and which custom, Captain B. says, is common the whole distance along the western shores of America, as far as California. I saw some specimens of this ornament, or rather deformity, which were worn by the natives at Millbank Sound.

The wealth of the lower Indians is estimated by the number of their wives, slaves, and canoes. Every Indian of any distinction takes as many wives as he is able to support, and his wealth is supposed to accord with the number. They are quite destitute of horses, and their almost only mode of traveling is in canoes; for the forests are so dense that they are nearly impenetrable, and they do not construct any roads. As the upper Indians excel in horsemanship, so these excel in the management of canoes, which are uncommonly well made, and of various sizes, from twelve to thirty feet long; the largest will carry as much as a good bateau. They are generally made of the fir tree. The bow and stern are raised high, so as to meet and ward off the boisterous waves, and the bow is sometimes decorated with figures of animals, and the upper edge of the canoe is ornamented with shells. Slaves are employed in propelling the canoes, but not exclusively; for often the chiefs will perform their part of the labor, and the women are equally expert with the men.

Their manufactures do not widely differ from those of the upper country, with the addition of hats and baskets of skilful workmanship, made of grass of superior quality, equal

to the Leghorn. The native hats are a flaring cone. Their
baskets are worked so closely as to hold water, and are
used for pails. Some of them are interwoven with various
colors and devices, fancifully representing men, horses, and
flowers.

The government of the Indian nations is in the hands of
chiefs, whose office is hereditary, or obtained by some special merit. Their only power is influence; and this in
proportion to their wisdom, benevolence, and courage.
They do not exercise authority by command, but influence
by persuasion, stating what in their judgment they believe
to be right and for the greatest good of their tribe or nation,
or of any family or community. The chiefs have no power of levying taxes, and they are so much in the habit of
contributing their own property for individual or public
good, that they are not generally wealthy. Their influence
however is great; for they rarely express an opinion or desire, which is not readily assented to and followed. Any
unreasonable dissent is subdued by the common voice of
the people. Probably there is no government upon earth
where there is so much personal and political freedom, and
at the same time so little anarchy; and I can unhesitatingly
say, that I have nowhere witnessed so much subordination,
peace, friendship, and confidence as exist among the Indians, in the Oregon Territory. The day may be rued, when
their order and harmony shall be interrupted by any instru-
mentality whatever.

There are exceptions, however, to the general fact of the
good conduct of the chiefs and the respect which is given
them. Cazenove, the first chief of the Chenook nation, is
one. He was a great warrior, and before the desolating
sickness, which commenced in the year 1829, could bring

a thousand warriors into action. He is a man of talents, and his personal appearance is noble, and ought to represent a nature kind and generous; but such is his character, that his influence is retained among his people more by fear than by affection. I saw him often, and several times at my room, while at Fort Vancouver. On Tuesday, February 2d, I attended the funeral of his only son, the heir to his chieftainship, a young man who had lingered under a protracted disease. Cazenove departed from the long established custom of his nation and fathers of depositing the dead in canoes, and had him buried in the cemetery of the Fort, in the decent manner of civilized people. He had the coffin made large for the purpose of putting into it clothing, blankets, and such other articles, as he supposed necessary for the comfort of his son in the world to which he was gone. Every thing connected with the ceremony of the interment was conducted with great propriety. I was not at the time furnished with an interpreter, but addressed those present who understood English. Cazenove expressed his satisfaction that an address was given, considering it a token of respect for his son; and appeared solemn in his affliction, indulging tears only, and not any loud lamentations. Had he conducted with equal propriety subsequently, he would have been worthy of commendation. But when he returned to his dwelling that evening, he attempted to kill the mother of this deceased son, who was the daughter of Concomly, and formerly the wife of Mr. McDougal. The chiefs say, that they and their sons are too great to die of themselves, and although they may be sick, and decline, and die, as others do, yet some person, or some evil spirit instigated by some one, is the invisible cause of their death; and therefore when a chief, or chief's son dies, the supposed author of the deed must be killed.   Cazenove, on this occasion, fixed on the mother of this son as the victim of his rage, notwithstanding she had been most assiduous in her attention to him, during his protracted sickness.   Of his several wives, she was the most beloved, and his misguided mind led him to believe, that the greater the sacrifice, the greater the manifestation of his attachment to his son, and the more propitiatory to his departed spirit.   She fled into the woods, and the next morning, when the gates were opened, came into this fort and implored protection. She was secreted here several days, until her friends at Chenook Bay heard of her situation, and came and secretly took her away.   Some days after this, a woman was found killed by the hand of violence, and it was supposed to have been done by Cazenove or some one in his employ.

CHAPTER XVIII.

Conversation with an intelligent Indian—meeting with Indians—
early and mild season—La Dalles Indians—their anxiety to receive
the gospel—Nootka humming bird—number and location of the
Indians in the lower country—Indians of the north—the agitated
question—solitariness.

A VERY intelligent and influential Indian from the Cascades called at my room, on the 8th of February, to enquire about God.   I endeavored to obtain from him his own
system of religion.   He said, he believed there is a God,
and he supposed he made all things, but he did not know
any thing more about him.   I questioned him in regard to
his belief of a future state, and what he expected would become of him when he died.   He said he did not know.   He
supposed that he should have an existence after death, but
did not know what it would be ; and wished me to tell him.
I endeavored to enlighten his mind, and to unfold to him
the great fundamental truths of God and eternity, and the
way to be saved.   He listened with attention, and appeared
sober.   He told me the Indians were growing better ; that
they did not kill each other in wars as in times past ; that
they did not rob and steal as heretofore.   I told him that
was good, but to be saved they must repent and receive the
Savior by faith, as the only hope for sinners.   So benighted
are the minds of these heathen, and so barren their language upon spiritual and invisible subjects, that I had to
use such illustrations as I judged best adapted to convey

truth to his mind, and I doubt not that he received some knowledge.

The next day he called again, and wished me to take his children and teach them how to read and write, and to worship God. I endeavored to explain to him the object of my tour, and that when I returned I would use my influence to have others come and live among them. But he wanted me to continue with them and instruct them. And when I told him I must go, and endeavor to get several to come and teach in different tribes, he wished to know how many sleeps it would take me to go, and how many sleeps before others would come. I told him it would be a great number. He wished to know if it would be moons. I answered in the affirmative, and told him it would be at least two snows. He paused and looked sorrowful. His very look affected me ; he arose and went out.

Sabbath, 14th. I attended service as usual in English. There were many Indians from the La Dalles who wished to know if they might be present. We told them there would not be sufficient room in the hall, but a few of their chiefs might attend, and after the English service I would meet with them ; which I accordingly did in the afternoon.

They were punctual at the hour, and came in single file, the first chief leading the way. When I prayed with them, they all kneeled down except two or three, and these were reprimanded by the chief for impropriety of conduct. As on other similar occasions, I endeavored to instruct them in the first principles of our revealed religion, to which they gave strict attention. The first chief, at the close of service wished to speak ; and on receiving permission, spoke a short time to his people, and then told me he had prayed much to the Great Spirit, and found his heart was no better, but worse. He said, a white man gave them a flag, and told them to set it up on a pole, on Sundays, and meet and pray, sing their songs, and dance around the pole bearing the flag; and that they had done so a long time. He wished to know if it was right,* I told him it was right to meet and pray, and sing, and talk about God, but to dance on the Sabbath was very wrong, and would offend God. I added farther, that they needed some person to teach them the right way to worship God and to be saved. He was affected, and kneeled down and with tears in his eyes said, if you must go away, do send us some one to teach us the right way to serve God. We will now throw away what the man said to us about dancing. We will go to our people and tell them what you have said, and worship God as you have taught us. I never felt so much like weeping over the heathen, as on this occasion ; to see this poor benighted Indian chief upon his knees, with tears in his eyes pleading for some one to come and teach them the way to heaven. What a spectacle!

March 1st. We have many indications of the presence of spring. The mildness of the climate, and the soft temperature of the season west of the mountains, render it one of the most delightful portions of our continent. The wide and sudden extremes of heat and cold, to which the eastern portions are subject, are almost unknown here, and while this is more agreeable, it is also more favorable to health. Those who have the charge of the farming establishment at this place, have commenced sowing thus early

---

* The reason assigned for including dancing in the services of the holy Sabbath, was the fear, that singing and praying without dancing, would not interest the Indians ; and to include it would not be so great a departure from their common practices, as to excite aversion to worship.

their spring crops; and the gardener is preparing his ground for the seeds. The grass in the yard begins to assume its beautiful, fresh green. The robin and blackbird have continued here through the winter, and now, with some others of their feathered brethren, resume their cheerful warblings in the fields and groves. During the winter, the thermometer has not fallen below 22° Fahrenheit, and to this point only three days. At this date, it stood at sunrise, at 37°; at noon, 46°; and at sunset, at 44°. The rains through the winter have been less constant and heavy than I anticipated; and snow has fallen only ten days, sometimes in trifling quantities, and at no one time over the depth of six inches, and has remained on the ground only a few days. Some have supposed, that the genial climate of the Oregon Territory is attributable to the proximity of the great Pacific, shedding the influence of its soft winds far into the interior. But the fact is, that almost the only winds through the winter are easterly winds, consequently coming direct from the regions of perpetual snow.

A number of the La Dalles Indians arrived to-day, who reside eighty miles distant. One of their chiefs stated to my friend Mr. T. that they had changed their mode of worship; that they do not now dance on the Sabbath, as they used to do, but they meet and sing, and pray; and that since they have been better acquainted with the way to worship God, He hears their prayers, and that now, when they and their wives and children are hungry, they pray for deer, and go out to hunt, and God sends them deer to satisfy their wants. It was interesting to know that they were disposed to do, as well as listen to what is taught them.

Sabbath, 13th. Besides the usual service in the hall in

English, I met the Indians from the La Dalles, and endeavored to exhibit to them the great truths of the Bible. They listened with deep interest to what I said, and then enquired whether they might expect, after I should go away, that some one would come and teach them. I could not promise, but replied, that I hoped it would not be more than two snows, before some one would be sent. They enquired if after one or two sleeps, I would let them come to my room and hear more about God. I appointed to meet them on Tuesday afternoon, and spoke with them several succeeding times before their departure.

It seems apparent to any observing Christian, that the present is the favorable time for the introduction of the gospel and civilization among the natives of this wide interior. Soon the cupidity and avarice of men will make aggressions here, and the deadly influence of frontier vices will interpose a barrier to the religion which they now are so anxious to embrace and practice. Every circumstance combines to point out the time when this work should begin, and one of the most important is that these Indians are enlisted in favor of white men, and feel that their condition, in all respects, for this world, as well as the coming one, is better than their own. A well-established Christian influence among these tribes, would surely be respected by those who otherwise would invade their rights, and deprive them of a home as dear to them as our own is to us.

March 24th. The season is progressing in delightful mildness. Flowering shrubbery and plants are beginning to send forth their fragrance ; and the Nootka humming bird has arrived, and is seen darting from bush to bush, feeding upon the open flowers. This most splendid species is not known east of the mountains. The whole of the upper part of the body is rufous, the head greenish, the throat cupreous and metalloidal crimson, varying according to the incidence of light. The throat of this species resembles that of the common, except, that it is even more gorgeous in its colors, and in presenting the metallic feathers, forms a broad ruff in the inferior part of the neck, instead of being wholly a component part of the plumage. The swallows made their appearance on the 12th, and a new species of blue bird of uncommonly beautiful plumage, arrived on the 14th. The swan, several species of geese, and the sand hill crane, are passing to the north for incubation. Their screaming notes are constantly heard, and in the night are not the most favorable to repose.

Before leaving the lower country, it will be proper to present, in a connected view, the best information I have been able to obtain of the several nations, their locations, and numbers. There are several tribes, about whom my knowledge is too limited to make any definite statements. Among them are those about Pugets Sound, and the upper part of the Cowalitz ; also the Chiltz Indians, north of the mouth of the Columbia and Chealis rivers. And although I have seen many of the Klicatat nation, who reside at the north of the Cascades, yet I have not been able to learn of them any thing more definite, than that they are a large nation. The Chenook nation resides along upon the Columbia river, from the Cascades to its confluence with the ocean, and though once numerous and powerful, now number not more than fifteen hundred, or two thousand.*

The Calapooah nation are located south of the Chenooks, upon the Willamette river and its branches. They are di-

* Five persons are the supposed number of a family. The number of families is ascertained by their number of lodges or dwellings.

vided into seventeen different tribes, under their respective
chiefs, and number about eight thousand seven hundred and
eighty persons, who speak the same language, radically,
with only a little difference in dialect.   They are scattered
over a territory of two hundred miles north and south, and
sixty east and west.   Their country is uncommonly good.

South of the Calapooah is the Umbaquâ nation, residing
in a valley of the same name.   They are divided into six
tribes ; the Sconta, Chalula, Palakahu, Quattamya, and
Chastà.   Their number is about seven thousand.   South of
this nation and north of California, there was a very powerful nation called the Kinclá, which before the year 1829,
numbered four thousand warriors.   But if they have been
swept away by sickness, as the other nations of the lower
country have, it is probable their whole number of men,
women and children, would not now amount to more than
eight thousand.

Near the mouth of the Columbia, along the coast, are the
Killamooks, who are numerous, but their numbers are not
known.   South of these, and at the mouth of the Umbaquâ
river, there are the Saliûtla, and two other tribes, supposed
to number 2000 persons.

This estimate of the Indians, in the lower country, makes
the number of those known, to be about twenty-five thousand.   This is probably a low estimate.   It may safely be
concluded, from facts now collected, that there are, between
the 42° and 47° north latitude, in what we term the lower
country, as many as twenty-five thousand more, making
fifty thousand, who probably at the present moment would
gladly receive teachers.

Gentlemen of the Hudson Bay Company gave the following statements of the numbers of Indians north of Pugets

Sound, viz. at Millbank Sound, three tribes, numbering two thousand one hundred and eighty-six. At Hygàna Harbor, five tribes or bands, amounting to two thousand ninety-two. At Queen Charlottes Island, eleven tribes, numbering eight thousand six hundred persons. About Hanaga and Chatham Straits, there are nine tribes, containing six thousand one hundred and sixty persons. Making the whole number of inhabitants, at and about these places, between the 47° and 55° of north latitude, nineteen thousand thirty-eight. At Queen Charlottes Island there is a field of much promise for a missionary station, where the necessaries of life could be easily obtained, and for that high northern latitude, the climate is very mild.

Their summer and winter residences are built of split plank, similar to those of the Chenooks. It is said they are well supplied with fish, fowl, oil, berries, and potatoes of superior quality and in great abundance; and wild meat is sometimes obtained. Their dress is much the same as what has already been described. Polygamy prevails, and also slavery. They do not treat their slaves with as much kindness as the Indians in the lower country of the Oregon Territory treat theirs. When they kill their slaves, the loss of property is the only thing they regard. Sometimes, when one chief becomes offended with another, instead of challenging him to a duel, he goes home and kills a number of slaves, and challenges the other to kill as many. The challenged person, if he can, kills as many or more, and notifies the challenger of the number; and thus they proceed until one or the other gains the victory ; and the one who yields in this mode of combat ceases to be a gentleman. "The point of honor" with these barbarous gentry is fixed higher than in our Christian country, for here the

life of *one* satisfies the powerful principle, but there, blood
must flow profusely to quench the noble fire of high minded
revenge.   They are not unfrequently engaged in wars,
which are often very bloody.

They are much addicted to gambling, and dancing; and
it is said they excel in singing.   The country is mountainous, and is generally covered with dense forests, consisting
mostly of fir.

On and about McKenzie river there are six tribes of Indians, making a population of about four thousand two
hundred and seventy-five.   The climate is very cold and
unpleasant ; but uninviting as it is, the Hudson Bay Company have found men who are willing to reside there in sufficient numbers to make *six establishments*, for the purpose
of obtaining the peltries which the Indians collect.   Their
principal establishment, which is Fort Simpson, is on the
upper part of the river and is a place of much resort for
the Indians.

March 26th.   Rode down once more to the lower plains,
as they are called, and was delighted with the freshness of
the wheat fields, which are beginning to wave in the gentle
breezes, and the forest trees are beginning to show their
leaves, and their plants their flowers.   The sea fowl, which
through the winter covered these fields, are gone to their
summer residences, and the little feathered tribes are tuning
their notes, so full of melody.

The question, to whom does this country belong, has
been, and is becoming still more, a question of general interest, both in Great Britain and the United States.   The
aboriginal population claim it as their own, and say, they

merely permit white men to reside among them. Before
the first discovery of the noble river, which in itself and
its branches waters almost the whole territory, these natives had undisputed possession. But their claim is labori-
ously, extensively, and practically denied ; for authorities,
both of written law, and the opinion of living judges and
expositors of law, sanction the principle that "unsettled
habitation is not true and legal possession, and that nations
who inhabit fertile countries and disdain or refuse to cultivate them, deserve to be extirpated." It is made, then, a
question of enquiry, whose claim to this region is best established ? Our government claim exclusive dominion
against any foreign power, of all the country lying between
the 42nd and 49th degrees of north latitude, by treaties with
nations who claim possessions contiguous, and who have
relinquished their claims to the country included in the
the above parallels of latitude, except Great Britain ; by the
discovery of the principal river by Capt. Gray of the ship
Columbia, the 14th of May, 1792; and by interior exploration. Great Britain claims the Columbia river for her
southern boundary, by right of discovery. Capt. Broughton, of the ship Chatham, having ascended the river with
two boats, as far as where Fort Vancouver is now situated,
took possession of the river and country in the name of his
Britannic Majesty, on the 31st of October, 1792. Capt.
Broughton was associated with Capt. Vancouver of the ship
Discovery, on a voyage of discovery in the north Pacific, and
around the world. The possession was taken in his Britannic Majesty's name in due form. A friendly old chief,
who did not understand a word of their language, nor they
a word of his, was invited to join in the ceremony, and to
drink his Majesty's health. Captain Broughton says the

chief appeared much pleased with the transaction. But it may be a subject of enquiry, with which the old friendly chief was best pleased, the rum he drank on the occasion, or with the ceremony which was so full of import. And farther, did the chief, by partaking of his Majesty's rum and joining in the ceremony, cede all this country to be the *bona fide* property of a foreign nation ? Still Great Britain " does not set up any claim of exclusive jurisdiction or sovereignty therein, and denies the claim of the United States to any such sovereign jurisdiction," but professes to claim for its subjects the right of joint occupancy, indefinitely deferring the settlement of the question of exclusive dominion. But these intricate questions, so often asked, I leave to learned diplomatists to decide, after confessing that I am not able to discover why the nations who have, from time immemorial, occupied this country, and who, like other nations, have their territorial limits tolerably well defined among themselves, should not still possess the domain which our common Creator and Benefactor has kindly given them.

The time has arrived when I expect to resume the work of further exploration. The weeks and months which I have spent here have fled rapidly away, while I have been feebly endeavoring during the winter to benefit the people of the fort, and the Indians ; and to embrace all the opportunities that should present, to collect information in those particulars which pertain to the direct object of my tour. I shall wander for a length of time, yet future, among the wild scenes of nature, which have so gratified and delighted me in traversing the wilderness of forest and prairie ; but my heart looks back to a variety of interesting scenes of civilized life and cultivated society in my own far distant land, and I ardently desire to see the wide region before me brought under the same beauty and cultivation. All the social affections of our nature strongly desire the happiness, which refined and Christian society and its concomitant blessings can alone give. A feeling of solitariness, and of desolation comes over the mind as you stand on the banks of the noble Columbia, and perhaps for weeks, it may be for months, no whitened sail becomes visible to the gaze of your watching eye. At length a ship enters its waters, and the Indians hasten fifty miles to tell you that the white man's great canoe, with its three upright sticks, is on its way, to bring a new supply of blankets, beads, and tobacco. The most unimportant incidents become interesting events, where so much monotony exists.

Monday, 11th April. Having made arrangements to leave this place on the 14th, I called upon the chief clerk for my bill. He said the Company felt a pleasure in gratuitously conferring all they have done, for the benefit of the object in which I am engaged. In justice to my own feelings, and in gratitude to the honorable Company, I would bear testimony to their uniform politeness and generosity ; and while I do this, I would express my anxiety for their salvation, and that they may be rewarded in spiritual blessings. In addition to the civilities I had received as a guest, I had drawn upon their store for clothing, for goods to pay my Indians, whom I had employed to convey me in canoes, in my various journeyings, hundreds of miles ; to pay my guides and interpreters ; and upon their provision store for the support of these men while in my employ.

CHAPTER XIX.

APRIL 14th. Having exchanged farewells with the gentlemen of the fort, whose kindness I shall ever remember, I took passage in a canoe of an Indian chief belonging to the La Dalles. Our company consisted of the chief and his daughter, another Indian who took the bow, a half-blood, named Baptiste, who took the stern, and two white men, who, with the chief, helped to propel the canoe, making seven persons. These, with the baggage of several hundred weight, loaded the frail craft so heavily, that its sides were only about seven inches above water. This, upon a river averaging about a mile in width, with many rapids, and subject to winds, was not a pleasant undertaking. But at this season of the year, when the Indians are about to commence fishing, another canoe could not be obtained.

We proceeded up the river about twelve miles, to what are called the upper plains, on the north side of the river, and encamped. This is a rich and beautiful prairie of some miles in circumference, and at this early part of the spring was covered with a coat of fresh green grass five or six inches high. A little back from the river, there is a beautiful lake, the resort of water fowl, which are seen exhibiting their unsullied plumage; and in the rear are forests of fir, whither the deer, which crop the grass of the prairie, flee, when they see men ascend the river's bank. A gathering storm rendered the night dark, cold, and dreary; for as yet no friendly habitations are reared upon these fertile fields for the resort and comfort of man.

The rain continuing with some wind, we did not decamp on the morning of the 15th, until a late hour; after which we passed up into the mountainous part of the country below the Cascades, and encamped near the high Pillar rock which I have mentioned. Soon after leaving our encampment this morning, we met Captain W. with a small company of men in two canoes lashed together, on their way to Fort William upon Wâppatoo island. They were wet with the rain of the morning; and their meagre countenances and tattered garments did not speak much in favor of the happiness of mountain life, or indicate that they had found the hunter's elysium. But they were in good spirits and passed merrily on their way.

The basaltic rocks, which wall up the shores, in some places two and three hundred feet perpendicular, and in this place for miles, do not lose in interest by review. For more than half a mile the basalt presented the regular pentagons. Near these, where the shore was inaccessible, we found a deer almost exhausted with swimming in the cold water. Its helpless condition and its mild, large black eye, excited by fear, pleaded for the exercise of humanity; but our men, instead of rendering it that assistance which it needed, shot it, and stained the pure water of the river with its blood. I could not help feeling a sympathy for this poor, beautiful animal.

While the men, on the morning of the 16th, were engaged in taking the canoe up the rapids and the Cascades, I walked five miles, sometimes along the shore of the river, and sometimes climbing over precipices; and so laborious was the task to get the canoe above all the rapids and falls, that it occupied most of the day, giving me time for examining the scenery around. Almost every variety of volcanic production was seen, but basalt and amygdaloid predominated. Large quantities of petrified wood were scattered along the shores, some of which preserved its natural appearance; but the large blocks, when broken, presented the appearance of mineral coal. The scenery around is grand; yet such was the misty state of the atmosphere about the tops of the mountains, which were at this time covered with snow, and the chilliness accompanying, that the enjoyment was less than it would have been under other circumstances. After having finished the portage by the Cascades, we launched out upon the gentle current above, and proceeding up the river two miles, encamped upon the north side. Several Indians came to our encampment and manifested a kind and sociable disposition. They told us that Captain W. the day before, in *cordelling* his canoes down the Cascades, had lost one, and with it baggage, of which they had found some articles, that they would deliver to him when he should again pass this way. The Indians are coming in from their winter retreats, and are engaged in catching sturgeon.

The 17th being the Sabbath, we did not remove. It was a rainy day, and in the forenoon the rain came down in torrents, which is common about these mountains through the rainy season of the year. We were not able to make a fire for preparing food, until after twelve o'clock, when the storm began to abate.

On Monday the weather was more pleasant, and we made very good progress up the river, through a country of diversified scenery. Though less mountainous than about the Cascades, yet here were mountains of interesting forms; one was almost a perfect cone, a thousand feet high, rising at an angle of 45 degrees, beautifully smooth and covered with grass. We passed, a few miles above this, a bluff presenting a perpendicular semicircle, with fissures regularly radiating from the centre of the diameter. In different places there were red hills of the color of well-burnt brick. We encamped on the north side of the river, upon a pleasant spot just above a small Indian village, where we found a good supply of dry wood, which added to our comfort and convenience.

A wind which blew very fresh through the night, abated on the morning of the 19th, and we proceeded on our way with a gentle breeze, before which we spread a sail made of a blanket. The wind continued to increase until the middle of the day, which rendered navigation rather dangerous. We came to a large bend in the river, and to save the distance of coasting around, the men who rowed wished to pass over to the south side of the river, which was here more than a mile wide. This seemed a dangerous experiment, because the wind and waves were too high for our deep-laden canoe; but as they were anxious to save labor, I did not persist in my objections. We had not passed more than half way across, before the increasing wind raised waves which rolled and broke three times as high as our canoe, and threatened to overwhelm us. At length the men were not able to keep the canoe headed across the waves, and it turned sideways to them. It seemed that nothing short of a miraculous providence could save us. But by much exertion and some abatement of the wind, we again got the canoe upon our course, and across the waves, and safely arrived at the south shore. But our greatest danger was yet before us. After coasting a few miles along the south shore, we came to a promontory called Cape Horn, a name given it on account of the dangers of passing. It is of basaltic formation, rising, as I afterwards found by measurement, two hundred feet perpendicular upon the water's edge, extending about a mile in length, and the lower part projecting several hundred feet into the river. The wind had so far lulled, that we did not apprehend any danger in passing it, but when we had doubled the Cape, the wind drew around and increased to a gale. The foaming, breaking waves ran high, and we could not return against the wind, and to go forward against the current was to add to the danger of being filled, or dashed against shoreless rocks. Such was the force of the wind, and such the efforts of the men to keep the canoe across the waves and away from the rocks, that in the same instant of time, the bowman and steersman both broke their paddles, and the sail was torn away from the left fastening, and whirled over to the right side of the canoe. It seemed that all hope was gone. There were only three paddles remaining, two of which were immediately put into the hands of the steersman and bowman. It was impossible to return, and to make progress against the current with only such means, appeared equally impracticable. A watery grave seemed inevitable ; but by the protecting mercy of God, when the waves broke, it was just without the canoe. It was necessary to our safety to be collected and fearless, and we cleared the sail, and gave orders as though no danger was near. Contrary to our highest expectations, we continued to make headway up the river, assisted probably by one of those large eddies, which abound in this river, until we came to a bay with a sandy shore, where we safely moored our frail barque, and waited until the winds and weather became more favorable.

After the wind had somewhat abated, Indians came to us from the opposite shore, of whom we bought paddles, and being again equipped for our voyage, we proceeded up the river to the La Dalles, and as far through them as we could safely go. Here we landed and encamped on the north shore, and a number of Indians soon came to us, whom we engaged to carry us with horses, to the navigable water above the Falls. Near this was a very large eddy, where, two years previously, nine men were drowned. Their bateau was drawn into it and capsized, and only one man escaped, which he effected by clinging to a bag containing some empty kegs. He was carried a few miles down the river, and then taken up by Indians who were passing in a canoe.

The 20th was occupied in passing the La Dalles and the Falls, above which we encamped. This place affords a favorable location for missionaries. The Indians resort here in large numbers for fishing, and remain usually through the summer, and some of them through the year. An intercourse would be always open with surrounding tribes, and facilities would be at hand both to disseminate the truths of the gospel, and to obtain the means of comfortable subsistence.

As soon as we were encamped, the Indians, who are here in great numbers preparing for fishing, came around us and their first enquiry was for *pi pi*, (tobacco.) I am much disgusted with this noxious plant, and am resolved no longer to consider it necessary to conciliate the Indians by smoking the friendly pipe. If an Indian is suffering with hunger and nakedness, his first request is for tobacco. As we had parted with the Indians who came with us from Fort Vancouver, we here engaged two others to assist us as far as Walla Walla.

On the 21st, we took a bateau which we found here, and progressed slowly up the river against the current and frequent rapids. On the morning of the 22d, while encamped, and the men were making preparation for breakfast, I rambled into a little village in the neighborhood, and called at a lodge, whose inmates consisted of an aged woman, a younger one, and four little girls. I addressed them in the Chenook language, but they did not understand me. Being tolerably familiar with the language of signs, I enquired whose were those children. The younger woman signified that three of them were hers, but the eldest was an orphan, whom she had adopted for her own ; and in the most pathetic manner she proceeded to relate her history, but little of which was intelligible. The aged matron sitting on the ground of her movable lodge, with her head reclined upon her hand, occasionally introduced a few sentences to aid the narration ; and so sad and affecting was the whole accent and sound of their voices, that I freely sympathized with them, and nodded my assent to all they said. I regretted the necessity which compelled me to leave them without being able to point them to Him, who is touched with the feelings of our infirmities, and who binds up the broken in heart. I thought, as I walked slowly back to my breakfast, how little of the savage character was exhibited by these females, and on the contrary, how these amiable sensibilities would have done honor to any civilized society.

Our encampment on the 24th, was on the south side of

the river, at a place of great resort for the Indians, but they had not come in from their winter retreat. There were many canoes drawn up at a short distance from the shore, and left without any apprehensions of their being stolen, showing the confidence the Indians have in each others honesty. They do not need guards, nor bolts and bars, and prisons.

To secure ourselves from a strong, cold wind, we selected a place densely covered with wild broom corn of last year's growth yet standing, and in the rear of willows which here skirted the shore of the river. Two Indians came to our encampment, who were as miserable objects as I have seen. They were not more than half covered with tattered skins of rabbits patched together ; and were emaciated with starvation. To relieve the sufferings of such objects of pity, the traveler needs to carry with him a store of clothing and provisions. It is distressing to see them, without having the means of furnishing them substantial relief.

On the 25th, we made slow progress against the strong current with our poorly manned bateau, and failing of arriving at Walla Walla as we had hoped, encamped under the high basaltic rocks, where we found a small spot of soil furnishing some wood. The next morning we arrived at the fort, where I met at the landing a number of Nez Percé Indians waiting my arrival. I felt much satisfaction in seeing them, and in witnessing their tokens of affection. It was like meeting old friends ; and there appeared to be so much unfeigned pleasure in the reception they gave me, that it inspired the hope, that the disposition they express to learn the way of salvation is based on a foundation more permanent than novelty. I had told a band of the Cayuse Indians, on my way down the river last October, that I would meet them here in the spring, and inform them about God and the way to worship him. Many of them were here, ready to attend to the fulfilment of my promise, and undoubtedly my arrival at the appointed time, confirmed their confidence.

As the season is yet early, I judged it expedient to continue here a week or two and improve such opportunities as might offer for instructing the Indians residing near this place, and those who might come from more remote places; making the best use of such facilities as can be obtained, without waiting for the thorough knowledge of their language, which the prudence of some persons would consider indispensible to the commencement of teaching them the way of eternal life. Their anxious curiosity to know what the religion of the Bible is, cannot be kept awake while its gratification is postponed. The danger that delay will result in indifference or disgust, is as great as that an early attempt to impart instruction may be connected with imperfections.

During my continuance in this place, I preached on the Sabbath morning to the white people belonging to the fort, and in the afternoon to the Indians of the Cayuse, Walla Walla, and Nez Percé tribes. They always gave good attention, and some appeared to be much interested. An instance of opposition to the truths of the gospel occurred here, proving the truth of the scriptures, that the Savior is set for the fall and rising of those who hear. A chief of the Cayuses, who several times came to hear, disliked what was said about a plurality of wives. He said he would not part with any of his; for he had always lived in sin, and was going to the place of burning, and it was too late for him, now he was getting old, to repent and be saved;

and as he must go to that place, he would go in all his sins, and would not alter his life. Those who are familiar with the various methods to which sinners resort, to avoid the convictions of truth and conscience, may see in his deep hatred to holiness, that the operation of sin is the same in every unsanctified heart. This is the only instance of open opposition, that I witnessed among the Indians ; nor does it characterize the Cayuse tribe. They very much resemble the Nez Percés in their peaceable disposition, and desire to be instructed, and present in connection with the Walla Wallas, a promising field of missionary labor.

May 3d. I walked down to the passage of the Columbia through the basaltic mountain, two miles below the fort, to take a more particular view of the scenery, than can be obtained in a hasty passage on the river. I ascended the mountain, from the top of which I had a fine prospect of the country around, opening in every direction as far as the eye could reach. All parts were covered with the fresh green of spring vegetation. Very few forests were to be seen in any direction, excepting upon the Blue Mountains at the south, and these, instead of the fresh hues presented by forests at this season, were softened by the distance to a hazy blue. Even at this distance, the perpetual snows of Mount Hood, could be distinguished at the west, and at the northwest Mount Rainier near Pugets Sound ; and at the north and the east various parts of scattered mountains. After some time employed in looking around upon the vast expanse, I approached the perpendicular walls, between which the Columbia descends, which are about three hundred feet high, as I ascertained by the number of seconds occupied in the descent of large stones, projected from the brink of the precipice, which I distinctly heard when they struck upon the shore below. I found a great variety of scoria and lava, the latter varying much in color and density, some of it suf-ciently porous and light to swim upon water. Two thirds of the way down this deep channel, are two high eminences called the Pillars, to which, by a circuitous route, I de-scended. They stand upon conical bases, eighty or a hun-dred feet high above the river ; and above these bases rise nearly a hundred feet perpendicular. They are indeed re-markable ; but there are so many singular formations in this volcanic country, that curiosities become common. I returned, though much fatigued with my long walk over prairies, precipices, and mountains, yet gratified with the examination of the works of nature.

My horses and mule, which I had left with the Nez Percé Indians, were kept in their country, one hundred and thirty miles east of this place, and were in April brought into this neighborhood. To-day, May 5th, they were caught and brought to the fort. I was surprised to find them in fine order, with new coats, and in high spirits. They had run out on the prairies without any shelter from the storms, and with no food, except what the remains of the previous sum-mer's growth afforded, together with the early grass of spring. Who would have supposed, considering their worn down condition, when I left them in October, that with no other fare they would have fattened during the winter. This fact shows the superior mildness of the climate, and the nu-tritive quality of prairie grass, even after dried up with the summer drouth. Another evidence of the truth of this remark may be seen in the condition of the cattle kept at this fort. With nothing more to feed upon than what they find upon the prairies, they are now not only in good order, but some of them are actually fat, and in as

good condition for market, as oxen driven from the stalls of
New England.

I rode to-day with Mr. P. ten miles up the river to the
confluence of the Lewis, or as it is called, the Nez Percé
river, with the Columbia. They are both noble streams;
the Columbia is nearly three-fourths of a mile, and the
Nez Percé a half mile wide. The prospect around is delightful; the soil is good, as is evidenced by the fresh verdure
which is springing up luxuriantly, at this early season. A
large band of horses belonging to a Walla Walla chief, are
feeding here. It is a curious fact, that the Indian horses
do not often stray from the place where they are left; habit,
however produced, is as good a safeguard as inclosures.
Along upon the shores of the river, I found specimens of
calcedony and cornelian.

The sixth was a very warm day, the thermometer standing at noon, at 84°. Distant thunder was heard, which is
an unfrequent occurrence west of the great mountains.
Towards and through the night the wind blew very strongly, and shook the bastion which I occupied, so that it seemed as if it would be prostrated to the earth; but such wind
in this particular section of country is common.

During the time of my continuance here, I had more
frequent opportunities to address the Indians, and in greater
numbers, than I had anticipated. From the promise that
the word of God shall not return void, but shall accomplish
that whereunto it is sent, may not the hope be indulged, that
some good fruits will be the result of these labors. The
Walla Walla tribe, though the descendants of emancipated
slaves, are not inferior to other tribes, and are treated with
the same respect.

CHAPTER XX.

IN company with several Nez Percé Indians who had come down from their own country to escort me, I commenced my journey on the ninth, and pursued the same route by which I came last autumn. Nothing eventful marked our way, and we arrived at the Snake or Lewis river, the evening of the eleventh, where we found several lodges of the Nez Percés, who gave us a very cordial reception, and a warm-hearted shake of the hand, the common expression of Indian friendship. The night of our arrival a little girl, about six or seven years of age, died, and on the morning of the twelfth they buried her. Every thing relating to the burial was conducted with great propriety. The grave was only about two feet deep ; for they have no spades, and a sharpened stick was used to loosen the earth, and this was removed with the hands ; and with their hands they filled up the grave after the body was deposited in it. A mat was laid in the grave, then the body wrapped in its blanket, with the child's drinking cup and spoon made of horn ; then a mat of rushes spread over the whole, and filled up, as above described. In this instance they had prepared a cross to set up at the grave, most probably having been told to do so by some Iroquois Indians, a few of whom I saw west of the mountains, not in the capacity of teachers, but as trappers in the employ of the fur companies. One grave in the same village had a cross standing over it, which, together with this, were the only relics of the kind I saw, during my travels in the country. But as I viewed a cross of wood of no avail, to benefit either the dead or the living, and far more likely to operate as a salvo to a guilty conscience, or a stepping-stone to idolatry, than to be understood in its spiritual sense to refer to a crucifixion of our sins, I took this, which the Indians had prepared, and broke it in pieces. I then told them that we place a stone at the head and foot of the grave, only to mark the place ; and without a murmur, they cheerfully acquiesced, and adopted our custom.

As we proceeded up the river to the confluence of the Cooscootske, on account of the high water, we had to pass over the huge precipices of basalt, at the foot of which we traveled down last fall, and which I have mentioned. We were compelled often to approach very near the brink, where it seemed as if we were almost suspended over the dizzy depth of three hundred feet. We arrived at the Cooscootske early in the afternoon of the third day after leaving Walla Walla, making the distance about 120 miles. The whole country had put on the loveliness of spring, and divested itself of the dreariness of winter, and the grandeur of the mountain scenery appeared to rise before me with new freshness and delight. The Indians are assembling in great numbers from different and distant parts of the country, to enquire about the religion that is to guide them to God and heaven; and which they also think has power to elevate them in the scale of society in this world, and place them on a level with intelligent as well as Christian white men.

On the north of the confluence of these two rivers, and down the Nez Percé river, the country is diversified with hills and mountains of a great variety of forms, from five hundred to two thousand feet high. The volcanic and ar- gillaceous strata are generally horizontal, but in some places thrown into various degrees of inclination, from horizontal to perpendicular; in other places curved or waving. They have all the regularity of works of art, raised up by human skill; why should not then the power and skill of an Omnip- otent hand be acknowledged in these stupendous works?

After having been several months where the Indians of the lower country came daily under my observation, the contrast between them and these with whom I am now, is very noticeable. The former are more servile and abject, both in their manners and spirit; while the latter are truly dignified and respectable in their manners and general ap- pearance, far less enslaved to their appetites, or to those vices whose inevitable tendency is to degrade. They know enough to set some estimate upon character, and have much of the proud independence of freemen; and are desirous of possessing a consequence in the estimation of other people, and for this reason, wish to be taught, and they receive any instruction with remarkable docility.

Saturday, May 14th. Very many of the natives are coming in for the purpose of keeping the Sabbath with me; but as I have little prospect of the arrival of my interpreter, I shall probably be left to commiserate their anxiety, while it will be out of my power to do them good.

I have frequent applications to prescribe for the ophthal- my, with which the people are much afflicted, and which I should think is a prevalent endemic. Calomel, applied in about the quantity of one grain to each eye, once in twenty-four hours, I found to be an efficacious remedy. No injurious effects were known to have occurred from its use, and in most cases it was successful.

The Nez Percés have been celebrated for their skill and bravery in war. This they have mentioned to me, but say they now are afraid to go to war; for they no longer believe that all who fall in battle go to a happy country. They now believe that the only way to be happy here or hereafter, is by knowing and doing what God requires. They have learned enough to fear the consequences of dying unforgiven, but not sufficient to embrace the hopes and consolations of the gospel. I have been interested to see the reasonings of their minds, and the results of their reflections, amidst the dimness of so imperfect a knowledge as they yet possess. It demonstrates that they are not indifferent to what they hear; and that their minds are inquisitive, and capable of thought and investigation. They have obtained light sufficient, to show how great is the darkness in which they have been enveloped; and it is to be hoped, that these efforts to enlighten them will be followed by those still more efficient, until that meridian day foretold in prophecy, shall fully come, and these heathen be given to the Savior with all the remote ends of the earth for a possession.

Sabbath, 15th. The interpreter I had been expecting did not arrive, and consequently much of what I wished to say to these hundreds of Indians, could not be communicated for the want of a medium. I felt distressed for them. They desired to celebrate the Sabbath after a Christian manner. When the chiefs came and enquired what they should do, I told them to collect the people into an assembly and spend the hours of this sacred day in prayer and singing, and in conversation on those things about which I formerly in-

structed them. They did so, and it was truly affecting to
see their apparent reverence, order and devotion, while I
could not but know that their knowledge was limited indeed.
The voice of their singing echoed from the hills and vales,
and I could not but hope, that the time will not be greatly
future, when they will sing with the spirit and with the un-
derstanding. As a proof that they have acquired some
correct ideas of spiritual worship, in distinction from the
employment of mere outward forms, Kentuc, the Indian
who attended me so faithfully on my outward route, came
to me, anxious to describe the different manner in which he
regarded the worship of the two chiefs, Charlie and Teutàcus. He said Charlie prayed with his lips, but Teutàcus
prayed with his heart. Confession of sin appears to occupy
much of his prayers, and if there is one among this multitude, who it may be hoped, has been everlastingly benefited
by the gospel, I believe it is this man.

Monday, 16th. I had hitherto been somewhat undecided
what course to pursue in my future movements ; but came
to the conclusion to proceed to the place of Rendezvous, and
join the returning caravan, provided I could go by the way
of the Grand Round, and to the south-west of the Snake
river, and explore a part of the country which I had not
passed through the preceding autumn. But the Indians
chose to take the retired route of the Salmon river mountains, to avoid danger from hostile Indians, as it was well
ascertained that there was a party of Blackfeet warriors
ranging the territory west of the great mountains. I wished to explore the north-east branch of the Columbia, which
runs through an important part of the country, and upon
which, and its branches, many considerable tribes reside.

To return by the way my company would travel, and by

which I came, would be to leave the object of my tour only partially accomplished ; and after canvassing the subject as deliberately as I could, I concluded to return to Walla Walla, procure guides and assistants, and go up the Columbia as far as Colvile, which is the highest post of the Hudson Bay Company, about seven hundred miles, by the traveled route, from the Pacific ocean. I informed the Indians of my determination, who, though they evidently preferred that I should accompany them, acquiesced in the decision, and showed more kindness than I had expected. They readily appointed Haminilpilt, one of their young chiefs, to attend me on my return down the river. After writing several letters, to forward to the United States from Rendezvous, we turned our faces to our proposed destination, and at night arrived at the village on the Nez Percé river, where we had encamped on the eleventh.

At this place I was peculiarly gratified to notice the industry of these people. Some were engaged in catching fish, and gave me some excellent salmon ; the women and children were early out on horseback to procure the cowish root, which they often manufacture into bread ; and when we left, only a few old persons and very young children remained in their village. Five or six miles from this village, up a small branch of this river, we passed a spot, which some few years ago, was a battle-field between the Nez Percés and some other nation, whose name I could not with certainty ascertain, but probably it was the Tuelca. The ground was judiciously chosen by the invading party, which was just back of a point of land coming down near the stream of water, leaving only a narrow pass, around which they opened a fire, while the Nez Percés, not expecting the approach of a foe, were taken by surprise, and fifteen or twenty of their number were killed. The very spot where each individual fell, is now designated by heaps of stones raised three and four feet high.

The country over which we passed to-day, a distance of forty miles, was uncommonly pleasant, diversified with hills and valleys and covered with its self-provided carpet of lovely green. Several Indians came on after us and traveled in company. Near night we encamped in a rich valley, through which a considerable stream of water runs to the north. Before it was dark, a number more whom I recognized as former acquaintances, overtook us, apparently reluctant to separate from our company. I conversed with them about the practice so universal among the men, of using tobacco for smoking, a very expensive indulgence, for which they pay almost as much as for their whole list of comforts besides. In reply to my arguments to dissuade them from its use, they said, "white men smoke." I admitted the truth, but told them that all white men are not wise in every thing they do; that they have some practices which are not good, The Nez Percés call tobacco, smoke, and remarked, "we are better then than white men ; for they eat smoke,"—meaning tobacco—"we do not eat smoke." This to be sure was an argument of much shrewdness, and wholly unanswerable. Such is their attachment to this stupefying vegetable, that to obtain it, they will part with the last article of food or clothing, or even take down the poles which uphold their dwellings, and sell them for fuel. In this view I regard it as a vice, from which they should be rescued if practicable.

The 18th we continued our journey, and rode forty-five miles over a more fertile tract than we passed yesterday, and better supplied with wood. On the upper part of the

Walla Walla river is a delightful situation for a missionary establishment, having many advantages not found for some distance around. It is not, however, so central for either the Nez Percés, Cayuses, or Walla Wallas, as would be desirable, yet a mission located on this fertile field would draw around an interesting settlement, who would cultivate the soil, and be instructed. How easily might the plough go through these valleys, and what rich and abundant harvests might be gathered by the hand of industry. But even now the spontaneous productions of these vast plains, including millions of acres, are so profuse, that not the fiftieth part becomes the food of organic life. In some places bands of Indian horses are seen; the timid deer, or hare; the wary marmot, and the swift gazelle. But these, with other animals, consume so small a proportion, that these wide fields are comparatively unoccupied.

We experienced a long detention on the morning of the 19th, in consequence of our horses wandering into a ravine, to which retreat we could not easily trace them. They did not, however, violate their rule, of making our encampment, for the time being, their home. We rode twenty-two miles and arrived at Walla Walla. Most of the remainder of the week was occupied in necessary arrangements for my northeast tour, and in writing letters to friends. Mr. P. assisted in obtaining Indian guides, and designated two French *voyageurs* to be my assistants; one of whom could speak some English. I concluded to take horses, and go up through the Spokein country, leaving the great bend of the Columbia to the left some fifty or sixty miles, and on our return to take the river. This would give a more extended observation of the country, of the tribes who inhabit it, and of their condition in regard to prospects of establishing teachers among them.

On Sabbath, the 22d, we had worship as usual, and the following day commenced the journey for Colvile. Our course was in an easterly direction forty miles, and at night we found a new place to lay our heads for rest, in a valley presenting all the appearance of the farmer's grass fields, ready for the mower's hand, and from which he expects to receive a future gain. But the natives, not appreciating these sources of profit, neglect them altogether, and gather only a scanty living from a few esculent roots, which grow spontaneously in the waste.

CHAPTER XXI.

Paloose Indians—Pavilion river—extraordinary excavation—lost on
the prairie—Indian principle—Spokein woods and country—Indian
ferry—Spokein valley—granite—volcanic curiosities—fertile valley
—worship with the Spokeins—Mill river valley—arrival at Fort
Colvile—description of the place—leave Colvile for Fort Okanagan
—a mountain of marble—Grand Coulé, or old bed of the Columbia
—Okanagan described—Long rapids—arrive at Walla Walla.

THE morning of the 24th, we took a more northerly course,
and after traveling five hours over a somewhat high but
diversified country, descended into a fertile valley, through
which flowed a small tributary of the Snake river. Here
we found a village of Paloose Indians who are a band of the
Nez Percés. We hired them to assist us in crossing the
river, which here is a half mile wide, and has a rapid current. We had only a small canoe, which the strength of
the current carried more than a half mile down the river
before we could gain the opposite shore. Three times we
had to encounter the stream, before every thing was safely
over ; and the horses made a strong effort to swim to the
opposite shore. This, together with refitting, employed several hours. We traveled up the Pavilion river, which comes
from the high lands that divide the waters of this and the
Spokein river. This river is walled up with basalt, generally high and perpendicular, in various windings and forms,
for the distance of fifteen or twenty miles. In some places
the walls are spread out so widely as to enclose large spaces
of rich interval ; in other places so closing upon the river

as to leave only space sufficient for it to pass. The night was cold, the thermometer standing on the morning of the 25th, at 34°.

We pursued our way over hills and valleys of an entire prairie, until we came to the south part of the Spokein country. Near the summit level which divides the waters of the Snake and Spokein rivers, there is an interesting excavation, walled within by basaltic rocks. The pillars are regular pentagons from two to four feet in diameter, in sections of various lengths, standing erect and closely joined, making a wall from fifty to one hundred feet high. The excavated enclosure, though not in a regular form, is yet nearly entire, containing fifty or more acres. On the outside of this wall, the earth is as high as the pillars, and gradually slopes off in hills and dales. By what agency was this excavation formed? There is no appearance, as in many other places, of volcanic craters, unless it is itself a crater, and there are no signs of the action of water. May it not have been a subsidence? I passed through it leisurely, and surveyed with admiration these huge crystals, of dark materials truly, but showing not the less for that circumstance, that certain laws govern the mineral world, as well as the animal or vegetable. We passed to-day several small villages of the Nez Percé and Spokein nations. They all manifested a perfectly friendly disposition, but appeared to be poor, evidently in want of a comfortable subsistence. We stopped for the night, after a ride of fifty miles, near one of these villages of Spokeins. Their language differs almost entirely from that of any tribe or nation I have yet seen. One of my Indian guides was sufficiently acquainted with it to inform them of the object of my tour through their country, with which they were not only satisfied, but apparently interested.

We took an early departure on the morning of the 26th, but traveled only a few hours before my Indian guides lost the track and the course they should pursue. Becoming confident that they were not right, I alighted and set my pocket compass, and discovered that instead of a north-east direction, they were going west. Enquiring of them if they knew where to find our trail again, one of them, a young chief, putting his hand to his head, and with gestures expressing the confusion of his mind, answered, *waiitu en soko,* "I do not know." Our situation was rather embarrassing. We had very injudiciously left our rifles behind, and at about an equal distance from Walla Walla and Colvile, on a widely extended prairie, with provisions adequate to our wants only for two days, and no probable means for obtaining more until we should arrive at the fort; to be lost under these circumstances was no pleasant affair. The point of a high mountain we had passed was in view, and we might retrace our path, and therefore I was determined not to lose sight of this land-mark, until we should find the trail leading to the Spokein river. While my guides went off in search of it, I could hardly fail to find even in our circumstances, some amusement in the apathy of my two Frenchmen. They are so confiding in Indian skill to find their way through any country, as by intuition, that they will sing or go to sleep with the same heedless indifference when lost in a wide wilderness, as when launched upon the waters of a well known river, or performing the duties of the fort. They appear wholly unconscious of danger on the approach of hunger and starvation, until long after the last morsel is consumed, and never borrow from futurity to add to the evils

that afflict them to-day. On this occasion these men spent
the time of our detention in calm repose. After some time
our guides returned and told me they had found some Spokein Indians about a mile distant, who were traveling towards the south, but had stopped to refresh their horses.
We proceeded to the place, and I engaged one of them to
assist us in finding the way to the main trail, or to the Spokein river. He was a tall, intelligent looking man. He
mounted his horse, and set off with such speed, that, jaded
as our horses were, it was with difficulty we could keep up
with him. After going at this rate more than an hour, he
stopped, and pointed us to a lake, and said we should find
the great trail on the east side. Lest we should again lose
our way, I was anxious to have him conduct us to their village on the river, but could not prevail upon him to go any
farther, although I offered him a large compensation. His
only, and unvarying answer was, that he had done for us
all that was needed, and why should he perform any unnecessary labor for us and take pay. It appeared to be a
principle with him, that it would be wrong for him to take
pay for what we did not need. I was astonished at the honesty of this heathen, and his steadfast adherence to it, when
I remembered how many there are in civilized lands, who
to be well paid, would lengthen a service to an unnecessary
extent, and artfully deceive you to make you believe it very
important. For his faithfulness and *honesty* I not only paid
him on the spot to his satisfaction, but afterwards sent him
a present of powder and balls, articles highly valued.

Without any farther difficulty, we arrived at the Spokein
river, at four o'clock, P. M. A few miles after we left the
lake, we entered the Spokein woods which are very extensive, consisting of yellow pitch and elastic pine, some hem-

loc, spruce and fir, together with various shrubbery. These are the woods in which Ross Cox was lost, about the circumstances of which he gives a very interesting description, but which, so far as I have yet had an opportunity to judge, contains far more fiction than truth. But his multitude of growling bears, and howling wolves, and alarming rattle-snakes, of which I have seen only one, may yet come out from their lurking places in hostile array.

When we came to the river, which is about thirty rods wide, we hallooed a long time for the Indian who keeps a canoe ferry, but without success. At length two women came to the river, and with uncommonly pleasant voices, together with the language of signs, the latter of which only I could understand, informed us that the ferryman was gone upon a short hunt, would return in the evening, and the next morning at sun two hours high, he would come and take us over. I never heard voices more expressive of kindness. I requested them to paddle the canoe over to us, and my men would perform the labor of ferrying over our baggage. They declined on account of the rapidity and strength of the current, the river being in full freshet. Therefore we had to encamp and wait for the morning.

This is a very pleasant, open valley, though not extensively wide. The North-west Company had a trading post here, one bastion of which is still standing. These woods present a fine range for the ornithologist. The magpie is seen in great numbers, flying from tree to tree, vociferating its chattering notes. Also thrushes, warblers, and wrens are numerous, cheering those otherwise solitary wilds with their delightful songs, grateful to the weary traveler. Their carols appear to be designed to animate each other in their intervals of labor, while constructing their habitations so admirably adapted for their tender offspring ; on an examination of which, the most infidel philosopher must be astonished, and be constrained to acknowledge, that God has manifested himsef in supplying, instead of reason, a mysterious, unerring instinct, always sufficient for the end to be accomplished.

On the 27th, about the time in the morning mentioned by the two women, the Indian ferryman came, and crossed the river in his canoe. His appearance, together with that of his canoe, reminded me of Æneas' ferryman, who carried him over the Stygian lake.

> "Canites inculta jacet;
> Sordidus ex humeris nodo dependet amictus,
> Cœruleam advertit cymbam, ripæque propinquat."

After the river, we crossed the valley of level alluvial soil, where it is about a mile and a quarter wide, and the east side especially is very fertile. Here the village of the Spokeins is located, and one of their number has commenced the cultivation of a small field or garden, which he has planted with potatoes, peas, and beans, and some other vegetables ; all of which were flourishing, and were the first I had seen springing up under Indian industry west of the mountains. Our ferryman conducted us through the valley to the foot of the mountain on the east, and pointed out the trail we should pursue. As we wound our way up the mountain, 1 looked down into the valley we had crossed, and which stretches along the winding river, and drew in my imagination a picture of what it will be, when this people are brought under the influence of Christianity and civilization. This section of country presents less appearance of volcanic operation ; and in several places I found granite in its natural form and position, resembling that found in the Eastern States. When we had arrived at the summit of this mountain, we came to a sandy plain, several miles wide, covered with yellow pine forming an open forest. Over parts of this plain were scattered volcanic eruptions of singular formation. Hundreds of regular cones of various magnitudes, from those of only a few feet in diameter and height, to those a hundred in diameter and sixty feet high. They all had the same appearance, differing only in magnitude, and were composed of broken granite, in angular pieces, from those that were very small, to six or eight inches in diameter, and on the outside were nearly black, as if colored with rising smoke. They had more the appearance of being broken by manual labor, and piled up for future use in constructing roads or wharves, than the result of internal fires, and yet no other cause but the latter can be assigned. The sandy plain around them was undisturbed, and large pine trees were growing about them as in other places. At the south of these were large rocks of granite, and in one place a basaltic dyke extending a hundred rods or more.

After passing this plain, we descended and came again to the Spokein river, which makes a bend around to the north-east. In this place the valley is less extensive, and the mountains more precipitous. We again ascended the mountain, upon which granite and mica slate prevail, without any volcanic appearances. From this we descended into a rich valley, which was covered with a luxuriant growth of grass, though but just springing up. This valley has the appearance of having been a lake filled up with mountain deposits. In the centre is a small lake, from which proceeds a rivulet passing out at the south-west. Leaving this place, we wound around a mountain in a northerly direction, down a valley less fertile but more extensive, and at four in the afternoon came to a stream of water, coming from the mountains at the east, where our guides said we must stop for the night.

Near evening, several companies of Spokein and some Nez Percé Indians came riding into the place of our encampment, and turned out their horses with ours in the half wood and prairie. The Spokeins, who had seen me on my way, and had learned who I was, sent information out to the various hunting parties, that a minister was passing through their country, and as it was the first time one was ever among them, they wished to see him and hear what he had to say to them. They brought with them a good interpreter, a young man of their nation, who had been in the school at the Red river settlement on the east side of the mountain, and had obtained a very good knowledge of English. We had public worship that evening in the Spokein and Nez Percé languages. One of the Nez Percés, a chief who understood the Spokein language, collected his people, a little to the left of the Spokeins, and translated the discourse as it was delivered, into the language of his people, without any interruption to the service. This was a plan of their own devising. All the circumstances combined were to me unusually interesting. Providences above my control had delayed me three several times, and thus given them an opportunity to collect their people and overtake me. Some of them had pursued my path a day and a half, and were unwilling to return, being resolved to accompany me to Colvile. These benighted Indians manifested the same solicitude to hear the gospel that others had done before. And as a most affecting proof that the impressions then made on their minds

were not momentary, they went home and erected in their
village a church, constructed of rude materials surely, but
designed, as they said, to furnish a place, that when the next
missionary should arrive, he might stop and teach them.*

The morning of the 28th was cloudy and some rain fell,
but this did not prevent our early departure; for it was necessary to be on our way, as my men had the evening before
consumed their entire stock of provisions, and, whatever
might occur, we could procure no more until we should
reach Colvile. We could not obtain any game, for being
advised by the superintendent at Walla Walla not to en-
cumber ourselves with rifles, we had unwisely left them
behind. After traveling a few miles in an easterly direction we came to a very fertile valley, well adapted to cultivation, extending north and south at least fifty miles, and of
various extent in width, from a half mile to two miles. The
valley is an open prairie well supplied with grass, and even
in this high latitude of 48°, cattle could do well through the
whole year, without the labor of cutting hay. The hills on
each side are covered with woods. As we proceeded down
this valley, we came to villages of Indians who understood
the Spokein language, but belonged to another tribe, probably to the Cœur d'Aléne. Near their principal village
we came to Mill river, which was in full freshet. They had
no canoes, and we found difficulty in getting my baggage
across. But the Nez Percé chief took part of it upon his
shoulder, mounted his horse, and swam over, and crossed
and re-crossed until all was upon the other side. I then

---

* The name of this nation is generally written Spokan, sometimes
Spokane. I called them Spokans, but they corrected my pronunciation, and said Spokein, and this they repeated several times, until I
was convinced that to give their name a correct pronunciation it
should be written Spokein.

crossed upon a pole, which was not the most desirable method, but still it was preferable to a cold bathing on horseback.
After pursuing our course a few miles farther, I divided my
remaining stock of eatables with my destitute French and
Indian attendants, leaving the anticipation of our next meal
to the time when, after a long day's industrious travel, we
should find ourselves safely at Colvile.

Towards the lower part of the valley, through which we
were passing, the land is remarkably fertile. A missionary located here, would have easy access to the Spokein, Sap-
well, Sintou-tou-oulish, Kettle falls, Lake, Cœur d'Aléne,
and Pondera Indians. I know not of so important a field
within two hundred miles, presenting the natural advantages of mild climate, good soil, and forests.

We arrived at Fort Colvile late in the afternoon, after a
weary journey of sixty miles. The situation of this fort is
on an elevated spot, about fifty rods from the river, surrounded by an alluvial plain of rich soil, and opening in
every direction an extended prospect of mountain scenery;
and a half mile below are Kettle falls, above which the
river spreads out widely, and moves slowly, but just above
the precipice it contracts into a narrow channel, and disappears from the view of the spectator at the fort, until
seen winding its way among rocks below. This establishment is built for defense and is well stoccaded, but so friendly have the natives always been, that no wars have ever
occurred among them. It is occupied by some half dozen
men with Indian families, and is well supplied with the
useful animals and fowls common to farming establishments. The winter and summer grains, together with garden vegetables, are cultivated with success and in profusion.
This place does not suffer with summer drouth, like many

other parts of this country, and rains are of frequent occurrence; the seasons here are not divided, as on the lower parts of the Columbia, into wet and dry.

I was much disappointed in not finding Mr. McDonald, the superintendent of the fort, at home. He had left a few days before with a brigade for Fort Vancouver; but the kindest attention was paid me by those who had the charge of the fort. I found here an old man, who thirty years before accompanied Lewis and Clarke across the continent, and had for several years past taken up his residence here. He is in the employ of the fur company, and acts as interpreter to the neighboring Indians.

On Sabbath the 29th, the people of the fort who understood English, assembled, and we worshiped the God of our lives, who had protected us hitherto, and from different nations had collected us in a little group in this region of the world. The Indians too came about me and expressed great anxiety to be taught the revealed will of God. They endeavored to make me understand what their former traditionary belief and practices had been, and to let me know, that what they had learned from me was reasonable and satisfactory to them, and that they wished to know all that related to so important and momentous a subject. But our medium of communication was inadequate to a full disclosure of that most interesting truth, that God so loved the world that he gave his only Son to die for its redemption.

Wherever I have met with the natives of this distant region they have invariably, with earnestness and importunity, asked the gift of the gospel from the hands of Christians. But how little of the faith, and love, and liberality of the church is invested in the most profitable of all enterprises,

the conversion of the world. Should some one propose the
construction of a rail road from the Atlantic to the Pacific,
and demonstrate the practicability of the measure, and show
that nature has interposed no effectual barrier, and that it
would concentrate not only the whole internal, but also the
China trade, and the stock would produce annually a rich
dividend, how soon would Christians engage in it.

Monday the 30th of May, we commenced our journey
down the Columbia. The brigade having taken all the
boats from this place on their late passage to Fort Vancouver, we were compelled to take horses for Okanagan. I
changed my guides for two others ; one a Spokein, and the
other a Paloose ; retaining my two *voyageurs*. As we left
Fort Colvile we had a fine view of Kettle falls. The Columbia was in its freshet, and as it rolled down in a broken
cataract for the distance of one hundred feet, it was a sublime spectacle. The whole scenery as we proceeded down
the river was marked by variety, wildness, and romantic
grandeur, as if the hand of nature, in decking these remote
regions, had consulted for her own amusement some of her
most playful and tasteful fancies. The mountains around
are constructed on a scale of magnificence, presenting almost all the varieties of elevation, precipice, and forest.
This is the country which by more than one of my prede-
cessors in travel, has been celebrated as the abode of wolves,
bears, and rattle-snakes, to an extent that renders it almost
impenetrable, by ordinary courage ; but we found no indications of the presence of these animals before this evening, when the distant barking of a prairie wolf, for once
interrupted the universal silence by which we were surrounded.

After a few hours ride, on the morning of the 31st, we

re-crossed the Spokein river just above its entrance into the Columbia. This large valley is capable of supporting a much more numerous population than now obtain a subsistence by hunting and fishing. The Indians residing here afforded us very cheerfully all the assistance we needed in ferrying the river. In the neighborhood of this place I discovered a mountain of rich and very beautiful saccharine marble, situated on the south side of the Columbia river; some sections are pure white, while others are beautifully clouded with blue and brown. It effervesced freely with sulphuric acid. This will in time become very valuable, for being upon navigable waters, it can be transported into various countries. Several miles below this marble location I was interested with the juxtaposition of granite and basalt. It was on an elevated piece of land one hundred and fifty feet above the river. Near the river there were large quantities of solid granite in its natural position, without any appearance of having undergone an igneous influence, and near by to the left was a stupendous dyke of basalt rising two hundred feet, presenting the appearance of having been thrown up by several successive volcanic eruptions; the earth on the back side gradually rising to a mountain.

At this place we left the river, to save traversing a great bend, and took a westerly course, expecting to reach it again before night. We pursued our way over an elevated prairie, destitute of wood and water. It became evident that night would overtake us before we could reach the river, unless we should urge forward with all the speed that humanity for our horses would permit. Before five o'clock we came near the great gulf walled up with basalt, which as we supposed, embosomed the deep-flowing Columbia. Our

next object was to find a place where we could descend to
its shores. After ranging along two or three miles, we
found a descent by a ravine ; but to our disappointment
discovered that it was the Grand Coulé, which was undoubtedly the former channel of the river. With considerable difficulty we wound our way into it, and found it well
covered with grass, and by searching, obtained a small
supply of water. This quondam channel of the river is
nearly a mile wide, with a level bottom, and studded with
islands. Its sides are lined, as the river itself is in many
places, with basaltic rocks, two and three hundred feet perpendicular. This Coulé separates to the left from the present channel of the Columbia, about one hundred miles below Colvile, and is about one hundred miles in length, when
it again unites with the river. The basaltic appearances
are exhibited here as in other places, furnishing evidences
of eruptions at different periods of time. A peculiarity in
this instance was a stratum of yellow earth, eight or ten
feet in thickness between the strata of basalt. Those who
have traveled through the whole length of the Coulé, represent it as having the same general features throughout,
while the whole distance of the river around to the place
where it again unites, as I know from personal observation,
has not the peculiarity of a deep channel, cut through the
rocks.

We left the Grand Coulé early on the morning of the 1st
of June, and with difficulty ascended the western bank.
Before noon my guides lost the way to Okanagan, and wan-
dered far out upon the wide prairie where there was no
water. Losing my confidence in their knowledge of the
country, except on some frequented routes, I directed my
course for the river ; and perceiving a snow-topped moun-

tain in the distance, I concluded the river must lie between it and ourselves, and accordingly made it my land-mark. Pursuing this direction a few hours with rapid speed, we came to a slope which gradually narrowed into a ravine, and introduced us at length to a spring of water. Our thirsty horses rushed into it, and it was with difficulty we could control their excess in drinking. We followed this ravine, the water of which continually gained accessions until it became a large stream, with a rich valley of alluvial bottom, and united its waters with the Columbia, a few miles above Fort Okanagan, the place of our destination.

Fort Okanagan is situated on the north side of the Columbia, above the confluence of the Okanagan river, from which, and from the Indians residing in its vicinity, the fort takes its name. It was first built by Mr. David Stuart, a partner of the American Fur Company, in 1811. There is an open space of considerable extent around; the soil is of an inferior quality, hard and gravelly, but producing grass to supply the cattle and horses belonging to the station. A few fertile spots of alluvial soil are found in the vicinity. The Columbia does not appear to have continued so long in its present channel, since leaving the Grand Coule, as to form those extensive alluvial bottoms, which exist in many other parts of its course. After leaving the Spokein woods there is very little forest to supply timber for fuel, fencing or building. They are dependent on flood-wood which descends the river for their ordinary fuel, and the freshets generally furnish a large supply. Not far distant, at the north there are snow-topped mountains, yet the country here is not remarkably mountainous. At this place I had an opportunity to see some of the Okanagan tribe. Their personal appearance is less noble than the Spokeins, but they are not less peaceable, friendly and honest in their dispositions. This is evident from the fact that the charge of the fort in the absence of Capt. Ogden, the superinten- dent, was committed temporarily to a Frenchman, and sev- eral of the Indians. This tribe with the Shooshaps number about two thousand persons. They are much employed in the salmon fishery, and large quantities are prepared by drying for the winter's use. Their country does not abound in game, and hunting occupies but little of their time. The climate here, as in other parts of the Oregon Territory, is very mild and salubrious.

Wishing to pursue my way down the river, I hired two Indians to assist my two Frenchmen in navigating a bateau which we obtained at this place ; and committed our horses to my Indian guides to take them across the country to Walla Walla. My confidence in the honesty of these men was without any suspicion, and I could trust them with our six horses, saddles and bridles, to go on any enterprise with- in their capacity to accomplish. They have so much self- respect that they would not on any account commit a crime, which would expel them from their people, induce them to seek concealment, or abridge their liberties as free- men.

We embarked in our boat, June 2d, to perform a voyage of four hundred miles, with the river in full freshet ; and its strong current increased by high water, secured to us a ve- locity beyond the ordinary. We passed several rapids, and dashed over the breaking surges, where the least misman- agement would have caused inevitable submersion without any prospect of escape. But my *voyageurs* showed by their adroitness at the oar, that they were upon their favor- ite element, and their gayety and songs began to revive, on being relieved from the rough, and to them unpleasant journey on horseback, over hills and down ravines, and through forests. The elasticity of their native character was almost immediately apparent, and we glided on with celerity, making a voyage of one hundred miles before it was necessary to seek our safety for the night on shore. The country through which we passed to-day was rather mountainous. I saw many locations of granite in its natural state, but as we proceeded, volcanic operations began to appear, and the granite exhibited the effects of intense heat, until it wholly disappeared, and breccia, amygdaloid, basalt, and lava took its place. In the afternoon we passed a perpendicular section of rock, two hundred and fifty feet high; half way to the top of which, a petrified tree of considerable magnitude is suspended. It appears to be retained in its place by having its roots inserted in the crevices of the rocks, between the layers of different eruptions. How it procured its elevated situation is quite a mystery. It could not have vegetated there, unless at the time of its growth, it was supported by a surface upon which to rise; and taking the present condition of the rocks, it could not be deposited there by any floods of the river, and certainly it could not in such case, intertwine its roots in the crevices of the rocks. Gentlemen of the Hudson Bay Company, and others who navigate this river, have amused themselves by shooting off pieces with their rifles, and they assured me it was wholly a petrifaction. Our encampment this evening was a few miles above the Long Rapids, which extend nine miles.

On the 3d, as we approached the Long Rapids about fifty miles above Walla Walla they presented the appearance of waves rolling under a strong breeze of wind, and their distant murmur broke upon the stillness of the morning. To

pass them without fear, is an undertaking which requires
courage and self-possession ; but knowing that these inland
navigators are experienced in all the dangers of boating excursions, I had but little drawback upon the pleasure I anticipated in a swift descent over them.   With much care
and exertion of my men we safely outrode them, a distance
of nine miles, in forty minutes.   It is this variety of falls,
cascades, and rapids, together with the ever-varying scenery of nature's wildest and grandest forms, that keeps the
mind from wearying, and awakens almost perpetually some
new emotions and energies, while performing a voyage of
several hundred miles in open bateaux or light canoes.   Not
unfrequently in the stillness and solitude of the river, when
it assumed its more placid features, such a sense of security
is enjoyed, that a resort to books, to assist in a profitable
disposition of time, is pleasant.

My *voyageurs* called my attention to a red lurid aspect
of the atmosphere in the south, and said we should have a
strong wind from that quarter.   Their prognostication was
soon realized.   The gale did not last long, and the only
remarkable feature was, that when it subsided, it was almost instantaneously.

Through the distance of about one hundred miles, which
we passed to-day, the country is level and destitute of wood.
I observed a bank of clay in layers of diversified structure, such as I have often noticed.   The different sections
were of various colors ; some dusky red, some yellow, and
blue, and others white, making an upright elevation of one
hundred feet or more.

Salmon are ascending the river in great numbers, and
groups of Indians are scattered along pursuing the employment of catching them.   Wherever we passed them, they

came off in their canoes, bringing salmon to sell, some of which were roasted in the best manner, and served up on broad pieces of bark, which answered a good purpose in the absence of plates ; and often large leaves of plants were spread neatly upon the bark. Upon these we dined, without bread, vegetables, or salt. My *voyageurs* found sufficient employment in the gratification of their appetites, to interrupt for a while their anecdote and song. We arrived at Walla Walla at evening, just in season to find shelter from one of the most violent thunder storms, accompanied with wind, which I have witnessed in this country. Such storms are of rare occurrence west of the mountains.

CHAPTER XXII.

A summary of the Indians of the Upper country—names of the tribes, their locations and numbers—leave Walla Walla for Fort Vancouver—swift passage down the river—run the Falls—Cascades—dangerous eddy—arrive at Vancouver—steam boat excursion.

HAVING traveled over the most important parts of the upper country, and collected the facts of its physical condition, together with the location, character, and condition of the most numerous tribes of Indians; before leaving this section of the territory west of the Rocky Mountains, it may be proper to give a connected summary of these particulars. On the south part of the Oregon Territory, adjoining Upper California, are located the Shoshones or Snake Indians. I was not able to gain knowledge of their definite numbers, but the general estimate is that they are more than ten thousand. Their country is decidedly the most barren, west of the mountains; most parts being covered with scoria and other volcanic productions. These Indians are poor, and as indicative of their condition and their resources, they are called Snake Indians, and Root-diggers. Some of them go to the mountains and hunt buffalo, and they very generally resort to the river in the season of fishing. They have a tolerable supply of horses. When they go to Rendezvous they make a great display, advancing on horseback, dressed in their most fantastic manner, exhibiting all their ornaments of feathers, beads, wolf-tails, teeth and claws of animals, arranged according to their notions of good taste. The warriors are armed, hideously painted, and those who have been wounded in battle are very fond of showing their scars. After coursing around and through the camp of Rendezvous for some time, they dismount and go through the ceremony of shaking hands. I had also an opportunity of seeing many of the Utaws at Rendezvous. Their country is situated to the east and south-east of the Shoshones, about the Salt Lake and on the head waters of the Colorado river, which empties into the gulf of California. They number nearly four thousand persons, and appear to be a mild and peaceable people, honest, kind, and hospitable to strangers, and affectionate among themselves. They live by hunting, fishing, and gathering roots and berries. Their dress is plain, and their manners are unassuming. Their country being in latitude about 41°, has a fine climate, and good soil.

Proceeding north, we come to the country of the Nez Percés, which has many fertile parts adapted to tillage and is throughout a fine grazing country. They number about two thousand five hundred ; but they have already been often mentioned.

The Cayuses are situated to the west of the Nez Percés, and very much resemble them in person, dress, habits and morals. They are equally peaceable, honest and hospitable to strangers. They number more than two thousand persons. Their wealth consist in horses, which are unusually fine and numerous ; it being no uncommon thing for one man to own several hundred. Their country, especially that about the Grand Round, is uncommonly fertile, producing spontaneously cammas in great abundance, upon which, with fish and some game, they principally subsist. They express the same anxiety to be instructed as the Nez Percés and Flatheads.

The Walla Walla Indians inhabit the country about the river of the same name, and range some distance below, along the Columbia river. The number of persons in this tribe is about five hundred. In their character, employments and moral habits, they do not materially differ from the last named tribes.

The Paloose tribe are properly a part of the Nez Percés, and in all respects are like them. Their residence is along the Nez Percé river and up the Pavilion. They number about three hundred. The four last named tribes speak the same language with a little dialectical difference.

North-east of the Palooses are the Spokein nation. They number about eight hundred persons, besides some small tribes adjoining them who might be counted a part of their nation. I have so fully described them that it is unnecessary to enlarge upon their character. Their country is much diversified with mountains and valleys, prairie and woods, and a large part is of primitive formation, and some parts are very fertile. They denominate themselves the children of the sun, which in their language is *Spokein.* Their main dependence for subsistence is upon fishing and hunting, together with gathering roots and berries. I have stated that a commencement is made in agriculture, which it is to be hoped will be generally adopted, so that their present precarious mode of living may give place to that which will be substantial. They have many horses, but not so numerous as their neighbors farther south.

East of these are the Cœur d'Aléne Indians, whose numbers are about seven hundred, and who are characterized by civility, honesty, and kindness. Their country is more open than the Spokeins', and equally, if not better adapted to agriculture.

The country of the Flatheads is still farther east and south-east, and extends to the Rocky Mountains. They are a very interesting tribe ; dignified in their persons, noble, frank, and generous in their dispositions, and have always shown a firm attachment to white men. They number about eight hundred persons, and live a wandering life. For subsistence they follow the buffalo upon the head waters of Clarke and Salmon rivers, and often pass over to the head waters of the Missouri. They have become a small tribe by constant wars with the Blackfeet Indians, though they themselves are not of a ferocious or hostile disposition. Being averse to war, they wish to settle upon their lands, and are only waiting to be instructed in the arts of civilization, and in Christianity.

Their country is mountainous, but intersected with pleasant, fertile valleys, large portions of which are prairie. The mountains are cold, but in the valleys the climate is mild.

An anecdote was related by a chief of this nation, which illustrates their native character, and the propensity of Indians to imitation. He said the first white men he saw, was when he was young. It was summer. He said, " These are a new people, they look cold, their faces are white and red ; go make a large fire, and I will ask them to come and warm them." In a short time his people had made a fire, and brought new buffalo robes. The white men came into his lodge and he wrapped them in the robes and seated them by the fire that they might be warm. The robes slipped off; he replaced them. Soon the white men made signs to smoke their pipe. The chief thought they asked for food, and brought them meat. The white men gave him the pipe, and he and his people smoked,

" and after this they loved smoke, and they loved the white men, and said they were good."

The Ponderas are so like the Flatheads in person, manners, and character, that a particular description of them may be passed over. They number about two thousand two hundred, and live on the north of Clarke's river, and on a lake which takes its name from the tribe. Their country has many fertile parts, and would soon be put under cultivation, if they could obtain instructors to teach them agriculture and to impart to them a knowledge of those things which are necessary to constitute a happy and prosperous community. Their language is the same as the Spokeins' and Flatheads'. The Cootanies inhabit a section of country to the north of the Ponderas along M'Gillivray's river, and are represented as an uncommonly interesting people. They speak a language distinct from all the tribes about them, open and sonorous, and free from gutturals, which are common in the language of the surrounding tribes. They are neat in their persons and lodges, candid and honest, and kind to each other. I could not ascertain their numbers, but probably they are not over a thousand.

There are several other tribes of Indians, whose countries are situated upon the waters of the north-east branch of the Columbia river, resembling each other so nearly in their customs, morals, manners, and mode of living, that it is unnecessary to go into a separate and particular description of each. I will mention the names, locations, and number of some of the principal tribes. North of the Cootanies are the Carriers, whose number is estimated to be four thousand. South of these are the Lake Indians, so named from their place of residence, which is about the Arrow Lakes. They are about five hundred in number. At the south, and about

Colvile, are the Kettle Falls Indians, who number five hundred and sixty. West of these are the Sinpauēlish, one thousand in number; and below these are the Shooshaps, having a population of five hundred and seventy-five. At the west and north-west, next in order are the Okanagans, numbering one thousand fifty. To the north and west are several tribes, about whom I obtained no definite information. Between Okanagan and the Long Rapids are detachments of Indians, who appear poor, and wanting in that manly and active spirit, which characterizes the tribes above named. South of the Long Rapids, to the confluence of Lewis' river with the Columbia, are the Yookoomans, a more active people, numbering about seven hundred. The whole number of the above named Indians is thirty-two thousand five hundred and eighty-five. This is probably a low estimate, and in the number, the Fall and La Dalles Indians are not included, nor many other numerous tribes residing at the north and south of the Falls of the Columbia, whose numbers, I could not with certainty ascertain. We might more than double this number, and probably still come below the population of the upper country.

The Indians to whom our horses were entrusted, came in safely, as I expected. After resting on the Sabbath, we renewed, on Monday the 6th, our voyage down the river, having Fort Vancouver for our next destination. We exchanged the bateau for a large canoe, retaining the men who attended me from Okanagan. Assisted by the high water, we made rapid progress until three in the afternoon, when a strong head wind compelled us to take to the land for the remainder of the day, having gone seventy-five miles. The Indians as usual came to us in their friendly manner, offering us salmon, and asking for tobacco, which they esteem more highly than either gold or silver. They have been accustomed to traffic in this commodity, until they expect it of every passing traveler.

The morning of the 7th was more calm, and we got under way at an early hour, but with the rising day the wind again increased to such a degree, that we were obliged to suspend our voyage. After a strenuous endeavor to effect a landing on the north, we were at length, without the power of controlling our canoe, and in much danger, driven across to the opposite shore ; and here for the first time in all my travels, I found it impossible to pitch my tent, such being the strength of the wind, that it would have been carried away. The canoe was drawn upon the shore, and wrapping myself in my blankets and buffalo robes, I laid me down in safety by the side of the canoe. We had here, as at all our other landing places, the usual friendly visit from the neighboring Indians.

The following day we were able to resume our journey, and passed the rapids, which in the tempest of yesterday looked so forbidding. A little caution on the part of my experienced Frenchmen in regard to the numerous islands and eddies, enabled us to effect the passage in perfect safety. In a short time we approached the falls of the Columbia, which, in low water, are twenty feet perpendicular, followed by raging rapids below. Bousheau, my steersman, proposed to run the falls, saying that there was no danger in full freshet, and that it would save a portage. We were then passing a section of the river where the banks were walled up with basalt; and while I was revolving in my mind the chances of safety, I had concluded, that when we should come to the great basin below, I would be set on shore ; but when we came to the basin, the water of the river, rushing from the mural shores, formed impassable breakers on the right and on the left, and onward we must go, let consequences be what they would. We kept near the middle of the river, which was free from breakers, though not from high surges. Soon, with amazing velocity, we were over the cataract of the mighty waters, and made our way into a bay at the head of the first portage of the La Dalles. The accumulation of water from those stupendous mountains above, was so great, that the narrow channel of the La Dalles, studded with basaltic islands, so obstructed the passage of the river, that the falls were almost lost in the depth.

Such were the eddies and surging of the water among the rocky islands in the narrow broken channel of the La Dalles, that we had to make three portages. Our canoe was so large that twenty Indians were not too many to carry it safely. Their mode of carrying is to invert it upon their heads and shoulders, and then it is with difficulty and danger that they pass the steep and rocky ravines. When we came to the last portage, the Indians were not willing to take hold again unless we would pay them in powder and balls; and although their demands were reasonable, yet our stores were not adequate to meet them, and they would not perform the labor without the required articles. I engaged Sopelay, and another influential chief, to induce their men to perform the labor of making this last portage, and promised that I would send them the demand from Fort Vancouver, and for their security I would give them a talking paper. They stated to their people my proposal, and were about to succeed, when Tilkī, the first chief, who had become familiar with an American trader, laughed at their credulity. Sopelay, however, stated to the people, that he

had seen me at the fort, and that he heard me teach the Indians good things, and did not believe I would deceive them.
He prevailed, and the men took hold of the work ; and in
four hours from passing the falls we were beyond the raging
water, where we made our morning repast upon very fine
salmon.

Our passage during the remainder of the day was pleasant ; we passed Cape Horn without difficulty, and landed for
the night twelve miles above the Cascades. In this high
state of the water, very few of the trees of the submerged
forest were to be seen.

On the morning of the 9th, we passed the Cascades by
hiring Indians to *cordelle* the canoe down them, exclusive of
one short portage, the distance of two miles to the great
basin, or rather the great whirlpool below. This labor is
attended with some danger, and cases, though not numerous,
have occurred of the loss of lives and property. As I walked along the shores, and over precipices, I saw the wrecks
of several canoes and bateaux strewed upon the rocks. We
embarked upon the great basin, at the lower part of which
we passed into a rapid, where the main current took a dia-
gonal course from the north towards the south shore. On
both sides of this current there were heavy breakers, and as
the only course of safety, we took the middle. We had not
proceeded far before a large whirlpool, with a deep, devour-
ing vortex formed almost directly before us, and as we were
going forward very swiftly, it seemed impossible to avoid its
circling current. I said to my steersman, bear a little to
the right. " O don't speak here," was his reply. As we
approached the vortex, it filled after the manner of smaller
eddies, and we soon felt the influence of its waters rolling
out from the centre, and all our strength was required to

resist them, lest we should be thrown upon the breakers. We passed with the rapidity of the wind, and in a short time were upon the smooth surface of the tide waters below.

The sensations excited in descending these Cascades are of that peculiar character, which are best understood by experience. The sensation of fear is no sooner awakened than it subsides before the power and magnificence of the rolling surges, the circling vortices, and the roaring breakers. Let those whose dormant energies, either of body or mind, need arousing, try the navigation of the Columbia in high water, and their powers will be invigorated for almost any future enterprise. Such is the fascinating power, I had almost said magic of these scenes, that those who are accustomed to be employed upon these waters, though far away from home and kindred, become attached to this mode of life, and are reluctant to abandon it for any other. Each time the scenery of these interesting Cascades is beheld, new wonders unfold themselves. Niagara itself, if we except its unbroken fall of one hundred and fifty feet, cannot bear a comparison with the superior style of nature's works here. Nor are these things created merely to attract our momentary admiration. Science in very many of its departments, may find subjects for investigation.

While the ornithologist listens to the songsters of the forest, and in these enchanting solitudes follows them with his eye as they dart from bough to bough; his attention is arrested by the noble and majestic white headed eagle, as he takes his favorite perch upon the loftiest heights of some needle-pointed rock, or the summit of some leafless tree, or as he darts from thence upon his prey; or his attention may be arrested by the daring fish-hawk in his rapid descent upon the finny tribe. An amusing occurrence took place in

my view. A fish-hawk seized upon a fish of such magnitude, that the contest for a long time was doubtful, as the
splashing water indicated, which should exchange its native
element.   The resistance was so great, that a disengage-
ment was deemed the best policy.

Here also the botanist, while he forbears to ascend the
lofty mountains, which for him present an aspect of too
much dreariness, may retire into the narrow receding valleys, or wind his way over sunny hills in search of new
genera of plants, or at least new species, with which to im-
mortalize his name, and add to the stores of his favorite
science.

The geologist, while he admires the stupendous monuments of volcanic operations before him, may also find
much to interest him in examining more minute formations.
Along the rugged shores are scattered specimens of calcedony, jasper, agate and cornelian.   He may examine the
cellules of the immense masses of amygdaloid ; the columnar basalt, and the mountains shooting up their denticulated
forms and needle-points.   His attention will be drawn to the
examination of the lava, breccia, and trachyte ; and he will
be interested in finding many dendrolites.   When he looks
at the deep channel through which the Columbia river finds
its onward way to the Pacific ocean, if he doubts the agency of God in forming the courses of the rivers, he may indulge his imagination in computing how long it has taken
this river to wear down the immensely hard basalt a thousand feet ; and having ascertained how long it takes to
wear any given depth, he may then make his mathematical
conclusions how long the process has been going on.   But if
he is a Christian philosopher, while he admits second causes, he may look up to the great first Cause, and admire and

adore; and not regarding baseless theories, may exclaim, "How wonderful are thy works, in wisdom hast thou made them all."

As we passed out of the mountain country about the Cascades, we found the wide valley below so inundated, as to present the appearance of an inland sea. I arrived safely at the fort, found my friends well, and exchanged cordial congratulations.

Sabbath, June 12th, I preached to the people of the fort, and in the evening had a third service, in which as heretofore, an opportunity was given to those present, to propose questions on any subject of religion about which they wished information. I was particularly gratified to find, that during my absence, public worship had been maintained, and an effort had been made to bring the French Canadians to attend upon religious instruction. They are assembled twice on the Sabbath, and a portion of scripture and a sermon in French, are read to them by Dr. McLaughlin.

I was favored with an opportunity to send to Sopelay the promised powder and balls, by Capt. Black, a gentleman of the Company, who in a few days was to leave Vancouver for his station north of Fort Okanagan.

On the 14th, we took a water excursion in the steam-boat Beaver, Capt. Home, down the Columbia to the confluence of the western branch of the Multnomah; up this river into the Willamette, and then into the middle branch of the Multnomah, and through it into the Columbia, and back to the fort. All the low lands were overflowed with the annual freshet, and presented the appearance of an immense bay, extending far into the country. The day was pleasant and our company cheerful. The novelty of a steam-boat on the Columbia, awakened a train of prospective reflections upon

the probable changes which would take place in these remote regions, in a very few years. It was wholly an un-
thought of thing when I first contemplated this enterprise.
that I should find here this forerunner of commerce and business.   The gayety which prevailed was often suspended,
while we conversed of coming days, when with civilized
men, all the rapid improvements in the arts of life, should
be introduced over this new world, and when cities and villages shall spring up on the west, as they are springing up
on the east of the great mountains, and a new empire be
added to the kingdoms of the earth.

The Columbia is the only river of magnitude in the Oregon Territory, and this is navigable for ships but one hundred and thirty miles to the Cascades; and it is the only
one which affords a harbor for large ships on the coast, from
California to the 49° of north latitude.   For bateaux and
various other light craft, the Columbia and its branches are
navigable a thousand miles.   The internal navigation could
not be much improved, unless at great expense, by canals
around the rapids and falls, which are so numerous that
ascending the river is now difficult.   Still a considerable
interior trade is carried on by means of these waters, and
the ingenuity of men on the west, when it shall be more
extensively populated, will contrive facilities, as on the east,
for greatly improving the intercourse of remote and different portions of this territory.

CHAPTER XXIII.

Geology.

HAVING remarked on the features of the country through which I passed, as I proceeded, I shall now give a more connected and summary view of facts, the result of my observations in relation to the geology of that hitherto unexplored region. In remarking, however, on the observed facts, it cannot be expected that I should be able to give a complete view of the geology of so extensive a territory; it being greater than the whole of the United States east of the Alleghany Mountains. The complexity, too, must be considered, of plainly marked phenomena, resulting from long continued igneous action, where both ancient and comparatively recent products are so blended, that time and much experience alone can resolve appearances, at first view inexplicable. Let the reader also add to this the circumstances under which the author was compelled to note the data of his conclusions. He regrets that in his brief stay in the country, where many years are requisite fully to investigate all its interesting phenomena, and in a field so rich, he could make but few measurements, and only judge in most cases by approximate modes. As to the strict scientific accuracy of his statements, he deems it no more than just to say, that while he doubts not that the facts he details are worthy the attention of scientific men, and are correct *in re*, so that perfect reliance may be placed on them, yet he feels himself to have wanted that almost intuitive knowledge, which he alone possesses who has long been a field-laborer.

With these considerations the author presents the result of his observations, hoping the reader may find much that is valuable respecting these regions of the setting sun, replete as they are with interest, arising from grandeur both of scenery, and of developments of the modes and effects of the operations of the great geological agents ; especially of that element, which in time past has wrought such changes, and is yet gradually and more unperceivedly producing them ; where it has played all its frantic freaks, and then quietly left this spot with so few superimposed materials, that well developed phenomena may be leisurely examined.

My design is first to give a general view of the rocks of Oregon—then state a few facts in the form of remarks or descriptions—and then add a brief catalogue of minerals found in this Territory.

After leaving the great secondary valley of the Mississippi, near the Black Hills, which are a range of lesser mountains, east of the Rocky Mountains, the geologist begins to find rocks of the Carboniferous Group, obscurely manifest beneath the deep soil, and anthracite coal in loose fragments on the banks of streams running into the Platte. Among and beyond the Black Hills, the carboniferous strata are clearly seen, the coal "cropping out" and presenting precisely the same features as did the Wilksbarre beds in Pennsylvania, when I saw them, before they were worked. Here, for several days, we rode over rocks, interspersed now and then with anthracite, and having marks of the presence of iron, as is usual in regular coal deposits.

Passing this, the geologist next reaches another group,

either the upper secondary, or more recent rocks, lying at the foot of the Rocky Mountains. I was inclined to believe, from the fact that I was apparently geologically rising, as well as really ascending above the level of the ocean, that they were the latter. Red Shale, or sandstone, I found in what are termed the Red Butes. Perhaps this is New Red Sandstone.

Reaching the Rocky Mountains, which are a continuation of the Andes, depressed in Mexico, Granite becomes abundant, and other primary rocks, extending to an unknown distance north and south, and more than a hundred miles east and west. This section, mostly covered with perpetual snow, affords ample space for the study of glacial geological action, a subject now eliciting much attention. The valley through which we passed remarkably indicates the overruling hand of Providence, in providing an easy pass, where no serious obstacle presents itself to the construction of a rail-road. This and other valleys would undoubtedly, with facilities for observation, give equal opportunities to discover the formation of this vast chain, as has been done in regard to the great rocky ranges of the Eastern Continent.

Advancing westward, and emerging from the Rocky Mountains, there is found immediately at their base Secondary Rocks ; but as we approach the borders of one of the great volcanic furnaces of the world, they are much broken and tilted up, presenting some singular phenomena which I have mentioned in the journal, such as the formation of narrow ridges with the strata at different angles. In some places these dyke-like ridges are nearly regular in size and distance, as though cracked by an upheaving force, and the fissures filled afterwards with earth ; and in other places existing in wedge-form masses, interspersed between other rocks, and having other varieties of dislocation. The lithological character of the tract, over which we rode for two days, corresponds with that of the new red sandstone of the valley of the Connecticut. There are deposits both of the red and slaty colored strata—and their depth seems to be quite great, as is evinced by bluffs. But, as I observed no organic remains, my inclination to believe that these rocks are the new red sandstone, is founded only on their mineral character, and the fact, a very important one, that they appear directly to underlay the saliferous rocks, or to lie immediately above them. Should these rocks, which are quite extensive, prove to be new red sandstone, it adds no little to the interest of the geology of a country so rich in other respects. Perhaps, as red rocks of the same kind lie on each side of the Rocky Mountains, it may be proved hereafter, that the range was elevated through a deposit of shale or new red sandstone.

Directly after leaving the red sandstone, and passing a belt of volcanic operations, which also are found among the red and slaty rocks just described, (as will be seen by reference to the *Trois Tetons*, the Butes, and other conical mountains, as exhibited on the map,) Saliferous Rocks are seen. Here is Native Salt, *Chloride of Sodium*, and red, green, brown, and white strata of indurated marl, agreeing in character with the geological features of the Bochnia and Wieliezka mines of Poland. These rocks also occupy quite a tract of country, as we were several days in passing them, and they seemed to reach both north and south of the locality of rock salt, as is proved by the existence of the great Salt Lake at the south ; and travelers assert that native rock salt is found to the north, and especially far to the south, near the Rocky Mountain range.*

We have now arrived at Oregon proper, and find it a vast amphitheatre of volcanic operations, where are exhibited in unexcelled magnificence, variety and distinctness, the productions of several periods.

The Greenstone, found in connexion with the new red sandstone and saline rocks, undoubtedly belongs to the same period as that of other countries.

The Columnar Basalt, corresponding as it does with other similar eruptions in the eastern world, is probably cotemporaneous with them. The same identity of time may be traced in regard to the trachyte, obsidian, clinkstone or phonolite, and other products, after allowing for difference of circumstances of pressure, and rapidity of refrigeration. Recent eruptions also have taken place.

The traces of igneous action, commencing near the Rocky Mountains, or mountains adjacent to them, in the secondary rocks, are evinced by the disturbed state of these rocks, as already described, and grow more and more evident until almost the whole region exhibits volcanic products. In other places, the Primary of the Rocky Mountains, or mountains west of this range, first begins to be cracked and injected with dykes, then farther west terminates in the vast volcanic field of upper and lower Oregon.

It is in vain to attempt fully to describe the volcanic operations here presented. Mountains of amygdaloid, the cavities of which are mostly vacant ; volcanic conglomerate, detritus, columnar basalt, and disintegrated lava, every where abound, together with other less frequent produc-

---

* See Ures' Geology, page 373, and Professor Rogers' Report to the British Geological Association.

tions ; obsidian, clinkstone, pitchstone, and minerals found in the cavities of amygdaloid.   The tops of hills and mountains are sometimes spread out into horizontal plains, others terminate in conical peaks or are rounded like domes. Escarpments are frequently presented like that in the plate heading this chapter.   Regular craters, presenting themselves in the form of cones and concave depressions, are often found in plains, or capping the summits of mountains ; most of them, however, are more or less obscured by the lapse of time, but still as marked as the extinct craters of the Sandwich Islands.   The marked volcanic agency, manifesting itself in these and similar products, and completely occupying most of the country which we have termed upper and lower Oregon, continues to be evident until lost in the waters of the Pacific.   In some places the Primary rocks seem again to be found on the western coast.   Near the mouth of the Columbia I noticed a few Tertiary rocks lying *in situ*, and obtained a few shells belonging to this deposit. Whether there is on the North West Coast a regular Tertiary basin, partly on shore, and the rest under the ocean, remains to be determined.   Queen Charlottes island on the north is, at least in part, primary.   Primary rocks rise in various parts of the country, and are like islands in the vast volcanic field.   Such are the Salmon river mountains, and the granite near the Spokein river, and other places.

We have thus glanced at the rocks of Oregon as we pass westward.   In relation to their extent in a northerly and southerly direction, I am unable to say much.   There is evidence that igneous action has extended from Queen Charlottes island to California.   Of the extent of the Saliferous rocks, I have remarked.   That they extend from north of the locality where I found native salt, south into Mexico, appears quite certain.

Having remarked thus much in general terms, I will proceed to give a few facts without much order, some, if not all of which, might have been included in my description of the great changes in the rocks.

The plate at the head of this chapter demands a more definite explanation than has been given in former editions. It substantially describes a frequent escarpment of volcanic rocks, such as is found in nearly every part of Oregon.

The place designed to be represented by it is below the junction of the Cooscootske with the Lewis river. With some variations it is applicable to a mural escarpment several miles below the Cascades on the Columbia. Similar mural escarpments are found in the Spokein country, and at the Grand Coulé or ancient bed of the Columbia. The needle-points on the right of the plate are found most distinctly marked just below the Cascades, though they occur at numerous other places. Indeed this is not an unfrequent form of basalt west of the Rocky Mountains.

The first strata marked in the plate above what is intended for the shore of the river, is irregular massive amygdaloid. In some localities similar to that from which the plate is taken, there is found a conglomerate underlaying this strata. The next or second strata of the plate, is volcanic breccia or conglomerate, composed of detritus, and angular fragments mixed with earthy matter, and is perhaps what some call volcanic tufa. This brecciated layer is more or less hard and compact, varying however very much in different localities, and is in all cases only a few feet thick. The third strata is columnar basalt, regularly crystalized in pentagons about two feet in diameter. In other places

they vary in size from one to four or more feet in diameter.
It is in all the localities where I noticed it, closely jointed,
with the convex surface upwards, like the basalt of the Gi-
ants Causeway. The fourth is a brecciated layer. The
fifth on the left, is columnar basalt, and on the right, amygdaloid in juxtaposition with the basalt. The sixth is a brecciated layer. The seventh and uppermost is a semi-crystalized basalt on the left, and needle-pointed basalt on the
right. The semi-crystalized basalt very nearly resembles
the Palisades on the Hudson river, and the greenstone of
East and West Rocks at New Haven, and the more distinct
crystals found in Mt. Tom and Mt. Holyoke. For the latter
see Hitchcock's Geo. 1st ed. page 73.

In a description of bluffs and banks of rivers, where
there are mural escarpments similar to that from which the
plate is taken, I have numbered from ten to twenty strata of
amygdaloid, basalt, and brecciated layers, which appear to
have been thrown up in different periods, through craters,
fissures or chasms, rising in succession one above another.
In some locations the lowest formation is pudding stone; on
this amygdaloid, varying in thickness from a few feet to
twenty or thirty; and then above this a stratum of angular
fragments of basalt and amygdaloid, frequently intermixed
with lava, which I have termed the brecciated layer. This
strata generally appears to have been exposed for a period
to atmospheric agencies, until in some degree decomposed,
and upon this the alternating strata as described above, indicating so many different eruptions; the whole series rising
from fifty to several hundred feet. The brecciated layers
are only a few feet in depth, and appear to have been for a
long period the surface, after which a new eruption has
again overspread the whole. In one section of the high

Drawn by H.W. Parker.

Peabody, St. Ithaca, N.Y.

BASALTIC FORMATIONS of the COLUMBIA RIVER.

walls of the Grand Coulé, far up the sides, instead of the breccia is presented a depth of yellow earth of six or eight feet, and upon this several strata of basalt and amygdaloid, as above described, in like manner exhibiting proof that this section for a long time constituted the surface. Thus it appears that the internal fires have had long intervals of repose, and then have again sent forth their volcanic substances. The probability is, that they were thus in operation for centuries, but with a few exceptions, have ceased for centuries past, so that time has been given for atmospheric agencies to decompose the volcanic productions, sufficiently to form a soil covering most parts of the country. The enquiry naturally arises, whether it may not be on account of the great internal fires of this country, that the temperature is so much warmer on the west side of the mountains than on the east; for it is an interesting fact, that the eastern side of North America, in given parallels of latitude, is the coldest, while the western in the same parallels, is the warmest part of the world. And may not this arise from the comparative recency, as well as extent and depth of the volcanic operations which have pervaded this whole region of the setting sun.* The length of time, which immense masses of lava and other volcanic matter retain heat, is well known, and needs no remark. May not the climate thus be affected in Oregon ?

Among other localities of columnar basalt, the columns

---

* By reference to the annexed meteorological table it will be seen, from observations taken between the 45th and 46th degrees of north latitude, that in the winter of 1835—6, the greatest cold was but 10° below the freezing point, and this for three mornings only—and during the month of March there were but two mornings in which there was any frost.

of which are regular crystalized pentagons, a distinguished one is on the high lands dividing the waters of the Snake and Spokein rivers. The formations of this locality have many interesting characteristics, as described on page 290. Another below the Cascades of the Columbia, where the regular pentagonal columns wall up the north side for the distance of half a mile. Here are also found all the varieties of volcanic productions;—volcanic peaks, as diversified in their forms as they are numerous, being conical, denticulated, and needle-pointed; varying in magnitudes, and rising one above another from ten feet to fifteen hundred feet. These occur almost entirely upon the south side. There are also numerous islands of basalt in the Columbia river and its branches, elevated often much above high freshet water. These are numerous in the La Dalles, and in the ancient bed of the Columbia, or Grand Coulé. These islands are the same in form and substance as the dykes which exist in various parts of the country. There is something similar to these Needles in what I have termed the Pillars, where one or two such needles occur alone, and rise some hundred feet. They are basalt, and so hard and comparatively smooth, that I can account in no other way for their production, than that they are dykes that have been injected into soft rock, or soil, which has since been removed by other agencies. The most remarkable instance of this is the PillarRock at the lower part of the rapids, below the Cascades, at the head of the tide water of the Columbia. It is about five hundred feet high; and is perpendicular on the river side, and nearly so on the other sides; and is wholly isolated upon a narrow strip of bottom land, with a small base, and its appearance resembles a vast monument. Another such needle is found in the river near the mouth of the Columbia, and standing alone makes a very conspicuous object.

Another result of volcanic agency is seen in the Primary rocks, which are cracks or fissures, through which gaseous products have escaped, without forming a crater, and indeed without ejecting any igneous solid matter. One locality of this kind presents a result somewhat peculiar. It is on elevated land near the Spokein river. Here are hundreds of regular cones, varying from a few feet in diameter and height, to a hundred or more in diameter at their base, and fifty or sixty feet high. They are made up of angular fragments of granite, from an inch to six or eight inches in size, and stand on a sandy plain now covered with yellow pine, apparently disturbed only at the places where these cones have broken through it. At a short distance south was granite *in situ.* Beside these cones was a dyke visible a hundred rods or more, the only other evidence of a disturbing force. These piles of fragments seem to have been made by the escape of steam or gas, for they appear as if smoked by a fire from within the cones. The Salmon river mountains afford another example similar to this. An irregular circular space of a hundred acres or more is covered with immense quantities of granite broken into cubical and angular fragments, as though prepared for Macadamizing the future turnpikes of Oregon.

These mountains, though mere islands of mica slate and granite in the great volcanic field, are quite extensive, and in addition to the breaking up of the granite by igneous forces, are also perforated by vents or chimneys, through which lava has escaped. One of the highest points of the mountains which lay in my route, was one of these. It is a granite mountain with the top capped by a volcanic cone, rising like an immense pyramid. The passage in some places of granite into basalt, is easily traced, and the first igneous appearance is not a change of the structure, but multiplied fractures increase, until you find the granite broken into large fragments, and these diminishing in size, until they disappear in the distinct characteristics of volcanic agency, in which it is changed into a substance resembling trachyte; if it has not become trachyte itself, while *in situ*. Smaller sections of granite are scattered over the country in forms of less dimensions, protruding from the earth; but these are of somewhat rare occurrence.

We have said that recent igneous action has taken place. A well authenticated instance occurred in August 1831. There was at this time at Fort Vancouver and vicinity, an uncommonly dark day which was thought to have been caused by an eruption of a volcano. The whole day was nearly as dark as night, except a slight red, lurid appearance, which was perceptible until near night. Lighted candles were necessary through the day. The atmosphere was filled with ashes which were very light, like the white ashes of wood; all having the appearance of being produced by great fires, and yet none were known to have been in any part of the whole region around. The day was perfectly calm, without any wind. For a few days after, the fires out of doors were noticed to burn with a bluish flame, as though mixed with sulphur. There were no earthquakes. By observations which were made after the atmosphere became clear, it was thought the pure, white, perpetual snow upon Mount St. Helens was discolored, presenting a brown appearance, and therefore it was concluded, that there had been upon it a slight eruption. The Indians say they have seen fires in the chasms of Mount Hood. Tilkī, the first chief of the La Dalles Indians, who is a man of more than ordinary talents, said he had frequently seen fires in the fissures of rocks in the last named mountain.*

Though I have improved every opportunity which has been presented to make observations, and have also made many enquiries of men who have traveled extensively and for a long time in different parts of this country, some of whom are men of science, yet no evidence of fossil remains have been noticed, with the exception of a very few specimens. 1 saw a small shell, a *Turritella*, which was found in a mountain south of Mount Hood, in the Callapooa country. Also a few miles up the Columbia river, on the south shore of the bay, I found some very large petrified bivalve shells, embedded in calcarious sandstone of the Tertiary formation. The largest specimens which I took, measure, longitudinally, four and a half inches from the hinge, and transversely, five. They are very perfect, beautifully scalloped, and have all the lustre of living shells.

Since the channel of the Columbia, in many parts, is walled up on its sides and studded with islands of basaltic rocks, rising in perpendicular height from twenty to four hundred feet; the question forces itself upon the mind, what agency formed the channel of the Columbia and other rivers flowing through ridges and mountains of hard basalt? Undoubtedly the action of water has worn the rock very considerably and effected changes, but perhaps by no principle of its action can it be supposed, that it has *produced* so long and so deep a channel, as the one through which the river

---

* Since the publication of the above in other editions, I have been credibly informed that lava was ejected at that time from Mount St. Helens.

flows, and through such solid rock formations, differing but little from iron in hardness. That the channels of rivers owe their existence to other causes than the action of water, is no new idea. Indeed very many are now described as formed otherwise. In relation to the channels of the Connecticut and its branches, see Prof. Hitchcock's Geo. page 167, 1st edit. While I believe that Providence operates by means, yet I doubt not there are phenomena which are, and ever may remain unresolved. While conversing in relation to the channel of the Columbia with some literary gentlemen who had frequently passed up and down this river, after several theories were proposed, none of which could bear the test even of probability, one of them remarked, he had been reminded of his boyish sports, when he had dammed up water, and then with his finger drawn a channel through the sand for the water to run ; so it seemed to him that God had drawn a channel for the Columbia.

If we do not keep in view the overruling hand of God as a landmark in our investigations, but look to nature, at work in her great laboratory, the earth, as our only guide to teach us precisely how the earth was formed, we shall, at least, be in danger of wandering into mazes from which we shall not be able to extricate ourselves.

The condition of the country on the western side of the Rocky Mountains, differing as it does in the species of its animals, birds, and plants, from that of the eastern side, gives us a view which shows what may be the truth in relation to regions of the earth now buried, and which perhaps are regarded as belonging to different Periods, though in fact contemporaneous. Yet in all such cases marks of isochronism, or the want of it, doubtless could be found, and with proper care would convince the experienced geologist of their diversity or identity in time. Compare the two sides of North America as they now are, and notice the difference which exists in their animals and productions. Let now the whole of the northern part of this continent be submerged, and after a long time be again elevated to its present position, and let future generations examine its fossil remains, and by the rules very generally laid down, would they not conclude that the section on the east side, and that on the west side of the mountains, indicate two different periods of submersion, and that there was a long intermediate period of tranquility between them? Would not the different genera and species of vegetables and animals lead to this conclusion? Would they not, from the evident difference of temperature of climate in the same latitudes on the east and on the west, conclude, if there was not a careful search made for other marks to show disparity or identity of time, that the western section was submerged, at a period when the earth was much warmer than at a period when the eastern section was submerged? This would be a rational and legitimate conclusion from the rule, that in strata of the same class, dissimilar organic remains belong to a different period of time, and were deposited under a different condition of the globe. And the gigantic balsam firs, found in the west and not found in the east, would as clearly prove a different climate in the same latitude, and therefore a different period of submersion, as the gigantic ferns prove a different temperature of the earth, and of course a different period of time, in which they were deposited.

On the west side, the enormous balsam firs, measuring from five to eight feet in diameter, and between one and two hundred feet in height, would be found so numerous as to constitute whole forests. Also the alder of various diameters, from the small to those of two feet, and proportionably tall ; and the rush varying from four to ten feet long, and proportionably large. While the fir, the alder, and rush, would be found on the east side, they would be mere dwarfs in comparison with those on the west, and also very sparse. And many genera of trees and plants would be found on the one side, which would not be found on the other. On the west there would be no walnut, chestnut, sugar maple, elm, and many other kinds of trees. And of animals, there would not be found any of the present fossils of the east, nor the ox, the ass, the swine, nor common sheep—the buffalo would be found east and in the mountains, but hardly beyond. To what strange conclusions, without great care and close examination, should we come, if such data simply were received ! If such is now the difference of vegetables and animals, between the country on the east, and the country on the west of our continent, and in the same latitude, may not mistakes be made in regard to different formations, and different periods of time in which they have taken place. Especially when periods are so remote, and the minute exploration of the earth confined to so small limits.

Far the greatest part of the soil of Oregon is formed from decomposed lava and other like substances, reduced by atmospheric agencies, which forms a fine rich black mold. Some parts, however, are in a different condition ; such as the great desert of the Shoshones or Snake country, which lies between two ranges of mountains, and extends three hundred or more miles in a southeasterly direction, with an average width of about one hundred miles. This desert, occupying as it does so many square miles, is to a great extent covered with scoria and other volcanic matter, which from their nature renders it a barren region. Other tracts of country are argillaceous. In several localities, escarpments of clay, diversified in structure, are presented. The layers are from a few inches, to twenty feet in thickness. Their colors are dusky red, brown, blue, green, yellow, and in some instances pure white, and not unfrequently more or less indurated. Still, other tracts are calcarious ; and some parts, especially near the Rocky Mountains, are covered with a silicious sand, mixed with volcanic detritus; while few, and only few parts of the country afford vegetable mold.

By reference to the map between Okanagan and Walla Walla, the dotted line, as will be seen, describes the Grand Coulé. By some cause the Columbia has been turned from its ancient bed, and made to take a new and more circuitous course. The old channel has islands rising above what was once the level of the water ; and as previously mentioned, high mural escarpments are found on its sides.

Another fact worthy to be mentioned, is the subsidence on the Columbia. It is twenty or more miles long, and about a mile wide. See page 141.

What I suppose to be another subsidence occurs on the summit level which divides the waters of the Snake and Spokein rivers. See page 290.

Rivers are found which disappear and again reappear from under volcanic products, which is no new phenomena in other volcanic countries. Two such rivers are put down on the map south of Henry's Fork.

Limestone does not abound here ; indeed it is questionable whether it exists except in very detached and small quantities. One location of magnesian limestone, I observed in the neighborhood of the Sulphur Spring, which I have

already described. The lime used at Fort Vancouver, is
made of rock coral, imported for ballast in vessels returning from the Sandwich Islands. In the vicinity of the Sulphur Spring was a quantity, though not very extensive, of
gypsum. The only marble I noticed was a mountain situated a short distance below the confluence of the Spokein
with the Columbia. In parts which I examined, I discovered it to be saccharine white, and variegated blue. A specimen of the first I have preserved. Situated as it is on a
navigable river, it will most probably become in time a
source of wealth.

In the region of Pierre's Hole, and still farther west, there
is clinkstone of marked and distinctive character, in great
abundance, and in the same vicinity obsidian in large quantities. From the dark color of this, and also of basalt generally, I detected the presence of augite. Obsidian is found
in very many places throughout the country, and towards
the ocean, in small quantities, it is a resinous white.

Lava is abundant in many places, in all the varieties of
color in which it is usually found, sometimes dusky red,
yellowish, gray, and black, of different degrees of hardness
and gravity, some being compact, some cellular, and often
so light as to float upon water. Trachyte is also found
among the varieties of lava.

Most of the varieties of the precious stones, such as calcedony, agate, jasper, and cornelian, are found upon the
shores of the Columbia, Willamette, and the large branches
of these rivers. While they vary in size, forms, and colors,
many of them are very pure and beautiful, and might·be
improved to great brilliancy in the hands of the artist. Por-
phyry of different textures and quality is frequently met with,
some of which resembles the precious stones in fineness.

I saw no anthracite coal after leaving the region of the Black Hills on the east of the mountains; bituminous coal, of which I saw a quantity, is obtained from a locality near Pugets Sound, and brought for use to Fort Vancouver.

It is an interesting fact that Mineral Rock Salt exists in its native state, in a section of mountains on the south side of the Salmon river, before entering the Salmon river mountains. It crops out from the side of a mountain, a little above the base. I saw the mine and examined specimens of it, and took of it for future use. It is pure and white, and contains less of the water of crystalization than common salt. The geological formations in the immediate vicinity, so nearly resemble those described in the neighborhood of the mineral salt mines of Poland, as to induce the belief that it exists in great abundance. It was peculiarly grateful to me in the circumstances in which I was placed, and the best testimony I can give to the quality is, that I found it very useful while compelled to subsist on game.

Salt is also found in a crystalized state upon the shores of the great Salt Lake, the waters of which are so strongly impregnated, that large quantities are deposited. How wise and kind is the disposition of the products of nature, and how well adapted to the wants of all his creatures has the hand of a beneficent Father distributed his blessings ; and here, at so great a remove from all the facilities of commerce, He has laid up in store one of the most necessary and useful articles of domestic use.

But few Mineral Springs have as yet been discovered. The most remarkable are, the Soda fountain on Bear river, about forty-five miles north of Salt Lake, remarkable for the quantity of carbonic acid gas which is evolved, but not having been analyzed, its particular mineral properties are not ascertained, and the general remark only can be made, that it greatly resembles the Saratoga waters ;—the Sulphur Spring to the south of the *Trois Tetons*, on a branch of Henry's fork, around which large quantities of pure sulphur are deposited, and from which sulphureted hydrogen escapes, and its annoying properties are perceptible more than eighty rods distant ;—and the hot springs in the great range of the Rocky Mountains, some of which are said to furnish the mountain men a convenient place to boil their food.

Sulphate of magnesia, (epsom salts) purely native, exists in immense quantities in and on both sides of the mountains. Lakes or pools, which the heat of summer principally evaporates, abound in this region, exhibiting crystalized salts in great quantities. Spicular crystals of the same salt shoot up on the surface of the ground, effloresced to such a degree as to present the appearance of fields whitened with snow.

No indications of Metalic Ores have yet been noticed in any part of Oregon Territory.

CHAPTER XXIV.

General remarks—Meteorological table.

HAVING explored the most important parts of this territory, and gained all the information within my reach, as to
the several objects proposed in my instructions from the
Board of Foreign Missions; and especially having ascertained to my entire satisfaction two most prominent facts,
namely, the entire practicability of penetrating with safety
to any and every portion of the vast interior, and the disposition of the natives in regard to my mission among them,
it remained that the most feasible and expeditious mode of
returning should next be consulted. I could expect to ac-
quire but little additional knowledge in traversing the route
to Rendezvous; and the necessary delay of several months,
it seemed could be avoided by a return by water. The
Hudson Bay Company were about to send a ship to the
Sandwich Islands, in which I was kindly offered a gratuitous passage. On the other hand, my friendship with
gentlemen of this establishment, my regard for the spiritual
welfare of the benighted men for whose good I had for
many a weary day pursued my object, over mountains and
plains, hills and valleys, through all the vicissitudes of climate and weather; and especially a desire to see in this
whitened field, the returning laborers I expected, and to be
able to give them personally, instead of by letter, the result
of my collected information, as a guide to them in their in-
cipient labors; all these held me riveted to the spot, and un-

decided as to my course. At length after consultation with my most judicious friends, I concluded to take passage in the barque Columbia for Oahu, in the hope that an early opportunity would present to return to the United States.

In taking leave of this country and the work in which I have so long been engaged, a train of reflections crowds upon my mind. The future condition of this noble race of men is a subject of interesting enquiry to many others as well as to myself. Whether the Indians are to pass away before the increasing power and numbers of white men, or whether enlightened and improved by their philanthropy, they shall arise in the scale of intellectual and moral existence, is a problem which time alone can solve. I entered on the work of exploring this field with no bias or preconceived opinion, and from critical and personal observation, I hesitate not to say that I can see no reason existing in the nature of things, or in their present condition, which necessarily dooms the race to annihilation on the one hand, or on the other, necessarily makes them objects of apprehension, as the future hordes who shall in coming time, like the northern barbarians of Roman days, be reserved as the scourge of an overgrown and decaying republic. If to do good be an object worthy of humanity or religion, I see not why a consistent and persevering attempt to raise a race of freemen from their depression, and to place them in the rank of intelligent men, be not an undertaking fraught with as much promise and encouragement, as it was in earlier days to elevate our ancestors. In favor of this opinion, we have the docility of the Indians in every thing pertaining to their improvement; in the sprightliness of their youth and children ; and in the amiableness of their native tempers and dispositions. I take nothing of this upon testimony.

In all my intercourse with them, I saw, with only one exception, no angry or malevolent passions in exercise in their
little communities.

I tremble for the consequences, when I reflect on the
wrongs inflicted upon this race of men. Able pens have
portrayed in vivid colors, their injuries and abuses, and humanity has wept. Were but the one hundredth part spread
out to view, we should recoil at the sight. The life of an
Indian, in the estimation of our border and refugee men who
visit their country, is nothing worth. Theirs is a land
where white men regard no law, but superior cunning, and
superior force, bear rule. It was related to me that Captain S., an English officer in half pay, while traveling
through the Indian country, lost a horse which he highly
valued, and believing it to be stolen by an Indian, offered
five hundred dollars for his head. One of a lawless band,
a half Indian who was present, went in pursuit, and returned
with the head of the person charged with the theft, and demanded his reward. To make out the sum Captain S. gave
him two horses, calling each $250. This ended the affair.
Mr. Wyeth in a memoir, embodied in a Report of a Com-
mittee of Congress, on the Oregon question, says "The
preponderance of bad character is so great amongst traders
and their people, that crime carries with it little or no shame.
I have heard it related among white American trappers, as
a good joke, that a trapper who had said he would shoot any
Indian, whom he could catch stealing his traps, was seen
one morning to kill one; and, on being asked if the Indian
had stolen his traps, he answered No, but he looked as if he
was going to." These are only specimens.

I have been much pleased to notice among the benevolent
operations of the present day, the formation of a society in

England, which I regard as among not the least benevolent, viz. "An Aborigines Protection Society," from whose "Plan and Objects," I quote, as expressing most fully my own sentiments. "Among these tribes, our imported diseases produce frightful ravages, our ardent spirits deprave and consume their population, our unjust laws exclude them from enjoying that first element of well-ordered societies, judical protection, as well as from the possibility of a timely incorporation with colonial communities ; while, in addition to all these evils, our neglect of suitable means and methods of improvement, prevents that adoption of civilized manners and customs to which they are inclined. It is impossible for us as men, patriots, philanthropists, or Christians, to behold without anxiety, the ruin of the people whom we are accessary in supplanting, unless our future modes of colonization be directed with greater humanity and wisdom than in times past."

I have in several places made mention of the superior mildness of the climate west of the Rocky Mountains, and that the seasons are divided into the wet and dry; the rainy season commencing about the first of November, and the dry about the first of May. The following meteorological table, which was taken with care, will give a general specimen.

METEOROLOGICAL TABLE.

The observations were taken at seven o'clock in the morning, at one o'clock in the afternoon, and at sunset.

1835—6.

OCT.	7 A. M.	1 P. M.	S. SET.	WEATHER. A. M.	WEATHER. P. M.
4	44°	60°	°	clear.	light clouds.
S. 5	50	76	75	clear.	clear.
6	51	70	68	cloudy.	cloudy and hazy.
7	53	72	66	clear.	hazy.
8	54	70	66	cloudy all day, and hazy.	cloudy and hazy.
9	51	56	62	do. do. do.	do. do.
10	50	68	60	do. do. do.	wind do.
11	51	70	58	do. do. do.	wind do.
S. 12	50	68	56	do. do. with rain.	do. showers.
13	51	65	54	do. do. all day.	cloudy with wind.
14	50	60	48	do. do. do.	do. with wind and rain.
15	46	54	50	wind and rain.	more clear—evening calm.
16				light wind.	a little rain.
17				do. do. and rain.	rain.

	°	°	°		
18	50	54	58	light wind—and rain.	rain.
S. 19	45	52	50	clear and cloudy alternately.	clear and cloudy alternately.
20	43	46	44	cloudy through the day.	cloudy.
21	38	43	38	do. do. do.	cloudy.
22	33	34	33	rain most of the day.	cloudy.
23	33	34	33	rainy, high winds.	a heavy sea in the bay, some snow.
24	34	36	33	snow and rain.	wind.
25	36	44	40	wind and rain.	but not as yesterday.
S. 26	35	50	42	heavy wind.	heavy wind and rain.
27	36	42	40	clear and pleasant.	wind and rain.
28	40	52	49	clear.	clear.
29	42	54	52	clear and cloudy alternately through the	day—evening rain.
30	40	49	45	rain.	light rain.
31	39	49	50	light rain.	light rain most of the day.
NOV.					
1	53	60	48	heavy rain through the day.	
S. 2	42	50	50	morning clear.	rain.
3	40	53	49	somewhat stormy.	somewhat stormy.
4	37	51	46	light rain most of the day.	light rain.
5	50	54	46	morning clear.	cloudy.

	48°	43°	48°		
6				light rain most of the day.	light rain.
7	44	50	40	clear.	light rain.
S. 8	33	43	38	light rain, most of the day	clear.
9	33	42	40	clear.	do.
10	32	41	38	do.	do.
11	32	45	40	do.	do.
12	39	48	44	do.	do.
13	32	46	37	do.	do.
14	34	37	36	a little snow.	rain.
15	38	41	40	rain all day.	
S. 16	38	42	36	hazy.	hazy.
17	40	46	38	cloudy.	rain.
18	32	38	32	cloudy.	rain.
19	30	35	33	snow and rain.	snow and rain.
20	35	40	38	rain most of the day.	
21	38	43	36	cloudy.	cloudy.
22	35	40	40	rain most of the day.	
S. 23	38	40	39	cloudy.	cloudy.
24	40	44	44	cloudy.	clear.
25	33	35	34	morning clear.	variable.

Date	32°	38°	36°		
26	34	41	37	clear.	variable.
27	38	43	38	fair a small part of the day.	as in forenoon.
28	31	34	36	cloudy.	cloudy.
29	33	45	40	cloudy.	cloudy.
S. 30				clear and	cloudy alternately.
DEC.					
1	31	35	40	cloudy, sun	sometimes seen.
2	33	35	32	clear and	cloudy alternately.
3	22	31	29	clear.	clear.
4	23	32	31	clear.	clear.
5	24	31	25	clear.	clear.
6	22	31	29	clear.	clear.
7	22	28	34	cloudy,	cloudy.
S. 8	33	34	37	cloudy, and	a little hail.
9	31	36	40	clear.	clear.
10	31	38	42	clear.	clear.
11	30	40	38	cloudy and	clear alternately.
12	35	44	45	cloudy and clear alternately.	sun sometimes seen.
S. 13	32	44	40	thin clouds.	thin clouds.
14	26	46	40	clear and	very pleasant.

	32°	44°	49°		
15				thin clouds and	some sunshine.
16	40	44	44	cloudy.	rain.
17	42	44	42	rain.	alternate rain and snow.
18	38	44	40	cloudy with intervals of sun.	a little snow in the night.
19	36	41	41	cloudy and	some rain.
S. 20	35	38	34	cloudy and a little snow, which	melts as fast as it falls.
21	28	30	31	cloudy, a mixture of	hail and rain.
22	33	34	32	cloudy and	some rain.
23	39	52	39	cloudy and rain.	pleasant, some thin clouds.
24	39	52	42	cloudy and rain.	wind—rain—clear.
25	42	45	44	cloudy and rain.	rainy.
26	52	57	52	changeable weather.	clouds—rain—clear and pleasant.
S. 27	56	56	56	cloudy and	rainy all day.
28	56	58	56	somewhat cloudy.	towards evening rain.
29	56	55	53	cloudy—sun.	cloudy—evening rain.
30	40	43	46	partially cloudy.	very thin clouds.
31	46	46	48	cloudy.	cloudy and rain.
				JANUARY, 1836.	JANUARY, 1836.
1	50	54	50	some clouds, but as	a whole very pleasant.
2	46	52	48	cloudy.	some rain.

	54°	50°	46°		
S. 3	46	48	46	heavy rain.	heavy rain.
4	44	50	46	some clouds, but pleasant.	some clouds, but pleasant.
5	40	46	44	alternately heavy rain	and pleasant sun.
6	40	44	43	cloudy and some rain.	cloudy and some rain.
7	38	42	40	cloudy.	cloudy.
8	30	38	36	cloudy.	cloudy.
9	32	38	38	clear and pleasant.	evening cloudy, snow.
S. 10	34	36	38	cloudy.	cloudy and rain.
11	34	42	37	cloudy most of	the time through the day.
12	30	32	30	cloudy most of	the time through the day
13	30	32	32	snow.	snow.
14	34	39	36	cloudy.	somewhat snowy.
15	36	42	36	cloudy partly.	cloudy, evening clear.
16	31	34	34	cloudy and	clear alternately.
S. 17	34	36	36	cloudy and	some snow.
18	34	36	38	cloudy.	rain.
19	31	38	33	some clouds in the morning.	clear and pleasant.
20	30	34	32	clear and	pleasant.
21	26	30	28	cloudy all day.	
22				snow.	cloudy.

	28°	29°	38°		
23				cloudy.	cloudy—some rain making ice.
S. 24	28	31	30	cloudy, and rain	which makes a crust.
25	32	36	34	cloudy.	some pleasant sun.
26	36	36	36	cloudy and	pleasant sun alternately.
27	30	40	36	cloudy and	pleasant sun alternately.
28	34	36	34	cloudy.	cloudy.
29	34	36	36	rain.	rain through the day.
30	34	44	40	some clouds, but	very pleasant.
S. 31	36	44	39	some rain.	some rain.
FEB.					
1	35	46	42	clear and pleasant day.	clear and pleasant day.
2	40	46	44	some rain.	cloudy.
3	38	48	42	some clouds,	middle of the day very pleasant.
4	39	48	46	thin clouds.	middle of the day pleasant.
5	38	42	40	thin clouds.	clear and pleasant.
6	28	41	46	white frost—clear.	clear and pleasant.
S. 7	30	40	39	thin clouds.	thin clouds.
8	31	38	38	cloudy morning,	clear—cloudy evening.
9	32	40	39	cloudy morning,	clear—cloudy evening.
10	32	38	33	much as yesterday,	but not quite as pleasant.

	28°	30°	28°			
11				the most snowy day we have had,		together with wind.
12	30	34	34	cloudy and some rain.		cloudy and some rain.
13	34	43	38	thin clouds.		some sun and pleasant.
S. 14	32	43	38	much as yesterday.		but more pleasant.
15	34	42	40	cloudy.		a little sunshine.
16	37	44	40	cloudy.		a little sunshine.
17	40	47	44	cloudy.		some rain.
18	38	50	49	cloudy.		some sunshine—cloudy.
19	46	54	51	cloudy.		pleasant—cloudy.
S. 20	40	52	46	pleasant.		a few thin clouds.
21	32	48	42	clear and pleasant.		clear and pleasant.
22	30	42	40	some more cloudy		than yesterday.
23	32	42	36	cloudy and		little snow—clear.
24	26	40	36	clear.		clear.
25	26	42	36	clear.		clear.
26	28	36	34	cloudy.		little snow.
S. 27	30	38	32	partly cloudy.		and clear.
28	26	36	33	cloudy and		clear alternately.
29	28	42	40	cloudy.		cloudy.

MAR.					
1	37°	46°	44°	cloudy.	some pleasant.
2	35	46	46	cloudy, and	little sun.
3	44	54	50	cloudy, and	little sun.
4	50	58	54	cloudy,	cloudy.
5	48	60	56	cloudy,	sunshine with some clouds.
S. 6	46	56	48	cloudy,	thin clouds.
7	46	58	56	thin clouds.	thin clouds.
8	50	60	56	thin clouds in the morning,	afternoon clear.
9	40	62	58	clear.	clear.
10	39	60	58	clear.	clear.
11	50	56	48	some showers.	some showers.
12	39	46	38	rainy.	rainy.
S. 13	36	46	42	night and morning rainy.	most of the day thin clouds and sun.
14	38	48	44	partly cloudy and sun.	partly cloudy and sun.
15	34	48	42	nearly clear.	light shower.
16	38	50	47	cloudy.	alternately clear and cloudy.
17	36	47	47	cloudy morning.	clear. clear.
18	35	52	44	cloudy morning—clear.	clear. clear.
19	32	58	84	light white frost; after 8 o'clock, clear	through the day.

	30°	64°	58°		
S. 20	36	66	57	clear	through the day.
21	34	60	58	clear	through the day.
22	45	55	48	clear.	clear—cloudy.
23	43	54	48	cloudy, some	rain—rain.
24	38	66	55	cloudy, interchanges	of clouds—clear—some rain.
25	34	64	58	cloudy—clear.	clear.
26	46	64	56	light frost—clear.	very thin clouds.
S. 27	46	62	54	cloudy.	cloudy.
28	44	58	52	cloudy, a little rain.	thin clouds.
29	46	60	56	changes of clear	and clouds, and showers.
30	49	65	57	cloudy.	thin clouds.
31				cloudy.	thin clouds.
APRIL					
1	52	58	56	cloudy.	somewhat rainy.
2	48	52	48	cloudy, and	some rain.
S. 3	42	54	48	cloudy, alternately	cloudy, clear, and sunshine.
4	48	60	54	cloudy.	mostly clear.
5	49	60	56	rain, alternately	clear and cloudy.
6	46	56	49	rain most	of the day.
7	46	58	54	rain—cloudy,	partly clear.

	48°	54°	50°		
8	48	54	50	cloudy.	thin clouds.
9	45	52	48	rainy.	showers.
S. 10	43	56	53	most of the day cloudy.	some part pleasant.
11	44	42	40	cloudy.	rain through after part of the day.
12	40	46	44	showers.	showers.
13	40	50	48	rain.	showers.
14	38	48	46	cloudy.	cloudy.
15	44	50	42	rain.	rain.
16	48	54	44	rainy.	rainy.
S. 17		44		very heavy rain all day.	cloudy.
18		50	46	cloudy.	very high wind.
19	46	56	50	some clouds.	most of the day.
20				clear,	pleasant.
21		62		pleasant.	pleasant.
22				pleasant.	clear.
23				considerable wind.	flying clouds and rain.
S. 24		60		much wind.	and pleasant.
25		62		some wind,	clear.
26		66		clear.	some clouds.
27		74		clear.	

	°	90°	°	Remarks
28		92		very warm. clear.
29	46	64		clouds. high winds.
30		64	62	clouds. rain.
MAY.				
S. 1	46	64	62	windy and some clouds.
2	50	66		warm. warm.
3	56	76	62	warm and clear through the day.
4	56	76	64	clear. a little wind.
5	56	76	68	clear. very warm.
6	58	84	76	clear. clouds, some lightning and distant thunder.
7	60	80	72	very thin clouds. clear.
S. 8	60	58	54	some rain. and very high wind.
9	50	52	38	wind and clear. wind.
10	34	68	58	clear and pleasant,
11	50	72		the morning was cloudy. clear.
12	66	80	66	clear. very warm, no wind.
13	58	60	57	cloudy, rain. rain, cloudy.
14	57	76	60	cloudy. clear. clear.
S. 15	65	76	62	cloudy, rain, and some thunder.

From this time the dry season commenced, in which there is but little variation of weather.

CHAPTER XXV.

On the 18th of June, according to previous arrangements, I took passage in the steam-ship Beaver for Fort George, to join the barque Columbia for the Sandwich Islands. As the Beaver was commencing her first voyage upon the Pacific, under the power of steam, destined for the northwest coast, the people of the fort, and those residing around, assembled upon the shore of the Columbia, and as she moved majestically from her anchorage, they saluted us with cheers, which were reciprocated by all on board, and they responded, " A happy voyage, a prosperous voyage." The ship anchored at night a little above Tongue Point; and the next day, after being detained upon a sand bar, from which the tide after awhile set us free, we arrived at Fort George. The next day, the 20th, my friend Mr. Finlayson, and a few others took a ramble on the shores below. The verdure of the trees and plants, the red indigenous clover in full sweetness in the desert, and the mildness of the season, all combined to make the scene enchanting. It was on the shore of this bay where I collected the large bivalve shell petrifactions, embedded in calcarious sandstone of the Tertiary formation, as described in the chapter foregoing. No volcanic appearances were visible in the immediate vicinity.

On the 21st, I embarked on board the Columbia, and we dropped down to the Chenook Bay, and anchored just above Cape Disappointment. Here for the want of favorable wind and tide, we were detained until the 28th. While we continued here, I made several excursions on shore; ascended the cape, which is probably about four hundred feet high, and from which a fine prospect of the Pacific and its shores is presented as far as the eye can reach. The shore is generally bold and rocky, furnishing no other harbor near. The country around is rocky and densely covered with forests, and the scenery is wild. Near the shore, on the west end of the cape, a large cave extends into the volcanic rocks the distance of one hundred and fifty feet. We penetrated into its gloomy recesses, and from the bones of animals strewed around within, we concluded it must be the retreat of some of those beasts of prey which inhabit these forests and coasts.

About the cape at different places, grow the large orange-yellow raspberries of a new species. The shrubbery often grows to the height of twenty feet, and more generally in the forests than in open places, and equally fruitful. They are more inviting to the eye than agreeable to the taste.

While we were detained here, our men belonging to the Columbia caught a large number of codfish. They taste

very much like, and resemble those taken upon the banks
of Newfoundland, excepting they are a little shorter. This
is the first time they were known to exist in these waters ;
the Indians knew nothing of them before, and they eagerly
took those we did not need.

On the 25th, the bar being smooth, with only a light wind,
though ahead, and the tide favoring, the Beaver weighed
anchor and put out to sea for her northern voyage. She
went over the bar finely, and could have towed us over,
but it being her first experiment, it was not thought advi-
sable.

On Tuesday the 28th, the wind and tide were favorable
for passing the bar, and we set sail at half past three in the
afternoon. There was a heavy rolling sea ; and every man
was at his post, one on each side of the ship constantly throwing the lead to take the sounding. Four fathoms and a half
was the least, and this was little enough considering the
heavy swell. The bar has a very bold termination ; for
we passed from seven fathoms to no sounding, where the
sea presented its dark blue. The land receded, and in a
few hours disappeared ; and nothing was to be seen but one
wide expanse of ocean. Our voyage to Oahu,* Sandwich
Islands, was attended with nothing remarkable, excepting that it was performed in much shorter time than usual,
being only sixteen days from the time we left the Columbia river, to our anchoring in the roads of Honolulu. We
took our direct course, and kept it without any variation,
and with a few exceptions without shortening a sail, the
distance of two thousand five hundred miles. An almost
entire uniformity marked our progress, and excepting the

* Pronounced Wauhoo.

common alternations of day and night, sunshine and clouds, nothing interrupted the monotony of the scene.

On the morning of the 14th of July, land was announced. The islands of Ranai and Morakai were near, and as we passed them, we had a near view of the latter. It is not so mountainous as most others of the group, and presented rather a sterile aspect. We soon after made Oahu, and passed on the east side around Diamond Hill to the harbor of Honolulu on the south. This harbor is the best and almost the only good one in any of the groups of the Polynesian islands. The entrance is somewhat intricate, and an experienced pilot is required to take ships in safely. Within the coral reefs the water is sufficiently deep for ships of almost any magnitude ; and this, with the long extended roads without the reefs which afford good anchorage, renders the port desirable, and the island, in a commercial point of view, the most important of any in this part of the Pacific ocean.

We went on shore, two o'clock in the afternoon, and I was invited by Rev. H. Bingham to his house, where I met several of the other missionaries, and felt much rejoiced to behold again a Christian community.

The heat of a vertical sun was very oppressive and enervating, and was it not for the refreshing effects of the daily north-east trade winds, it would be insupportable to a northern constitution.

On Sabbath 17th, I attended worship in the native church, and heard Rev. Mr. Bingham preach in the Hawaiian language to a very large assembly of natives, probably two thousand five hundred, who gave very good attention. They were all decently dressed, while some of them were in the European mode, the most of them were dressed in their native costume, and made a good appearance. Their conduct and attention were very becoming, and many listened with deep interest. Madam Kinau, the queen regent, and the royal family, were present; and although it was easy to distinguish them from the common people, yet they made no ostentatious display of royalty. Their dress was rich but plain, and they paid sober attention to the worship of God. The performance of the singers was good, but there was not that melody in their voices which characterizes the Indians.

The house of worship is large and commodious, one hundred and ninety feet long and sixty-two feet wide, built in the native style, with the roof and sides covered with thatch.

Oahu is the most northern of the Sandwich Islands, situated in north latitude 21° 18' and in west longitude 158° 38'. Its greatest length is forty-five miles from Koka on the south-east to Kakana on the north-west. The greatest portion of the island is on the north-east of this line. Its greatest breadth is twenty-eight miles from Kahuku on the north to Laeloa (Barber's Point) on the south; about four fifths of the island is on the east of this line. The island is very mountainous; the highest eminence is called Honahuanui, and is a little over four thousand feet. The Pari, at the upper end of the valley of Nuuanu, north of Honolulu, may be counted among the curiosities of the island; principally on account of its being a part of the main road, or rather the only one to Keneohe. It is one thousand one hundred and forty feet above the level of the sea, and six hundred feet nearly perpendicular. This is to be clambered up and down in passing from Honolulu to Kenehoe, and to a stranger it is a fearful undertaking, as it is necessary to have a native to assist in putting your feet into the crevices of the rocks.   And yet the natives pass up and down with their calabashes of *poi*, and their loads of melons, fish, and other commodities, without any difficulty more than fatigue.

Some years ago, in a war between Tamehameha and the king of Oahu, the final battle was fought here which decided the fate of the island.   The king of Oahu made a desperate struggle ; and one part of his routed army, numbering more than three hundred, were pursued to this precipice, forced down, and almost all were dashed to pieces.

On each side of this pass, needle-pointed mountains rise up two thousand feet forming a narrow chasm, through which the north-east trade winds rush with great violence. Before you, at the north, you have a very pleasing view of the fertile valley of Kolou ; and beyond is a fine prospect of the bay and wide spread ocean.   The valley between the Pari and Honolulu is seven miles long; the upper part of which is narrow and very picturesque.   Interesting cascades are seen dashing down the almost perpendicular mountains, and the whole scenery is covered with fresh foliage.   This was almost the only place where the cool and invigorating breezes gave me relief from the oppressive heat. The lower part of the valley is wide, and covered to a great extent with *taro* patches.

Taro is a bulbous plant of the genus *arum*, and is planted in hills upon patches of ground, so formed as to be partially flooded with water, somewhat after the manner of rice cultivation.   In eight or ten months after setting the plants, they are fit for use.   To prepare it for food, it is always necessary to roast it, to take out the pungency which is common to this genus, as found in the wild turnip.   It is frequently

eaten for bread with no other preparation except roasting ;
or it is converted into *poi* by pulverising and making it into
a stiff paste.   The natives prefer the *poi* after it has undergone the acetic fermentation.

East of this valley is another called Manoa, about five
miles in length, running north from Diamond Hill.   It is
well watered by streams descending from the mountains,
formed by showers of rain which frequently fall upon them,
and which sometimes extend to the valleys and plains.   Its
fertile soil is well cultivated with sweet potatoes, taro, and
melons.   At the upper end, Kaahumanu, the late queen regent, who died in 1832, had a house built for retirement
from the bustle of Honolulu, and for devotion, near a beautiful cool grove of *ohia* and *kukui* trees,* on an eminence
commanding a view of the valley below.   Near this dwelling, she caused a house to be built for the accommodation
of the missionaries, when they should wish for rest, and to
be refreshed with the invigorating air of the mountains.
The evidences of her Christian character were convincing.
Her piety was active.   She traveled through all the islands,
from time to time, to see that the people attended upon the
means of religious instruction, and the schools ; and to recommend the religion of the Bible to all classes of her subjects.   Her example, as well as her authority, was powerful in suppressing intemperance, and the many vices which
threatened the ruin of her country.   Her influence was felt
not only by her own people, but also by foreigners who re-
sorted to those islands.

When I visited this spot of remembrances, the buildings

---

* The *kukui* tree bears a nut as large as a black walnut, a string of
which is used for candles, and hence the tree is called the candle tree.

were far gone to decay ; but not the cherished regard of her piety and philanthropy. This spot presented a very pleasing view of the high and precipitous mountains around on every side ; excepting the south, which is open and exhibits to view the grandeur of the rolling ocean. The many cascades around upon the mountain sides added to the interest of the scenery. Among the variety of shrubbery, we found the coffee tree with its fruit in various stages of maturity ; the arrow root ; and the brake fern growing, in many instances, to the height of twenty feet. From a bulb, near the root, is taken what the natives call *hapuu*, a silky down, which makes excellent beds and cushions.

Honolulu is situated on the south side of the island, on a bay of the same name, and is the capital, and business place of all the islands. The land around, and on which the village is located is a dry barren, excepting on the north and north-west, which is moist and cultivated with taro patches, with some cocoa trees interspersed. The buildings generally are in the native style, thatched ; many are built with *doba* walls after the Spanish manner on the coast of Mexico and Peru, that is, with large sun-burnt bricks made about two feet long, eighteen inches wide, and ten inches thick. The clay is mixed with cut-straw to strengthen them, after the manner of the ancient Egyptians. Their enclosures are often built in the same manner. There are several good buildings made of rock coral in English style, some of which are spacious and well finished. The village contains about nine thousand inhabitants, three hundred of whom are English and Americans. Most of the commercial business and trade are carried on by foreigners, to a large amount, increased by the resort of whale ships, in the fall and spring, for repairs and fresh supplies, particularly vegetables ; it is the place where all other shipping touch which navigate this ocean from Europe and America, in the Chinese and East India trade. This place is constantly growing in importance, and must continue to do so from its local advantages.

Four miles south-east of Honolulu is the pleasant native village of Waititi, situated on the bay of the same name. It contains five or six hundred inhabitants, is situated in a beautiful grove of cocoa trees, which adds very much to its appearance and comfort. This place, if its cultivation was proportioned to the richness of the soil, might be made one of the most delightful spots on the island.

The only road, or any thing that deserves the name of a road in this island, is between this place and Honolulu.

About two miles east of this village are the remains of an old heathen temple, in which human sacrifices were offered; a part of the walls of the enclosure are still standing. Various methods were employed to obtain victims. One of which was to lay a *tabu* upon all the people in the whole region around, that no one for a certain period of time should go out of their dwellings, or make any fire in them, upon pain of death. If any violated the *tabu*, they were apprehended and sacrificed to their idols. If they were unsuccessful in obtaining victims in this way, they would send out men in a canoe, to range along between the coral reef and the shore, and to feign distress, and if any were decoyed out for their relief, they were apprehended and carried to the temple and offered in sacrifice.

It is a pleasing consideration, that the benign influence of the gospel has dispelled these bloody and cruel superstitions of heathenism. I had an opportunity of seeing an old man who had been a high priest in these bloody rites. He has no hope that he is interested in the salvation of the gospel, but he said it is *maitai*, (good,) and that the Christian religion is so firmly established in these islands, that their ancient idolatry can never again be revived. He saluted me with many *alohas*. Mr. Bingham gave him some account of my journey across the Rocky Mountains and the object. He replied that it was good, and that God was with me and preserved me. He said in their former religion, they were all ignorant—all was darkness, entire darkness, but now the light shines. He said that when Captain Vancouver visited these islands in the reign of Tamaha, he urged the king to renounce idolatry, and the king promised he would, when Christians would send from the land of light a minister to teach them in the right way. They waited until their king died without knowing the right way, and no one came until Mr. Bingham and his associates in the year 1820. This old heathen priest gave up his religion and his honors, took Mr. B. by the hand on his first arrival, and called him brother, and has ever since been friendly to the missionaries. His wife, whom I also saw, hopes that she has experienced the saving power of the gospel.

Fourteen miles west of Honolulu is Eva,* a village of considerable magnitude, but not very compact. It is situated on Pearl river, at the head of a large lagoon extending several miles inland, and is surrounded with a fertile valley reaching twelve miles north, which is two thirds of the distance to Waialua. The highest elevation between these places is about four hundred feet, and is intersected in various parts with deep ravines. Eva is the station which Rev. Artemus Bishop and wife occupy, whose prospects of usefulness are encouraging. When I was there, the na-

---

* Pronounced Āva.

tives were engaged in building a substantial and commodious house of worship, and appeared to take deep interest in the effort.

In the north-west part of the island, is the village of Waialua, where Rev. John S. Emerson and wife are stationed. The village is situated upon a wide spread bay, which would furnish an excellent harbor for any shipping, if there was sufficient water upon the bar at the entrance. The valley around is large and fertile, capable of being made very productive. On a Sabbath which I spent here, eight natives, six men, and two women, were received into the communion of the church, who appeared very intelligent and serious, and conducted with as much propriety as is seen in the most civilized parts of the world. I felt a satisfaction in joining with these redeemed heathen in the ordinance of the Lord's supper. Every part of divine service was conducted with Christian decorum. I was particularly pleased with the appearance of the native deacon, who was dignified in his person, dressed in good taste, and very devotional in his behavior.

The only remaining village of any considerable importance is Keneohe, where Rev. Benjamin W. Parker and wife are stationed. This village is in the fertile valley of Kolou, near the shore of a pleasant bay, which would afford an excellent harbor if there was sufficient water at the entrance over the coral bar. This village is about four miles north of the Pari, and is the most cool and refreshing retreat I found upon the island. The basaltic mountain on the south, three thousand feet high, and nearly vertical ; and the north-east trade winds give a temperate atmosphere, not found in any other part of the island sufficiently low for a village.

The greatest part of the island is mountainous, though but two ranges are of considerable magnitude. The largest, Koanahumanui, is on the east side, and runs parallel with the ocean, and its highest point is four thousand feet above the level of the sea. This range of mountains is diversified with cones, acute points, and paries. At the great Pari, the upper end of Nuuanu, the main chain turns to the west, and terminates towards Waialua. The north side of the range, west of the Pari, is very precipitous, having many spurs projecting to the north, including deep, pit-like ravines. The other range is on the west part of the island, called Kaala, running north and south, separating Waianae on the west, from the valley of Eva on the east. The highest point is three thousand eight hundred and fifty feet. There are many conical hills of different magnitudes in various parts of the island, which were evidently ancient craters; one six miles south-east of Honolulu, called Diamond Hill; and another a short distance north of Honolulu, called Fort Hill. They are open and concave at the top, with high walls, reeded down the sides, which appear to have been formed by streams of lava, and by the action of water, cutting ravines. There is an abundance of lava and other volcanic productions about these hills.

The Salt Lake, four miles west of Honolulu, is of the crateric form. It is a great curiosity, as well as a source of trade. It has undoubtedly a connection by some subterraneous passage with the ocean, near which it is situated. Its depth is not known, being nearly filled with excellent crystalized salt, which appears to be inexhaustible, and is taken out in large quantities for use and exportation. The lake appears as if covered with ice, a little sunken below the surface of the water.

The geological formations of this island, and all the others in the Pacific which I saw, and concerning which I obtained information, are volcanic and coraline to a great extent. Some have supposed that these islands have been thrown up in the first place by internal fires, and then enlarged by coraline additions. But there is too much argillaceous soil to favor the opinion; and to say the least, the supposition is without conclusive evidence. Much of the soil is formed of disintegrated and decomposed lava. The reefs lying off from the shores, and in some places immediately upon them, are coraline. The corals are divided into ancient and modern, the latter still increasing. Between these formations is a volcanic deposit. The ancient corals are found in many places forming the surface of the plains, elevated some six or eight feet above the present level of the ocean. As the zoophytes, which form coral, never work above water, it is evident that these islands have been elevated by some subterranean or submarine power, or the ocean is subsiding; and as this recession of the ocean is seen in various parts of the world, in nearly, if not the same degree, is it not probable that the waters of the ocean are gradually diminishing? Of the modern corals there are many species, from the rock, to the most beautiful kinds resembling trees and plants, and of various colors. The volcanic formations do not differ materially from those in Oregon Territory. Cellular lava is very common, often bordering upon pumice, and of various colors; brick red, ash colored, orange yellow, and green. No primitive rocks are found, nor any silicious sand; the sand upon the shores being formed either of disintegrated lava, scoria, or coral, but more generally combined of these three elements.

While I shall not attempt a minute enumeration of the

productions of these islands, the following are some of the principal. The cocoa tree, bread fruit, coa tree, which furnishes lumber nearly equal to mahogany; hybiscus, candle nut tree, mulberry, fig, cotton tree, which grows spontaneously and produces cotton of very fine quality; coffee tree, grape vines, oranges, lemons, limes, pine apples, melons of superior quality, squashes, sugar cane, arrow root; indigo plant, which grows finely without any care; the guâva, a fruit resembling mandrakes, but not agreeable to the taste of those not accustomed to them; taro, sweet and common potatoes, and bananas. There are many ferns of extraordinary size, and the *cactus opuntia*, familiarly known as the prickly pear, growing to the height of six or eight feet, is planted in hedge-rows for enclosures. All the most superb tropical flowering plants luxuriate in these islands, among which we find the oriental lilac, eight different species of mimosa, the pride of Barbadoes, several varieties of convolvulus, and mirabilis, the passiflora or passion flower, roses, the Spanish pink, Mexican pea, and many other beautiful genera. Also garden vegetables of various kinds.

These islands when discovered by Capt. Cook, contained but very few animals, and most of those now found upon them have been since introduced from the Mexican coast. There are now, horses, mules, neat cattle, goats, hogs, dogs, fowls. The birds which have their residence here, though not numerous, are of most beautiful plumage, and the favorite head ornament of the women, is made of the golden colored feathers of a native bird. The crow and raven, which are common in almost all parts of the world, have not found their way here. There are very few reptiles, but the green lizard is very common, and in the days of the idolatry of the Islanders was worshiped, and such is the influence of superstition, that they can hardly dismiss all feelings of reverence for this insignificant reptile. If one comes into their dwellings, they choose to let it take its own departure rather than molest it. Snakes are unknown, and the scorpion and centiped have within a very few years been brought here in vessels. The musquitoe was not known until recently, though now they are numerous and very annoying.

The government of these islands is absolute and heredi-tary, administered by the king, queen, and chiefs, whose will is the supreme law ; the common people are a nation of slaves. The lands belong to the government, and are leased to the people at high rents, and even then they have no security that they shall enjoy the avails of their labor ; for beside the stipulated rents, the government make any addi-tional demands they please, and the people are taught to obey without complaining. The persons of the chiefs are remarkable for their extraordinary size, towering quite above the height of the common people, and in corpulency preserving corresponding dimensions. The king secures his house and person by life guards. Very frequently on a Saturday morning, the queen regent, attended by her train and servants in equestrian style, visits her garden some two miles from Honolulu. Their appearance is fine, and they are well skilled in horsemanship. Her ordinary mode of riding is in a small, low-wheel carriage drawn by twenty servants. The Sandwich Islanders, or *Kanakas*, as the com-mon people are called, have less activity of body and mind than the Indians of our continent, and yet a phrenologist would say that their intellectual powers are well developed. In their present political condition, they are not expected to be otherwise than indolent and improvident. In their dress,

mode of living, and habitations generally, they have made
but little advance upon the days of heathenism ; some in
the interior, especially, wearing little more clothing than
their *maro*, and having their dwellings in caverns in volcanic rocks. The chiefs, and some of the people, have
good houses, dress in good fashion, and live comfortably.
The king, queen regent, and chiefs, gave a tea party, to
which with a few others I had the honor to be invited.
They were dressed richly and in good taste ; the table was
splendidly arrayed with silver plate and china ; the entertainment was both judiciously and tastefully arranged and
prepared, and all the etiquette and ceremony of such occasions was observed. The conversation was cheerful and
intelligent, without frivolity, and nothing occurred embarrassing to any one. At a suitable early hour, we were invited into a saloon well furnished, where, after a performance of music, both vocal and instrumental, the queen proposed that *prayer* should conclude our agreeable visit; after
which the company retired. I have seen but few parties
in Christian America conducted more on the principles of
rationality and religion.

An entertainment, however, is sometimes transacted in a
different style by some of our countrymen and other foreigners in those islands. A dog-feast, as it is there called,
was given by foreign resident gentlemen, on the 20th of
Sept. at the country seat of the American consul, in honor
of the officers of the American squadron, the Peacock and
Enterprise, then in the harbor of Honolulu. I extract from
the account published in the Sandwich Island Gazette as described at the time. "Food in native style was bountifully
served up—baked dog was among the dishes, and it was not
to be despised. Songs, toasts, cheers, bumpers, and speech-

es all came in their turn.   Among the toasts were, 'Commodore —— *our Commodore.*'   Commodore's reply, ' May you all live a thousand years, and may we always meet here.'   Doctor —— of the United States ship Peacock. ' Population and prosperity to the Sandwich Islands, and an end to all oppressive *tabus.*'   The party separated teeming with good spirits."

The population of these islands has been decreasing ever since an acquaintance has been had with them.   Captain Cook estimated the people at 400,000.   The present population is about 110,000.   A variety of causes have conspired to bring about this declension, and yet no one so prominent above the rest, as wholly to satisfy enquiry.   It is acknowledged by all observers, and has become evident to the government itself, that a change of things in the internal structure of their national affairs, is necessary to the prosperity of the people.   During my stay at Oahu, the heads of the nation had frequent meetings to discuss the subject of reform and improvement, and to adopt some new mode of administration which will give to the people the privileges of freemen, and thereby stimulate them to industry.   To effect this, the lands must be distributed among the people, a more equal mode of taxation must be adopted, industry must be encouraged, and progressive prosperity will follow in train.

The perpetuity of the independence of this nation, and with it their existence, is very problematical.   A disposition to possess these islands, has evidently been manifested by foreign powers.   Whether the paw of the Lion, or the talons of the Eagle, shall first make them its prey, or whether they shall be mutual checks upon each other, and thus prolong the life of this feeble nation, is not known.   The manner

in which the king and chiefs are often treated by the officers of foreign nations, the insults they often meet with,
would not pass with impunity from a more powerful people.
In fair and honorable negotiations, regard is had to mutual
rights, but here foreigners assume the style of dictation ;
" You shall, and you shall not." Assertions are made of
things existing in the laws and practices of England and
America, which neither government would tolerate. Lord
Russel, the commander of the Acteon, a British man of
war, obtained the signature to a certain instrument, by
assuring the Hawaiian government that if they refused
any longer to sign it, he would order all the English vessels to leave the harbor, and request all the American
shipping to withdraw ; and then bring his armed ship before their fort, and batter down the walls, and prostrate
their village. The king signed the instrument, and then,
together with the queen and chiefs, like some other people
who feel their feebleness before a mightier nation, had only
the poor resort of a public remonstrance. They accordingly
sent a remonstrance to the king of Great Britain, in which
they say, that " on account of their urging us so strongly ;
on account of said commanders assuring us that their
communication was from the king ; and on account of their
making preparation to fire upon us,—therefore we gave
our assent to the writing, without our being willing to
give our real approbation; for we were not pleased
with it." They feel incompetent to contend with naval
strength, and therefore submit to indignities from which
their feelings revolt. Why cannot the principles of justice and equity govern the intercourse of men with
men, where they are so well understood, and the painful necessity be spared of innocence and helplessness

supplicating that protection which Heaven grants to its children.

Much has been said of the character of the foreign residents, and of the counteracting influence they exert upon the labors of the missionaries in this field. The cause of their bitterness and opposition is well understood, and lest my own observations should seem partial to the missionaries, and invidious towards those who oppose them, I will embrace all I have to say on the subject in a quotation from a work published by Mr. J. N. Reynold of the voyage of the Potomac, an American man of war. He certainly cannot be accused of partiality to the missionaries who reside on these islands, for his remarks on them are somewhat acrimonious, but in regard to the foreign residents he says, "they are generally devoid of all religious principle, and practice the greatest frauds upon the natives in their dealings with them ; which tends to corrupt their morals, and to preclude all hopes of fairness in trade among them. It cannot be denied, and no one can regret it more than we do, that this whole population, generally speaking, are of the lowest order ; among whom every thing like decent restraint which civilized society imposes upon its members, is at war with their vicious propensities, and of course resisted by them to the extent of their power." He farther adds, "let us be distinctly understood in the remarks we have made in reference to the foreign residents and missionaries on this island. As to the question, which party is on the side of virtue and good order, there can be but one opinion, where there is not even room for comparison." I have been in communities where vice has been unblushingly indulged, but I have never witnessed direct enmity to

every thing morally good, in so much bitterness and power, as in Oahu.

Most of the foreign residents have native wives, and
manifest a regard for the education of their children ; and
send some of them to other countries for this purpose ; but
for most of them a *charity* school has been established, and
for its support a call is made upon the commanders and
officers of vessels who come into this port ; and they have
even sent to England and America for charitable aid.
Though some *poor* are taught here, yet I know not why the
benevolent should help, by way of *charity*, the consuls and
rich merchants in Oahu.

I visited the seamen's chapel and preached several times
for Rev. Mr. Diell.   While there are often several hundred
seamen in the port of Honolulu, there are frequently very
few attendants on the regular services of the chapel.   Rev.
Mr. Diell, their worthy chaplain, is however indefatigable
in his labors through the week, visiting sailors on ship
board, and wherever he can find them, endeavoring to promote their spiritual good.   Some conversions have crowned
his efforts.

On the occasion of the funeral of an infant of the Prin-
cess, whose husband is Leléiohoku, alias Wm. Pitt, I visited
the burial place of the kings and royal family.   This is a
stone building of rock coral, of the common size and structure of the houses of the village, and situated amongst them,
having nothing particularly distinguishable except an outward signal, by which is understood the number and rank
of the dead within.   They are encased first in lead, secured
from the admission of air, and then deposited in coffins of
elegant workmanship, covered with rich silk velvet or
crimson damask, and ornamented with silver or brass plate.

Here sleep the remains of Rihoriho, and Kamehamalu, who died on a visit to England, and several others lying in state; and in the same tomb, are interred a number of other members of the royal family.

The missionaries of the American Board of Commissioners for Foreign Missions in these islands, have done much to elevate the character of the population, by teaching and preaching the truths of Christianity, by schools, where the first rudiments of education are taught, by the press, and a translation of the entire bible ; they have exerted a salutary influence upon the morals of the whole nation, and raised a monument to the power and excellence of the gospel of Jesus Christ. They have also laid instrumentally, a broad foundation for the political, and social, and religious improvement of that people, unless thwarted by the interference and opposition of foreigners, and for the future and unending happiness of many redeemed souls in the world to come. I had frequent opportunities of witnessing the effect of their labors in the evidences of the moral renovation of these once idolaters, and of meeting with them in their great congregation on the Sabbath.

CHAPTER XXVI.

FROM July to November, no vessel departed from the
Sandwich Islands direct for the United States, and after
being detained about five months, waiting an opportunity to
return, I engaged a passage in the Phœnix, Allyn, from
New London, and embarked December 17th. The ship was
built for the China trade, of four hundred and ten tons,
manned with twenty-eight persons, besides five passengers.
The pilot boat left us well out at sea, at nine in the morning;
our course south-west. On the morning of the 21st, we encountered a strong wind, which in the afternoon had increased so much, that we were compelled to put two reefs
in the top-sails; and a squall split our jib and sprung our
foremast. I had no opportunity or disposition to enjoy the
grandeur of the rolling ocean, being confined to the cabin
by sea sickness. Our ship was engaged in the whaling
business, and I was furnished, for once, with an opportunity of seeing the experiment of taking a whale. The thing
has often been described, but the novelty of the manœu-
vre interested me. The experienced and skillful whalemen dispose of the dangerous process, with the tactics of
their profession, in a manner much beyond my conceptions
before witnessing it ; and the monster of the deep, though

mighty in his strength, is made to submit to inferior power, and to contribute largely to illuminate our evenings at home. When the whale is brought along side of the ship, the whalemen dissever the head from the body, and hoist it on deck, and while some are employed in perforating the scull, and with a bucket taking out the sperm, others make a spiral incision in the oily portion, beginning where the head was taken off, and by rope and hook suspended by a pulley twenty feet up the mainmast, draw up the oily part which cleaves from the flesh, while the body of the whale revolves in the water; and this process is continued until all that is valuable is secured. There are said to be thirty thousand men employed in this business in the Pacific, while only about four hundred are engaged in diffusing the light of life through the dark places of the earth.

January 12th, 1837. Through the whole of to-day we had strong gales from N. N. E. Our top-sails were close reefed,—split our main-top-sail. Headed to the E. close on the wind. Very bad sea—not able to take any observation of our latitude or longitude. These gales continued on the 13th until almost every sail was taken in, and we lay to on the wind. The last part of the day was more moderate, and we headed south. By observation taken to-day, our latitude was 14° 47′ south.

Sabbath, 15th. The winds subsided, and the weather was warm. In the morning we came near Tetuaroa, a small island of the Society group. It is low, the highest parts rising but a few feet above the level of the sea, is thinly inhabited, and adorned with large and beautiful groves of the cocoa tree extending even to the water's edge. The fresh verdure of this island in all the luxuriance of perpetual summer, was a delightful contrast to the constant view of the

water for nearly a month, and I felt as though these gems of
the ocean were scattered here to refresh the tired voyager,
and bring to his mind the recollection of his own dear home.
Like all the islands of this ocean which I have seen, it is surrounded with coral reefs, lying off at a little distance from
the shore, and upon which the sea constantly breaks.   In the
afternoon we approached the harbor of Papeeti, at the island
of Tahiti.   The pilot came off to us, and made an effort to
get the ship in, but did not succeed, the wind being too light,
and we had to bear off for the night.   The prospect as it
lay spread out before us was a combination of all that was
beautiful in nature.   Nor am I alone in the impression
which this little "Queen of the ocean" makes upon a stranger.   Others have described it with all the vividness which
its romantic and delightful scenery inspires.   The harbor
forms a gentle curve, and in the foreground, on a level tract
were scattered neat cottages built of thatch, or wood, plas-
tered and whitewashed with coral lime, situated together with
the church, in the midst of bread-fruit, cocoa, and orange
groves.   The back ground of the enchanting picture was
filled up with hills and valleys, and streams dashing their
way down the ravines, and then meandering through the
rich vale below, to the ocean, while the outline terminated
in steep and lofty mountains.   But not the least interesting
were the marks which the Christian religion and its attendant, civilization, have made.   Here was a church, and to
know that this people had lately been rescued from pagan-
ism, and all the hideous forms of idolatrous worship, raised
in my heart emotions of pleasure and gratitude, which not
even nature's fairest forms had power to awaken.   An immortal spirit elevated from the dust, and raised to heaven, a
monument of the Savior's grace—what can equal it?

Monday morning, the 16th, we passed safely into the harbor, where we found the Daniel Webster, Pierson, from Sag Harbor; on board of which were Rev. W. Richards and family, passengers for the United States.

We continued in this port four days, during which time I made several excursions about the island, and became acquainted with the English missionaries, of whose successful labors I had often heard and read; the Rev. Messrs. Wilson, Pritchard, and Darling, and their families. They appear happy in their work, and devoted to it. The Christian religion is the only religion acknowledged in these islands, and its influence is universally apparent. As the conversion of multitudes in the first ages of Christianity, has ever been considered as furnishing evidence of the truth of the gospel, so the "moral miracle" of the conversion of the islands of the sea, in our own day, is calculated, with all its attendant circumstances to confirm our faith, as well as to encourage us in prosecuting still farther those benevolent designs, which render the deserts, both naturally and morally, the garden of the Lord. Besides preaching on the Sabbath, the missionaries have religious service on other days of the week. At sun-rise every morning they have a public prayer meeting. They are doing much by their schools and the press; and most of the people can read. The performances of the natives in vocal music pleased me, their voices being very soft and musical, though less cultivated than those of the Sandwich Islanders. Their personal appearance, complexion, language, and dress are much the same as the natives of those islands. Their advances in the arts and in agriculture are less than might be expected of them, but in a climate where so many rich fruits vegetate spontaneously, the necesssity of cultivation is less imperious. While the harbor is not as good as that of Oahu, less is done by way of wharfing, or otherwise to facilitate business, or aid in repairing the shipping which visit this island. A good public road has been commenced to extend around the island, on which convicts, instead of being imprisoned, were employed, but it is now neglected, and all the bridges are broken down.

The government here is much the same as that of the Sandwich Islands, but is in some respects more free and systematized. Their judiciary is well organized, and justice is tolerably well administered. Their legislative body is composed of the queen, governors, chiefs, and two representatives from each district of the islands of Tahiti and Eimeo; the laws when framed are canvassed by the people, and if approved, receive the queen's signature. The young queen Pomare is of very prepossessing appearance, possesses talents, and decision of character; but her views of civilization are not so enlarged as those of Madam Kinau.

The American consul, of these islands, resides at Papeeti ; he is a Dutchman, and as he informed me, a native and citizen of Antwerp. His English is hardly intelligible, and his knowledge of the duties of his office is yet to be acquired.

The islands of Tahiti and Eimeo, like the other large islands of the Pacific, are volcanic and coraline. They are mountainous, many of which are high and steep, and many of the valleys are deep and narrow, extending far into the interior. To a considerable extent the soil is rich and productive ; oranges and all other tropical fruits being abundant, and requiring little labor or care. Such is the indolence of the inhabitants that they cultivate little besides sugar cane and a few vegetables. These islands are well supplied with forests, in which are several kinds of wood equal in value to mahogany for cabinet work.   The heat for the most part of the year is so oppressive that though many things are very pleasant, yet these islands come short of the paradise which some journalists have described.

These, like the other islands of the Pacific, have been diminishing in populousness.   Various causes, such as the introduction of foreign diseases, infanticide, human sacrifices, the means furnished by commerce of rendering wars destructive to human life, and the introduction of ardent spirits, have all contributed to this end.   It is estimated that only about twelve thousand people inhabit the two islands of Tahiti and Eimeo, and about forty thousand the Georgian and Society group.   The introduction of the Christian religion has banished many causes of their decline.

The cleanliness of the islanders is a subject worthy of remark.   Their practice of frequent ablutions and sea bathing, to which they are induced by the climate, and of which they are fond, including all descriptions of persons, and even children, is highly conducive to health, and promotes a taste for neatness in their persons not common to heathen nations.

Wednesday, 18th, I accompanied Mr. Pritchard in his pastoral labors, about seven miles, on horseback, where he preached to a congregation in a village in which the queen has her residence.   Queen Pomare was present, and an interesting audience appeared to listen as if they were hearing the word to obey it.   After the meeting we pursued our ride about seven miles farther, to Rev. Mr. Wilson's at Point Venus, a lovely spot, situated in orange groves and bananas.   Our way thither was around the base of hills and mountains which approached near the beach in precipices, and where the opening through the coral reefs permitted the sea to break on the shore with a noise like thunder, so that we had to watch the opportunity afforded by the receding waves to pass their points. Any horses, but those accustomed to the sight, would have denied us a safe passage. With these dear missionaries I partook of a cheerful dish of tea, while we talked of the interests of the kingdom of our common Redeemer, and of the time when fellow laborers from every part of our lost world, and from their different spheres of agency, when their work here is done, shall be gathered to their Father's home in heaven.

In the evening we returned to Mr. Pritchard's, on my part delighted with so refreshing an interview.

During my short stay, the queen and royal family of a neighboring island, paid a visit of friendship to Tahiti. This afforded me a very desirable opportunity of remarking the manners and customs of the people. A public feast was given in honor of the royal visitants; and the day was ushered in by firing rusty guns, of which they have a very few. The morning until ten o'clock was occupied in collecting together their cocoanuts, bananas, baked hogs, &c. Many were out to purchase calico scarfs of two or three yards in length to wear in the procession. A very large procession formed, the women taking the lead, and the men following in order. A female with an infant in her arms led the van. This was explained to me as done in honor of mothers; for here, as well as at the Sandwich Islands, women are regarded as in all respects on a par with men. All were well attired in European style, their heads adorned tastefully with garlands of most beautiful tropical flowers, with which their sea-girt isle abounds in profusion. After taking, in single file, a long and circuitous march, they arrived at their feasting bower, under a grove of cocoanut, bread-fruit, and orange trees, where near the centre, with an infant, sat the royal visitor; and each Tahitian as they passed, threw down at her feet their scarfs or some other present. It was the pleasure of the queen, however, not long to retain all these tokens of honor, for she seemed happy in generously giving them to others. After the procession had passed in respectful review, next came the refreshments, which were placed, some on the ground, others suspended on boughs of trees, which were taken and shared in little circles seated upon the grass, evidently enjoying the social interview. This is considered one of their most joyful holidays, and was managed without noise, confusion, or any apparent infraction of the rules of propriety. It must be recollected that this is a temperance island; all traffic in ardent spirits being prohibited by law.

In taking leave of these islands, I would not fail to mention the kind hospitality of Rev. G. Pritchard and family, and the satisfaction I had in seeing the other missionaries, and witnessing the interesting fruits of their labors under the blessing of God.

Our stay at Tahiti was employed by the ship's crew in disposing of our poor sulphureted water from the Sandwich Islands, and in re-supplying themselves with the pure mountain streams of this island, and in *"vegetating the ship,"* as they phrase it; that is, by collecting quantities, which are purchased of the natives, of oranges, bananas, sweet potatoes, limes, cocoanuts in abundance, bread-fruit, yams, and squashes. Here I collected for my cabinet, some choice specimens of coral, and shells of the ocean, which the natives dive to obtain, and sell to the ships which enter this port.

On the morning of Saturday 21st January, we left the

harbour of Tahiti with a light wind, and as we sailed around Eimeo, its mountains, with their densely wooded tops and precipitous sides, appeared in full prospect. On this island there is a high school for the children of the missionary families of the several islands.

We proceeded with a favorable wind until the 30th, when our latitude was 30° 27' south, and longitude 153° 10' west. I was here much gratified to witness the interesting phenomenon of a water spout. It first became visible to us about half a mile distant as it arose, and at that distance we had no apprehensions of danger from it, and yet it was sufficiently near to give a distinct view. It commenced in a small, dark, and nearly perpendicular column, enlarging its diameter as it rose, until it reached the region of the clouds, when apparently feeling the influence of the wind, it passed obliquely to the south-west. It continued in view some time, but as we were proceeding on our course, it gradually disappeared.

On the 4th of February, fresh breezes from the north-west took the place of the south-east trade winds, and our course was laid E. S. E.

On the 5th we had strong gales from the west. Put two reefs in the top-sails, and took in the mizzen-top-sail, and handed the main-sail. The sea was very heavy. On the 9th the wind was more moderate; and while engaged in spearing porpoises, one of the men fell overboard from the bow, and went directly under the ship, and came up under her stern. The life buoy was thrown over to him, but being an indifferent swimmer he was long in his efforts to seize it. By lowering the boat and rounding about the ship, he was recovered on board much exhausted, and almost overcome with the cold. Hundreds are daily, by a great variety of occurrences taken from the world, and the certain knowledge awakens but feeble sensations in our bosoms; but a solitary case of individual danger and suffering which we witness, arouses all our anxieties and sympathies, and we are grateful when relieved by the safety of the sufferer.

On the 16th and 17th, the gale was tremendous. We were in latitude about 47° south, and 120° west longitude. With nearly every sail taken in, we could only run before the wind, which was from the north-west, and the waves were constantly breaking over our bulwarks. Such was the roaring of the wind and breaking waves, that it was difficult for the orders of the captain to be heard, upon his loudest voice, from midship, forward or aft. The wind blew tons of water into the air and scattered them into ten thousand sprays. I never had such evidence of the power of wind and water, nor of the admirable manner the ship could live in such a gale. She would roll upon the waves and plunge and rise again upon the mountain billows. The whole scene was fraught with magnificence, terror, and grandeur. It was a great favor that we had a courageous and experienced captain; and a sober, active, and obedient crew; and above all the protection of Heaven. Two men were constantly at the wheel, selected from our best steersmen. We shipped a great quantity of water, and on the night of the 17th, the fore deck had scarcely at any time, less than a foot, or two feet of water, the waves breaking over faster than the water could pass through the scuppers. Two pumps were at work a large portion of the time to keep the ship clear, so much water was constantly finding its way down the closed hatches and other leakages of the deck. The two men at each pump labored so forcibly, that it was necessary to be relieved by others every three minutes. I reflected on the condition of those who were not prepared for death, and that even to a Christian a quiet deathbed would be preferable to leaving the world in such a scene of confusion. But we were spared in great kindness, and the following morning the wind began to abate. Captain Allyn, who had been into most of the principal seas, and around both of the great Capes, said he never saw, except in a typhoon which he encountered on the Japan coast, any gale which equalled this.

The gales continued with frequent squalls of hail and rain until the 28th, when we found we were driven to the 59° of south latitude, and 77° west longitude. This was farther south of Cape Horn than we wished to go. The weather was cold and thick, the thermometer ranging between 41° and 47° for several days. On the 1st of March we saw for the first time after leaving Tahiti, a sail to the windward heading south-west, but were unable to speak her. It was very pleasant to find our latitude lessening in our homeward course, though we were not up with the Cape until the third of March. During the gales, and especially in stormy weather, our vessel was very frequently visited by a bird which navigators call the Noddy, and which is easily taken by the hand. It is of the Tern genus, twelve inches long, slenderly formed; its plumage is a dark sooty brown, excepting the top of its head which is dusky white. The Albatross also was constantly flying about us, regardless of wind and waves. Our men caught several of them with a hook, the heads of which, when standing upon the deck, were four feet high; their aler measurement was ten feet. Although they are generally of a brown color, yet in the region of Cape Horn, they vary from a mixture of brown and white, to an almost entire white. They are the largest class of the feathered race.

We had for a long time an opportunity of observing the Magellanic clouds; which are three in number, two luminous and one black; about thirty degrees distant from each other, and fixed in their relative situations as are the fixed stars. Although I had noticed them, supposing them to be clouds, and wondering how an illuminated cloud should be seen at all times of the night, and preserve its position with an outline so well defined and so plainly marked, yet my mind was not wholly satisfied respecting them, until the Mate of the ship, who had seen them in previous voyages, and who possessed considerable astronomical knowledge, pointed out to me some of their characteristics. The weather in those high southern latitudes being so uniformly thick and cloudy, prevented our observing them so early, or carefully as we might otherwise have done. They were distinctly visible for weeks, keeping their relative situation, and their altitude above the southern horizon, lessening to the beholder according as his latitude diminished while he proceeded north. The forms of each are about five degrees in diameter. The luminous ones undoubtedly are formed by clusters of stars, so numerous and contiguous, and so distant as only to give a glimmering light like luminous clouds, which gives them their name; and the black one is very probably the entire absence of all light. I gazed at these, night after night, with wonder and admiration. It seemed to me, that looking at the dark one, was looking beyond created nature into infinite space.

Gales occurred occasionally after we doubled Cape Horn, but most of the time was pleasant and the winds favorable, until the 27th of March in south latitude 23° 27′, and west longitude 28° 34, the wind came around to the north, and continued to blow from a northerly direction for ten days, which retarded our progress, and carried us off our course to the east, until we were brought into 26° west longitude, where we changed our course west by north.   On the first of April, we spoke and East Indiaman.   She was a very large, fine-looking ship, of about eight hundred tons, well filled with men, women, and children, who probably were passengers for New Holland.   This was the first ship we had spoken after the Spartan, near the line on the other side of the continent.   It is difficult to imagine how pleasant it is to see and speak a ship after having been months at sea.   A few hours after, we saw another East Indiaman, but did not speak her.   By falling in with these ships, we found we were so near Africa, that we were in the track of ships from Europe to the Cape of Good Hope.

The same day we buried one of the seamen in the great deep.   He was a man who in early life was trained up in the care of pious parents, but whose after life was marked by vices, which in their consequences led to a comparatively early death.   It was a solemn scene when we committed his remains to the water grave.   The colors were raised half mast, the whole ship's company collected around ; the body, with weights attached, was laid upon a plank at the gang-way; and we paused to dwell for a moment on death and the dread scenes beyond.   I addressed them in a few remarks suggested by the occasion, and after a prayer, the plank was gently moved over the side of the ship, and the dead disappeared to be seen no more.

On the 2d, we made Martin Vass islands, which are five in number, composed wholly of volcanic rocks, without any soil ; some of them are cones, shooting up four or five hundred feet. Two are very small and needle pointed. They are all so precipitous, and the sea constantly breaking against them, that there is no landing. Their forms are fantastical ; one of them having the appearance of a fortification with bastions, about which are needle points resembling men on guard. They are in 20° 31′ south latitude, and 28° 38′ west longitude. By changing our course more westerly we made Trinidad, off against St. Roque, which is an island of considerable size, and in latitude 20° 28′, and longitude 29° 5′. Near evening we were fifteen miles from it, and wishing to land in the morning, we took in sail and lay off for the night. Some Portuguese once settled upon it, but it is so difficult of access, that they abandoned it, and it is now without any inhabitants.

On the morning of the 3d, we ran down to within three miles of the island, and manned three boats to go on shore ; but finding no place free from breakers, gave up the attempt, caught a few fish near the shores, and after being much annoyed with flies which came off to us, we returned to the ship, and with a favorable breeze pursued our course. This island is also volcanic, has an iron bound shore, and is mountainous, the highest part of which is about fifteen hundred, or two thousand feet. It is a place of resort for multitudes of birds and sea fowl, some of which are large. I had an opportunity to see, but not to examine, the man-of-war hawk. They are numerous here, and while they are handsome, they are also ravenous, always taking their prey upon the wing. There were many of the perfectly silky white species of the Tern, which hovered over us with great tameness, as though they wished to form an acquaintance with us, not suspecting any hostility.

Most of our nights as well as days for a long time were clear, and the stars were seen with remarkable brightness. What has been described by others of evenings at sea, in the southern hemisphere, I had an opportunity of observing with admiration.   The richest colors of red, orange, and yellow, are spread over the western sky after the setting sun, and often over the whole concave of heaven.   No pencil of art can imitate the tints and hues which blend in softness over this scene of beauty.   Nature's pencil only can lay on these delicate shades, and add to it the brilliancy, ever varying, of so much richness and splendor.

In the deep seas we did not see many fish; of the few which came under our observation, the *dorado*, or as commonly called, the dolphin, and the pilot fish excelled in the beauty of their colors.   The former, when taken upon deck, constantly changed its colors from the bright purple to the gold, the bluish green, and the silver white, and these spreading out into vanishing shades.   The pilot fish is equally beautiful, but is singular in the choice of company and employment; always being found with the shark, and conducting him to his prey, from which it derives its name.

The flying fish is a curiosity, furnished with powers for occupying both air and water, but finds no friend in either; pursued by the dolphin or some other fish, it swims with all speed until it can no longer escape its destructive enemy, and then takes to flight in the air, where the albatross and the man-of-war hawk hover to make it their prey.   In its flight it often falls upon the decks of ships, when *man* shows it no mercy.

On the 19th of April we passed the equator.   For a few days we had calms or only light winds with showers.   The heat was very intense, and to be becalmed under these circumstances is more to be dreaded than gales. But we were much favored, and soon found ourselves in north latitude, and it was with sensations of delight that I again beheld the North Star, though but just above the horizon. I hailed it as the harbinger of good, and the future guide to the long forsaken home and friends which I now realized that I was fast approaching.

All objects at sea are considered worthy of notice, and we observed the gulf weed in great abundance before we came to the gulf-stream. It is an aquatic plant of a peculiar light green color, and floats upon the service of the water. We entered and passed the stream on the 14th of May, in 36° 37' north latitude; and though a rough sea is generally expected here, yet we had a very pleasant time. The current is at the rate of three miles an hour, and the temperature seven degrees warmer than the adjacent water.

On the 17th of May, at three in the afternoon, we were cheered with the cry from the man at the mast head, "*Land ho! ahead.*" It proved to be Block Island. We came in sight of the light-house in the evening, but too late to attempt to get into the harbor before morning, and therefore lay off for the night. In the morning we found ourselves among various shipping bound to different ports. We passed Montauk Point and drew near to New London, where the sight of the city, the shipping in the harbor, the country around, and the islands dressed in green, were most grateful, especially to one so long conversant with heathen countries and a wide expanse of ocean. Passed up the Thames to the city, and I rejoiced to land once more upon Christian and civilized shores, my native land, my country! In taking leave of the Phœnix, I felt it due to the captain and crew to say, that I received from them every kind attention

I could wish, and being a temperance ship, I did not hear a profane word from any while on board. We had public worship, during the voyage on the Sabbath, and the word of God was blessed, as there was reason to believe, to the saving conversion of some souls. I found kind friends in New London, and after arranging my business, directed my way to Ithaca, where I arrived on the 23d of May, after an absence of more than two years and two months, and having accomplished a journey of twenty-eight thousand miles.

APPENDIX.

VOCABULARY OF INDIAN LANGUAGES.

English.	Indian.
God,	hemákis Tota.
Spirit,	koonapa.
Father,	tota.
Man,	hámá.
Woman,	iat.
Mother,	pēka.
Child,	mēaits.
Brother,	uskeep.
Sister,	axsip.
Husband,	hámá.
Wife,	waipna.
I,	ēn.
Thou,	ēm.
He,	emim.
She,	aiat.
It,	ke.
They,	eláhne tetokan.
People,	tetokan.
Heaven,	accompenaka.
Earth,	waitush.
Water,	coos.
Fire,	aula.
Snow,	maika.
Rain,	waikit.
Wood,	haitsu.
Grass,	pax.
Hell or bad spirit,	koonapa kapseish.

Horse,	shecum.
White Bear,	háháts.
Black Bear,	eakat.
Beaver,	taxpull.
Otter,	collas.
Deer,	enishnim.
Moose,	taissheep.
Buffalo,	cocoil.
Wolf,	siyah.
Salmon,	natso.
Trout,	wowalthum.
Gun,	temoon.
Powder,	pōpokes.
Ball,	saip.
Stone,	pishwa.
What is that?	ētu ke.
Who is that?	eshe ke.
There,	koone.
Here,	kēne.
Where,	mene.
When,	mowwa.
How many?	moits.
None,	sīou.
All,	oekalla.
Plenty,	elahne.
Near by,	keemta.
Great way off,	wyat.
This road,	iskit.
Stop,	collo.
Go,	coetuc.
Run,	willaikit.
Go fast,	haum teets.
Stop here,	collo kēne.
Encamp,	wispeix.
Sleep,	penemeek.

Eat,	hipsh.
I hear,	ēn amachish.
You hear,	ēm amachish.
I understand,	ēn amacus.
Come,	cōme.
I know,	en soko.
You know,	em soko.
He knows,	emim soko.
They know,	elahne tetokan soko.
I do not know,	waiitu en soko.
Talk,	tumtein.
Ride,	wyatcus.
Wait,	cōats.
Swim,	shuway.
Love,	aitou.
Hate,	waiitu aitou.
Kill,	wâpseou.
Alive,	waikus.
Make,	ainees.
Take,	enip.
Carry,	enip coeta.
Give,	enâhanim.
Pay,	tumaitcus.
Make fire,	ailix.
Worship,	tolla poosa.
Smoke,	keiēta.
Sun, moon,	hasumtooks.
Prairie,	paix.
Mountain,	mashum.
Friend,	sextua.
Chief,	mēōhōt.
Nez Perce,	nūmēpo.
Blackfoot,	quasne.
Bonnax,	tuelca.
American,	suēapo.

Frenchman,	allīma.
Head,	hooshus.
Hair,	hookoo.
Arm,	artum.
Leg,	waiu.
Foot,	akooa.
Cloth,	tahea.
Saddle,	supen sapoos.
Pack,	supen saps.
Beads,	collowin.
Good,	tois.
Bad,	kapsēis.
No,	waiitu.
Yes,	ái.
Great,	hemakis.
Small,	coots.
Sick,	comitsa.
Well,	penamina.
To-day,	tâx.
Yesterday,	wâtish.
Once more,	nox emaka.
White,	hihi.
Black,	cinmo cimmeo.
Red,	ilpelp.
Vermilion,	ailish.
Paint,	penasuet.

1	nox.	10	poetumpt.
2	lapeet.	11	nox tit.
3	metait.	12	lapeet tit.
4	pēēlep.	20	laap tit.
5	pahut.	30	metaip tit.
6	elaix.	40	pelap tit.
7	quoenapt.	50	pahap tit.
8	wemuttut.	100	pooetap tit.
9	quoies.		

VOCABULARY OF THE KLICATAT NATION, WHO INHABIT THE
COUNTRY NORTH OF THE CASCADES.

English.	*Indian.*
God,	Meyoh.
Evil spirit,	melah,
Sun,	ān.
Moon,	ulhigh'.
Stars,	kashlo.
Fire,	lokkowouks.
Earth,	te 'tsum.
Water,	chow wass.
Stone,	'p's swah.
Wood,	il quass.
House,	enneet.
Bread,	shappleel.
Fish,	t'kuinnat.
Deer,	owinnat.
Bird,	'hat 'hot.
Cow,	moos moos stun.
Horse,	kosee.
Dog,	kosikkosee.
Boat,	quâssass.
Man,	wince.
Woman,	iyet.
Girl,	p'teeniks.
Boy,	asswan.
Fingers,	pahhahtopat.
Foot,	wattekas.
Toe,	owhunghe.
Tongue,	melleese.
Ear,	misshu (plu.) pesahmisshu.
Mouth,	metolla'hhow.
Lip,	um, (plu.) pesah um.
Black,	chēmook.

White,	pillas.
Green,	láhm't.
Yellow,	penahkunnootowass.
Red,	klutsâh.
Good,	seyah.
Bad,	chilooeet.
High,	'quaahme.
Low,	mētee.
Many,	hugh'lâk.
Few,	millah.
Little,	iksiks.
Who?	sindewah.
What?	sinmisswah.
Knife,	hahbittelme.
Bow,	toominpass.
Arrow,	kiasso.
Gun,	toowinpass.
Sea,	attackass.
River,	wânnah.
Lake,	wattum.
Mountain,	'ke'h.
Hill,	pussque.
Valley,	'tkop.
Plain,	tâk.
Here,	itche.
There,	ekkone.
Near,	'tsahpah.
Far off,	weat'tpah.
Night,	'tset.
Day,	echoosah.
Where,	minnan.
When,	mittach.
I walk,	inikwenahsah.
I talk,	sinewesah.
None,	chahow.

I know,	assook sah.
I have known,	mewe sah sooh sah.
I see,	ēnahūkheno sah.
I hear,	innasick sah.
I taste,	quatas sah.
I smell,	annookse sah.
I,	sah.
Thou,	imk'.
He,	equak.
She,	equakiik.
Head,	chlamtukh.
Eye,	tats'k.
Back,	koopkoop.
Come,	winnum.
Go,	winnak.
Give,	annik.
Large,	'nche.
Smaller,	mi'nche.
Smallest,	ooksooks.
Beauty,	seeghewah.
All,	k'lhweek.
True,	chawnumsisk.
False,	t'sis.
Chief,	kool'ltup.
Common men,	wullumteen.
My father,	hahtootas.
My mother,	naheclas.
Elder brother,	nahnahnas.
Younger brother,	incoks.
Sister,	inchats.
Husband,	inman.
Yes,	deh.
No,	waht.
Beaver,	wispuss.
Rabbit,	sinwe.

Cat,	wâsswâss.
Wolf,	enahte.
Bear,	'hollees.
Otter,	nooksi.
Laziness,	ilkkah.
Sleep,	'tsotah.
Soft,	uquatuquat.
Strength,	h'too.
Swan,	wâhhalow.
Goat,	powyanin.
Beads,	k'pput.
Cold,	'tsoisah.
Hard,	k'ttet'k.

1	lah's,	12	neep'twâppena,
2	neep't,	13	mettaptwâppena,
3	mettapt',	20	neeptit,
4	peneep't,	30	mettâptit,
5	pahhat,	40	peneeptit,
6	p'tuhninis,	50	pahhâptit,
7	tooskâs,	60	p'tuhninsaptit,
8	pahhahhemaht,	70	tooskahsâptit,
9	'tsawlawsimkah,	80	pahhahtusap'tit,
10	hōtem,	90	'tsaulochsáptit,
11	lah'swappena.	100	potemtit.

VOCABULARY OE THE CALAPOOA NATION.

God,	'ntsompate.
Heaven,	ahlupklooah.
Evil Spirit,	ehwakehe.
Hell,	owievenah.
Sun,	'npeun.
Moon,	'ntope.
Stars,	'ntsalowah.
Fire,	ummi.
Earth,	umpullo.

Wind,	'ntolouh.
Water,	'mpahke.
Wood,	owâttuk.
Stone,	'ntâugh.
Bone,	'ntsa.
House,	ummi'.
Bread,	shappleel.
Fish,	'ntumuak.
Deer,	ammoke'.
Elk,	'ntokah.
Bird,	noknok.
Horse,	kuetan.
Cow,	moosmoos.
Dog,	'n'tul.
Boat,	'mpaw.
Man,	'noihee.
Woman,	ehwahktsut.
Boy,	ehwahpyah.
Girl,	'mpeena.
I,	tsa.
Thou,	mah.
He,	annoihe.
She,	ahwahkkotsut.
My father,	hum nee.
Your father,	makkan nee.
My mother,	sin nee.
Elder brother,	tâh.
Sister,	shetup.
Husband,	tahwahke.
Wife,	tahwahke.
Yes,	aw.
No,	kussowe.
Head,	unquâh.
Mouth,	tinte.
Chin,	'tlâk.

Teeth,	tinte.
Arm,	t'ntooque.
Hand,	t'lakquah.
Finger,	taw'nah.
Foot,	teuofoh.
Ear,	toandunkahtâh.
Black,	mo'.
White,	mow'.
Blue,	'mpulunk.
Green,	pitchish.
Red,	'tselow.
Good,	misso.
Bad,	kaskah.
High,	tshamayunk.
Low,	wâllah.
Many,	milloe.
Few,	'mponuk.
Large,	pellah.
Small,	ētoo.
Who,	me'eh.
What,	ânnikkee.
Knife,	'nkamistik.
Bow,	unchin.
Arrow,	un'owsuk.
Gun,	sukwâllahlah.
Sea,	mullak.
River,	'ntsok.
Lake,	wâssetnummeke.
Mountain,	peotahmefook.
Valley,	wâllah.
Night,	mooyoo.
Day,	'mpeyon.
Here,	m'hash.
There,	piefan.
Near,	'mchillah.

Far off,	m'lokkio.
Where,	mutchoo.
When,	tahnondeh.
To talk,	tanuk.
To walk,	owållowah.
None,	'nwa.
I see,	chats'onhot'n.
Beaver,	'nkipeah.
All,	teloh.
Chief,	'ntsombeek.
Common men,	anwoekee.
Come,	mahek.
Go,	tattea.
Give,	mahaque.
Swan,	mow.
Rabbit,	umpon.
Wolf,	molent.
Bear,	'mmo.
Sleep,	towi.
Hard,	'p'tsåkkolloo.
Soft,	'mput'l.
Boil,	liplip.

1	towneh,	10	teeneefeahåh,
2	kamah,	11	teenefeahpetownah.
3	peshin,	12	teenefeahpekamah.
4	tohwah,	20	keefotenefeah.
5	wul,	30	p'shintenefeah.
6	tåffo,	40	tohwatenefeah.
7	p'sinmewe,	50	wultenefeah.
8	ke'mewe.	100	tenefeah.
9	'quisteh,	1000	tumpeah.

VOCABULARY OF THE CHENOOK LANGUAGE AS SPOKEN
ABOUT FORT VANCOUVER.

God,	Cannum.
Heaven,	coosah,

Earth,	illaha.
Fire,	olaptska.
Water,	isuck.
Sea,	wecoma.
River,	ibolt.
Sun,	otlah.
Moon,	ootleum.
Evil spirit,	skokoom.
Hell,	skokoom.
Boat,	conim.
Knife,	ōpitsah.
Gun,	sucwàllâl.
Powder,	poolalla.
Ball,	coliētan.
Air,	kummataz.
I,	nīka.
Thou,	mīka.
He,	yahkah.
She,	yàhkah.
It or them,	klaska.
Chief,	tie.
Boy,	kaskas.
Girl,	l'kpho.
Sister,	áhts.
Father,	tilecummama.
Mother,	st'llmama.
People,	tilecum.
Yes,	ah, aha.
No,	wayick or wāke.
Good,	close.
Bad,	wake close.
Very bad,	mestsa.
Large,	hias.
Small,	tunas.
Far,	sia.

Little way,	tunas sia.
Great way,	hias sia.
To go fast,	clatua hiuc.
Not fast,	wake hiuc.
Black,	klaait.
White,	t'koop.
Blue,	spock.
Red,	pelpil.
Green,	peteish.
High,	saghalle.
Low,	kekulle.
Now,	witkă.
Much,	oghooway.
Little,	tunas.
Who,	'tkaksta.
What,	ikta.
Mountain,	saghalle illaha.
Valley,	kekulle illaha.
Where,	câh.
Here,	ookook.
Night,	pollakle.
None,	haloo.
Bear,	siano.
Beaver,	eena.
Fox,	tiskowkow.
Wolf,	leelō.
Deer,	moueech.
Horse,	kuetan.
Cow,	moosmoos.
Dog,	kamux.
Salmon,	quanagh.
Bird,	kallakalla.
Speak,	wâwâ.
I speak,	nica wâwâ.
Thou speakest,	mica wâwâ.

He speaks,	yâkkâ wâwâ.
They speak,	klaska wâwâ.
Make,	mammook,
I make,	nica mammook.
Thou makest,	mica mammook.
He makes,	yâkkâ mammook.
They make,	klaska mammook.
Come,	chawko.
Perhaps, or 1 do not know	clunas.
Understand,	cumetax.
I understand,	nica cumetax.
Now I understand,	alta nica cumetax.
Sleep,	moosom.
I have, or it is with me,	mitlit nica.
I walk,	nica clatuwa.
Long ago,	aunacotta.
See,	noneneech.
Eat,	mucamuc.

1	eght,	8	stoghtkin,
2	moxt,	9	quiitz,
3	none,	10	taughlelum,
4	ʻlăkit,	20	moxttâghlelum,
5	quinum,	40	ʻlakittâghlelum,
6	tohhum,	100	taughlelum taughlelum
7	sinnamox,		

The Philologist, by examining the specimens of the languages in the foregoing vocubularies, will notice how entirely distinct they are from each other, and may form his own opinions in regard to their origin. The languages of other Indian nations are equally distinct. The use of the commas, as in ʻkeʻh, mountain, ʻnoihee, man, is designed to designate a guttural sound, wholly inarticulate.